Economic Reform in Japan

Economic Reform in Japan

Can the Japanese Change?

Edited by

Craig Freedman

Director, Centre for Japanese Economic Studies
Macquarie University, Australia

IN ASSOCIATION WITH THE CENTRE FOR JAPANESE
ECONOMIC STUDIES, MACQUARIE UNIVERSITY,
AUSTRALIA

Edward Elgar
Cheltenham, UK • Northampton, MA, USA

Published by
Edward Elgar Publishing Limited
Glensanda House
Montpellier Parade
Cheltenham
Glos GL50 1UA
UK

Edward Elgar Publishing, Inc.
136 West Street
Suite 202
Northampton
Massachusetts 01060
USA

A catalogue record for this book
is available from the British Library

Library of Congress Cataloguing in Publication Data
Economic reform in Japan: can the Japanese change? / edited by Craig Freedman.
    p. cm.
    "In association with the Centre for Japanese Economic Studies, Macquarie
University, Australia."
    Includes index.
    1. Japan—Economic conditions—1945– 2. Japan—Economic policy—
1945– I. Freedman, Craig, 1950– II. Macquarie University. Centre for
Japanese Economic Studies.

    HC462.9 .E237 2001
    338.952—dc21

                        2001031363

ISBN 1 84064 509 1

Printed and bound in Great Britain by MPG Books Ltd, Bodmin, Cornwall

Contents

Figures and tables

FIGURE

TABLES

Contributors

James C. Abegglen
Asia Advisory Services, Tokyo Japan

Ronald Dore
Centre for Economic Performance, London School of Economics and Political Science

Craig Freedman
Centre for Japanese Economic Studies, Macquarie University

Noel Gaston
School of Business and Institute for Global Corporate Governance Studies, Bond University

Koichi Hamada
Economic Growth Center, Yale University

Aiko Ikeo
School of Commerce, Waseda University

Kazuhito Ikeo
Faculty of Economics, Keio University

Makoto Itoh
Faculty of Economics, Kokugakuin University

Masato Masuda
School of International Economics, Banking and Finance, Hosei University

Eileen Mauskopf
Board of Governers, Federal Reserve Bank, Washington, DC

Colin R. McKenzie
Osaka School of International Public Policy, Osaka University

Marcus Noland
Institute for International Economics, Washington, DC

Mikio Wakatsuki
Board of Counsellors, Japan Research Institute, Tokyo

Learning to live on a horizontal learning curve

To lose one parent, Mr. Worthing, may be regarded as a misfortune, to lose both looks like carelessness.
The Importance of Being Earnest – Oscar Wilde

Women friends like to tell me that giving birth more than once can be attributed to a form of programmed amnesia. (The initial plunge can be blamed on a sense of ingrained disbelief formed by novices when listening to first hand descriptions.) Evolution seems to find it advantageous to encourage women to blur or even to purge sharp memories of the sheer horrors surrounding the event. Instead, what memories remain no more than months after the blessed event are softly backlit by all those sentimental *Kodak*-type moments. The agony itself is soon lost in a sepia-toned haze of forgetfulness.

Like the trauma of childbirth (though in no way its equivalent), organizing one large-scale conference ought to be sufficient for anyone capable of rational thought. Amnesia must be my only possible defence. For while it may be a misfortune to organize one conference, to deliberately persist and arrange any such subsequent events can only be scorned as sheer carelessness.

It is true that my first attempt to stage an international conference in 1998 was motivated more out of sheer ignorance and unwonted high spirits than anything else. It was sadly reminiscent of all those ancient MGM musicals where Mickey Rooney and Judy Garland decide to put on a show in an empty barn. But once having discovered exactly what happens when you place your hand on top of that particular hot stove, the wise course of action would have been to retire discreetly into the background, allowing yet another foolish tyro to take my place.

Unfortunately, after leaving the edited volume of those proceedings to the tender mercies of my publisher, the logic of the next conference insinuated itself relentlessly into my consciousness much against my own inclinations. For after dissecting the reasons for Japan's dramatic stumble in 1998, the next step logically would require an examination into the consequences of such a stumble. Would Japan actually change and embrace the sort of regime of economic reforms that so many outside observers were now quite strenuously urging? When I thought of the issue and some of the possible presenters who might be willing to speak at a 2000 conference, my mind subconsciously shifted gear. I suddenly told myself that given what I had learned, the next conference would be in no way as difficult, thus proving that people are condemned not to learn the most important lessons that experience has to offer.

I must admit that, as always, I was encouraged by the ongoing political structure which continues to plague Japan. In particular, the Liberal Democratic Party (LDP) of Japan seems to conspire to make each conference I organize more interesting than the last. As such, it has proved each time to be my unwitting ally. I have come to rely on the tone-deaf approach so reliably exhibited by the functionaries of that party to support my own struggling efforts. In this case I owe a particular vote of thanks to Yoshiro Mori and his curious 2000 election campaign. For my own selfish reasons I would regret to see the LDP unceremoniously booted out and replaced by a political party more interested in governing than merely holding on to government. Though to be fair, the Japanese people may have their own, quite different, preferences.

With the LDP conspiring to maintain interest in the future of Japan, I once again started to plan for the 2000 conference by inviting some of those people who initially most influenced my own thinking about the Japanese, though over the years those views have been modified by events.[1] I started with the rule of thumb that what I would be interested in sitting and listening to might also intrigue a wider audience. In this particular instance I wondered what such established figures as James C. Abegglen or Ronald Dore might now think about Japan given the events of the 1990s? Had they largely reconsidered their former views or could they somehow square such events with the frameworks which they had so carefully erected over decades of research and analysis? To stir debate I looked for individuals who might present quite different views on the same subject. By heightening such contrasts, I hoped some insight would flow. I also made sure to frame the topic of the conference in the strongest possible terms in order to elicit bold, as opposed to overly cautious, responses. As always, it is left to the reader to decide to what degree I accomplished my goal.

One quick clarification which may help to explain some of the material in this volume. Readers will find that after each chapter (with the exception of that by Mikkio Wakatsuki – a lunchtime address – and James C. Abegglen – the discussant self-vaporized) there are comments by a designated discussant. All participants, both presenters and discussants, were allowed to revise their remarks subsequent to the actual conference. Naturally, the revisions were made based on those original remarks and presentations rather than on any subsequent altered versions. So there is the inevitable possibility that some of the discussants' comments will seem vaguely out of sync. Fortunately for the reader, I doubt that this has in fact caused any noticeable disparities in the final versions presented here.

As always, there are many people to thank and even a few who deserve tender apologies. It would be impossible to cover all who so kindly assisted this process, such as the cab driver who at 6.30 a.m., while I was trying desperately to make it to the conference hotel, was tuned to a Mozart concerto rather than the standard offerings of breakfast radio. However, there is no doubt that the conference would not have happened at all but for the efforts of Elaine Kent. Without people attending a conference, no reason for its existence remains. Elaine has the fortunate knack of convincing people, much to their own surprise, that they actually would like nothing better than to sit through a number of people talking at length about Japan. There is also the matter of funding. Bills after all have to be paid and these large events are in no way self-funding. Fortunately, Sony (Australia), under the forward-looking leadership of Haruyuki Machida, kindly stepped in to assist with some of those pesky bills. Jenny Geddes of Sony (Australia) also proved to be an ideal person to turn to for any assistance in these matters, never put off by a momentary difficulty. Nobutake Odano, Consul-General of Japan, was kind enough to take an interest in our efforts and, by extending his hospitality, provided a memorable ending to the conference itself. Meanwhile, Edward Elgar continues to be a perfect gentleman, perhaps illustrating the difference between a publisher and a media mogul. Nor could I ask more from his sometime changing but always diligent publishing crew.

Lastly I owe a series of apologies to my family who found me to be absent without leave for so many months in both the lead up to and the aftermath of the conference. My two six-year-old girls continue to be mystified by what I do for so much of my time, almost as mystified as I am myself.

Craig Freedman
December 2000

NOTE

1. When asked why he seemed so often to change his mind, it is reported that Keynes replied, 'When the facts change, I change my mind. What do you do?' I hope that I have over the years managed to escape the worst pitfalls of dogmatism.

1. When change is not reform: transforming the Japanese economy

Craig Freedman

And so these men of Hindostan
Disputed loud and long
Each of his own opinion
Exceeding stiff and strong
Though each was partly in the right
And all were in the wrong
(Saxe 1961:200)

When I was quite young, the educational theory of the day somehow deemed it to be a good thing (moral and uplifting) for young children first to commit to memory and then publicly to declaim bits of well-known verse. I leave it to the reader to debate the merits of such a character-building approach. The consequences though are less in doubt. Even to this very day, I can still stand up, throw back my head and do at least the first verse of 'Abou Ben Adem' to the great annoyance of anyone within a listening radius.

Perhaps more than any other poem (be it by Robert Louis Stevenson, A.A. Milne or any of the varied denizens inhabiting *A Child's Garden of Poetry*), I can best recall a poem which vividly painted the reaction of ten blind sages of India confronting an elephant for the first time. Each precise description given depended entirely upon the exact part of the elephant each wise man had happened to fix his inquisitive hands around. From each individual's own particular position (*vis-à-vis* the elephant), the logic of his description was unassailable. The problem that each one of these venerated sages had failed to grasp was that each had managed to fix on a quite different part of the same elephant.[1]

These days, whenever I am fortunate enough to have the opportunity of listening to, or reading, an analysis of modern day Japan (especially a discussion attempting to probe the ever-elusive future of that country), those verses of my youth immediately provide me with a cautionary warning. Never mistake a partial view for a panoramic outlook; learn to examine all such arguments critically and carefully. Every expert has in front of him or

1

her (we are blessed with wise women these days as well as the standard issue of wise men) the same collection of information, the same data and an identical set of statistics. Nonetheless, each analyst seems most often drawn only to one particular subset out of the whole available range, namely that which most clearly delineates and supports a specific point of view.

When our modern day wise men (especially those bearing the name 'economist') tackle the equally perplexing elephant that is modern day Japan, it often appears that what they see may depend upon whether they subscribe to a market or more idiosyncratic, institutional view of an economy. (Are similarities more important than differences?) It is true that a consensus view today, given recent history, would tend to focus on the dominant role played by markets (especially global markets, as any commentator permitted within the proximity of a keyboard feels compelled to remind us).

But, by falling in with the market consensus too easily, we are in danger of cheerfully embracing a popular form of amnesia. In the 1980s, a substantial contingent of commentators (mostly composed of other faces than those prominent today, but including some who simply like to ride bandwagons) equally felt compelled to explain why Japan did not fit into the models promoted by standard economic theory. Oscillating between these two extremes[2] (predicated entirely on the prevailing economic environment) seems to promote a partisan debate that is bound to be limited in its fruitfulness. Either approach can easily provide the grist for the sort of satire best embodied by the tailors of Laputa,[3] who cared more for theoretical niceties (and precision) than empirical fit.

This type of intellectual sparring inevitably leads to exaggeration on either side of a controversy, confounding rather than clarifying the issues at hand. So it was in the 1980s, so it was in the 1990s and so it seems to continue these days as well. One thing though is very certain in life. If an economy falters, there will never be any lack of critics eager to explain why what was previously done was quite wrong, and why the following laundry list of reforms has to be implemented immediately to achieve salvation. There is of course an element of barely suppressed glee added into the mix if previously the pitiable failure had been a roaring, and perhaps even an arrogant, success.[4]

Japan then finds itself with no lack of Job-like sympathizers. These legions are largely populated by many mainstream economists and commentators who grew increasingly exasperated in the 1980s with the idea that Japan could succeed without seeming to adhere to a textbook economic regime. These grumblers have now had the opportunity to voice the ultimate 'I told you so'. (Revisionism is always a thriving academic cottage industry.) They have certainly not passed up the chance to explain (at length) why Japanese post-war prosperity occurred in spite of Japan's industrial policy and post-war institutions. The boldest might want to go so far as to say that Japan's performance would have been even brighter had it hewn to a standard approach reflecting the tenets of economic liberalism.

These same critics are quite capable of incisively pointing out why Japan's post-war aura of invincible success was in fact nothing but an illusion. A fair-minded observer would conclude that the best of this work contains a great deal that can easily be supported and justified (no matter what the underlying objective of the author might be). It is seemingly undeniable (though someone is always ready to deny the obvious) that Japan does need to change, though whether it needs to change radically is an entirely different, though related, question. Even accepting the need for radical change does not automatically mean an irresistible and inevitable convergence to the Anglo-American model of corporate governance and economic management. That is why a careful and considered debate over economic reform is essential if one hopes to understand the status of Japan today and plot out, to some extent, its future course.

If we are then going to question whether the Japanese can change in order to put in place much needed economic reform, we are left with two basic difficulties. It is not entirely clear what version of economic reform is necessary (though it would be difficult to find anyone claiming that there is no need for any whatsoever). Nor is there anything like a consensus on how the Japanese themselves must change. At its most radical level, the Japanese would have to engage in a self-transformation, becoming in fact something quite different from what they have been, ceasing to be Japanese (fundamentally rather than in some superficial sense). At a more trivial level, change is, of course, inevitable. It is hard to imagine a modern society or economy remaining static.[5]

So the real question is not whether the Japanese have changed (of course they have).[6] It is not even whether they have changed more than some subset of other countries. The important issue is whether they have changed sufficiently and in the right direction so as to prosper in their current economic environment. (Defining that right direction will, almost inevitably, spark controversy.) Does Japan need to make deep-rooted changes in those institutions providing the basic bedrock of the economy? Ideally institutions should foster beliefs and behaviour that nurture economic growth and development. But should these same institutions and the economic reality they mediate become out of sync, then the very same set of institutions may become impediments rather than lubricants to economic wealth and progress.

It might safely be argued that the Japanese have yet to undergo a radical transformation, for all the wonderful adaptation the world marvelled at first during the Meiji Restoration or subsequently in the post-war period. (Though, whether they should or can is another matter.) Many of the feudal relationships and mindsets, characteristic of the Tokugawa shogunate, have continued to dominate the last century and a half of Japanese history.[7] Technological catch-up or economic growth has been finely balanced against more distributional issues. Relational rather than purely market contracting, to some extent, has dominated Japan's economy and society. Although the political, economic and social landscape of Japan in those years leading to its forcible opening looked radically different from the Japan of fifty years later, fundamentally Japan retained many of its feudal attitudes, conventions and institutions. These were merely adapted to Japan's new environment rather than being swept away.

Attempts to plant the seeds of what we might label the dominant aspects of Anglo-American capitalism (a reliance on market contracting and individual decision making) were almost inevitably short-lived and often ruthlessly suppressed and eliminated.[8] The long tradition of banging in any stray nails with the temerity to stick out aided and abetted this process. But a strong preference for the status quo and a pronounced risk averseness[9] seemed to favour, over the years, the more conservative elements of society, whether represented by the military, business or farming.

The problem, when discussing deep-rooted changes and a transformation of Japan, lies in distinguishing the traditional baby from the less desirable bath water. In the present Japanese system, what is in fact worth preserving in order to ensure the future well being of the people of Japan? Even if some neat distinction can be made, the two elements may not be so clearly separable. The baby may cease to thrive if deprived of its bath water environment. Or, a sudsy residue can still remain and inhibit development despite all the well-meant, vigorous towelling conceivable. The Japanese have throughout their history shown themselves capable (when sufficiently pressed by outside realities) of adopting foreign practices and technology. In doing so they have yet to abandon what can be seen as distinctly Japanese patterns. There is no reason to believe that they will change in this regard.[10]

US firms in the 1980s adopted numerous production and organizational techniques perfected by the Japanese. Yet it would be a stretch of the imagination to claim that these firms (or the workers maintaining them) grew to resemble the Japanese or adopted specific Japanese institutions or conventions. Such an objective would come close to being a contradiction in terms. History and development limit our choices. To think otherwise would be erroneously to dismiss the importance of sunk costs. Assets, whether physical or non-tangible, cannot be transferred costlessly from one use to another. The very idea of making real choices is that they constrain future opportunities. Otherwise, choosing would itself represent the ultimate illusion.

Just as the US of the 1980s did not converge to the Japanese model, it is perhaps foolish to anticipate a similar convergence by Japan to the US model, simply because recent events have turned the tables as to relative success. Historically, it would be difficult to find a country where a radical transformation, similar to that suggested as being the key to future Japanese success, has occurred.[11] This does not however negate the argument that Japan is a historically special case, having endured somewhat less of a radical transformation than other comparable countries.

What would in fact constitute an economic shock of sufficient magnitude, one that would be capable of shifting Japan away from its traditional structures and institutions?[12] Even the aftermath of a devastating wartime defeat, forcing the Japanese to face a future seemingly stripped of resources, proved insufficient. What Noguchi (1998) has labelled the 1940 system was essentially resurrected during this post-war period. But Noguchi for completeness needs to extend his thesis backward as well as forward.[13] The system he so carefully delineates wasn't simply created and imposed on the Japanese people when a military regime successfully gained power in the 1930s (only to be resurrected almost immediately after a subsequent disastrous military defeat). The roots of this set of institutional relationships go back much further in Japanese history.

The key addition that the post-war version offered was the promise of a significantly greater widespread economic prosperity. The mass of people would continue to toil diligently based on this premise of a rising standard of living, the coming of the guaranteed middle-class society. Every man may not have aspired to become an emperor, but every citizen now could believe in his or her right to the bourgeois life.[14] The basis for this low risk, middle-class society rested upon an essentially unsustainable level of economic growth. The stagnant 1990s undermined the assumption that Japan would be able simply to grow its way out of any economic difficulties.

If, as seems likely, Japan's institutions and national myths have become largely out of sync with its current economic environment, then what adjustment process will prove ultimately capable of bringing these two aspects back in line once more? To a large degree, the authors in this volume tackle, in quite contrasting ways, the question of why structure and environment ceased to synchronize and what needs to be done to align them once more.

The core of Japan's problem today lies in its overwhelming post-war success (as Hamada points out clearly in this volume). All organizations are by nature backward looking. For this reason, success is far more difficult to manage intelligently than failure. Failure sends out a clear and useful

signal. ('Do something immediately or repeat past mistakes.') But an unam-
biguous triumph is less informative. It provides no reliable guide as to what
course will yield future success. Instead, it appeals to the natural conser-
vatism of any corporate body. 'Why tinker with a winning formula?'
Victorious generals restage their last war. Corporations preserve the status
quo, more concerned with conserving what has been accomplished than in
achieving new success. With the lapse of sufficient time, successful corporations must face an additional difficulty. Time creates constituencies with
stakes in that existing structure. Given the inherent uncertainty surrounding any significant change, these groups will quite logically dig in their heels
to resist any more than small changes at the margin.

Unfortunately, institutions and economic structures are time and place
specific, which means that the economic efficiency arising from a given set
of circumstances is similarly constrained. The most common and dangerous error that organizations commit is to confuse a specific solution with a
more general one. As a result, much of the Japanese leadership still seems
stunned. Even after a decade of economic disarray, they, for the most part,
lack a clear-cut idea of how to proceed. Or if they do, they are paralysed
by the potential cost of making radical changes. At times, Japan appears to
be almost wallowing in its recent disillusionment and despair, providing a
perfect counterpoint to the self-confidence displayed in the 1980s.[15] Much
of the senior leadership (whether political, business or bureaucratic) is
prosperous and near retirement. A natural inclination would be to try to
conserve one's gains and one's hold on government, rather than taking the
much riskier course of actually trying to govern.

This is then where any serious discussion must begin. All of our authors
agree that Japan made mistakes in the 1980s. No one has a good word to
say about the asset bubble which hijacked the economy in that same decade
(or at least in the last half). But this particular colloquium of Aesops has
no easy time agreeing on the moral to be drawn from the fable of the
bubble. In each of the first three sections of this volume, the authors seem
distinctly at odds in describing Japan, past and present. There is however
at least one constant. All would agree that whatever Japan's economic
problem might be, the root problem is to a great degree political. To say
much that is positive when describing the current political structure, long
dominated by the Liberal Democratic Party, remains a distinct challenge.

We begin then with two overviews of Japan. Both turn out to be surprisingly upbeat, but they seem to be describing two quite different Japans.
What becomes decisive, here and in the chapters which follow, is the degree
to which each author finds economic liberalism (the diet of markets and
unfettered individual choice) to be congenial. That seems to provide the
basis for deciding whether or not reform, modelled after Western standards,

is to be welcomed. Few would go so far as completely to disown those structures and practices that created the world's second largest economy. The real issue is the degree to which Japan must take up Anglo-American[16] ideas of corporate governance, employment and regulation.

Mikio Wakatsuki has long been a bureaucratic insider, holding a series of key positions at the Bank of Japan during the rise and demise of the now infamous asset bubble. In his concise depiction of how Japan went wrong and how the reform process is putting the country back on track, Mr Wakatsuki takes a very mainstream approach towards economic reform and economic liberalism. So we start off with some obligatory hand wringing and an acknowledgement that policy, especially financial policy, was ill advised.

Attempts to accelerate the pace of reform (move rapidly, at least in Japanese terms) under the Hashimoto government proved too much for the Japanese to stomach. What followed can best be viewed as a period of necessary consolidation under Mr Hashimoto's successor, Mr Obuchi. While Mr Wakatsuki thinks that the emergency spending measures of the late 1990s were a necessary measure to deter the worst scenarios created by the threat of a deflationary economy, he does feel that the Japanese government needs to refocus on Western-style reform. Still, he firmly thinks that recent business response to yet another new international challenge is already creating an irresistible pressure for such reforms to take place. Does Mr Wakatsuki see a convergence with Western ideas of economic liberalism? Not entirely. Japan is adopting those elements that best suit its system and will not entirely lose its comparative strength in creating a cooperative workplace. Yet the current pattern of change will go a long way in aligning Japan's workplace and corporate boardrooms with those that distinguish Anglo-American economies. Japan therefore is not only changing, but also changing in the right direction and (after a few years of stumbling) changing at an appropriate speed. Mr Wakatsuki remains guardedly optimistic.

For that matter so does Ronald Dore, who established his name by pointing out the differences (and the superiority in many cases) of the Japanese approach relative to a more market-oriented practice.[17] Where economic liberalism would insist that government should best shrink to some minimum sustainable level, Dore demonstrated that much of Japan's success lay in the strategic activism of the government sector. Bureaucrats and businessmen could freely cooperate based on a foundation of mutual trust that formed the bedrock of Japanese society.[18]

These days, Dore goes so far as permitting himself to believe in some degree of (what he would see as necessary) reform. To be fair, few would object to most of his personal laundry list of desirable changes (many would support them all). But the reforms Dore supports, though in some cases not dissimilar from those championed by economic liberals, have attached to them a particular twist. Dore would see those practices (needing either elimination or reform) as somehow, at heart, not Japanese. By redistributing income to wealthy special interest groups, they fly in the face of a Japan that at its core is focused on building a fair society based on community rather than individual values. As Dore admits, he is far more certain about his moral than economic concepts.

Japan then does not essentially have to change, especially not if it is to continue being the sort of country that Dore (and the Japanese people Dore likes and admires) can recognize as being congenial to their own tastes and proclivities. I suspect that Dore regards the current fad for reform as just that, a sort of Noh dramatization which the Japanese feel obliged to stage for foreign observers.[19] Fortunately, according to Dore, Japan remains a dynamic society that will move ahead without in any clear way coming to resemble Anglo-American economies.

Whether Dore's 'steady as she goes' approach is correct depends to a good deal on a point he incisively made in his previous work. Dore's (1986) insight as to how the Japanese succeeded in making a set of post-war constraints into strengths has a good deal of allure as well as explanatory power. Much of Japan's post-war success can be explained in just this way. (Japan's history has revolved around making do with what superficially would seem to be a very limited potential.) However, given a real seismic shift in the prevailing economic environment, one wonders whether it is now those same rigidities that have come to dominate Japan's previous flexibility. That vaunted flexibility of Japanese firms seems particularly conducive and thus limited to a specific economic environment. It is understandable that Dore should warn against casually abandoning the cooperative spirit that has always been Japan's greatest strength. This is the classic baby's bath water argument. But at its weakest, the argument can become overburdened with too much *fin de siecle* sentimentality. In fact, the Japanese, over the centuries, can credibly be described as one of the least sentimental people imaginable.[20]

The issue can then be stated as to whether the Japanese ended up believing their own rhetoric. Did they somehow convince themselves that they had discovered the solution to the fundamental economic puzzle (the same sort of self-infatuation witnessed in the US these days)? Efficiency (and thus success) will always be a very time- and place-specific concept. Japan should be given all the credit in the world for developing an effective approach that served it well for the two immediate post-war decades. But it is misleading to stop at that point. It is similarly necessary to recognize that the same country failed to correct its course when (almost inevitably) the economic environment changed in ways that were both unanticipated and not conducive to Japan's own institutional structure.

Both Kazuhito Ikeo and Makoto Itoh make this point, though in quite different ways, when analysing Japan's financial structure and history. These financial institutions have been much studied in recent years since they do seem to hold the key to Japan's problems in the past as well as in the future. Ikeo provides a very persuasive take on the problem. Following Noguchi (1998), he sees the financial structure as a continuation of the wartime regime. Both during the war and in the post-war period, the paramount problem continued to be one of ensuring that available funds would efficiently flow to the proper industrial sectors. Though of grave importance to any economy, it was essential that Japan's capital-constrained system in no way misused or even wasted these limited flows of funds. Despite Eileen Mauskopf's objections (provided in her own interesting commentary), it is undoubtedly the case that Japan's development went wonderfully well given the financial system in place. In such a supply-constrained environment, getting the money out of the door and into corporate coffers becomes the dominant priority. This will be true even if the way loans are allocated tends to raise questions as to whether a proper estimation of risk is attached to the outstanding and ever growing volume of loans.

The real test occurred (at least for Ikeo) in the early 1970s when Japan's economic development neared completion. Newly faced with a demand-constrained economy, making fundamental changes to the financial system became more than just another option to contemplate. But, as Ikeo clearly indicates, a system, once established, gathers its own built-in inertia. Financial structures like any other system ever devised, give no thought to their own ultimate dismantling and disestablishment. Faced with a growing threat posed to Japan's successful and established order, the existing system did change. It changed, however, only in order to protect and sustain the status quo, not to shift the focus that had become the defining characteristic of the Japanese economy. Changes were made premised on the assumption that the economy would always grow its way out of any difficulty, no matter how fundamental the problem faced. Jumping to this conclusion was quite effortless, a simple extrapolation of the post-war experience.

By choosing to shore up existing structures and institutions at this point (the shift from a developing to a developed economy) an opportunity was almost casually surrendered. What followed was a collection of ad-hoc attempts to buttress and expand Japan's past successes. Ikeo sums up his major thesis by arguing that Japan did change, but unfortunately entirely in the wrong direction. The asset bubble that destroyed the illusion of Japan's invincibility (particularly an ability to grow out of any economic difficulty) is in Ikeo's view an almost inevitable result of dodging basic financial reform in the 1970s. Interim measures delayed the consequences, without removing the critical faults of the system. Banks continued to focus on channelling funds to borrowers, largely disregarding underlying lending risks. These lenders acted as though the economy was still supply constrained. When traditional corporate (*keiretsu*) borrowers deserted the banking sector, bankers simply substituted increasingly high-risk alternatives. As Ikeo notes, given the subsequent institutional lock-in (an inability to adopt a more appropriate financial system), Japan might have been wiser to have modelled its initial post war approach in a way that reflected traditional Anglo-American verities. (This despite the vital role played by banks in Japan's rapid development and growth.)

Where Ikeo would conclude that Japan needed to embrace Western financial practices when it achieved economic maturity, Makoto Itoh claims that Japan's clumsy embrace of those same principles characterizing economic liberalism in fact caused the Japanese financial system to self-destruct. This failure arises not because Japan employed those principles half-heartedly (or not at all) but because it couldn't resist the temptation to turn away from such principles entirely. Unfortunately, one is left unclear as to whether the Japanese, in Itoh's mind, made the wrong sort of changes in the 1970s as Ikeo contends. Does Itoh perhaps see Japanese missteps as only commencing with the start of the 1980s? As Masato Masuda points out, in his discussion, Itoh is far clearer when dissecting the wrong trajectory implemented by economic liberals, than when describing his own benchmark for an effective financial system. It is far simpler to see that Ikeo perceives the Japanese government as being too intrusive than to be sure that Itoh would prefer more or less strenuous government intervention (or perhaps intervention based on an alternative economic model).

Ikeo finishes in much the same way that Wakatsuki does in the piece already mentioned. He is determined to be upbeat about the result of the reforms now being implemented. Yet at the same time he is dubious about the financial merger movement which seems to be transforming the landscape of Japan.[21] No one has yet explained satisfactorily how combining two badly run banks will lead to an improved financial performance.[22] We can only sincerely embrace such a future, if we leave the realm of economics and take up residence in the land of fables where spinning straw into gold is all in a day's work. Itoh lacks even the guarded level of enthusiasm that Ikeo displays for the current position of the banking sector. Itoh would naturally look askance at any attempts to incorporate further the standard precepts of economic liberalism. (He sees this as a cause of, rather than a solution to, financial instability.) Still, the financial sector remains fragile and a continuing drag on economic growth.

In what is perhaps the most interesting of all the uniformly insightful articles, Koichi Hamada takes some of the ideas already suggested by Itoh and Ikeo a step forward. Japan benefited from a specific set of favourable circumstances in the post-war era. The Japanese were able to exploit these circumstances by constructing institutions and structures highly attuned to this particular environment. (Many of these institutions simply adopted elements from already existing structures.) Emboldened by an overwhelming degree of success, Japan tried to extend its time- and place-specific system to the furthest limits of its capacity. As Hamada remarks:

> Any excessive adaptation to a specific stimulus can make an institution too fragile effectively to respond to different kinds of shock. In that sense, success can prove to be fatal. A successful experience, if over-emphasized, can cause an organization to lose the flexibility required to cope with adverse shocks (p. 147).

Both Hamada and Abegglen (when he also takes up the state of the Japanese firm) recognize the need to have the right set of cultural institutions in place. These structures must allow the economic egg to nestle in, and be sustained by, the appropriate institutional nest. The argument, best exemplified by these two chapters, is whether and to what extent the traditional Japanese bower is worth saving.

It is at this point that the two analysts widely diverge. James Abegglen has achieved a good deal of well-deserved and hard-earned recognition as one of the few Westerners who understand and can explain how the Japanese firm works to a wider audience. (His co-authored volume *Kaisha* (1982) is a particularly good example of this ability.) The real difficulty lies in trying to read the current evidence to forecast future trends. After carefully considering the arguments by both Abegglen and Hamada, the reader may have a sneaking suspicion that necromancy would do just as well.

If we, like Hamada, adopt Aoki's (1990) J-firm/A-firm dichotomy, the question is whether the J-firm's days are numbered.[23] According to a consensus of authoritative commentators, the demise of the Japanese firm (at least as far as Japan is concerned) is now inevitable (as it has been for the last two decades). At the same time, one of the latest management theories (focusing on the comparative advantage of female managers) emphasizes a particular type of cooperative behaviour built on trust. This approach ends up sounding suspiciously like recycled J-firm analysis.[24]

When Abegglen looks at the Japanese corporate sector these days, he sees more evidence of continuity with past practices than either a need for radical reform or an inevitable convergence with Westernized routines. He rejects and reinterprets the standard signs so often cited as evidence of reform and change in corporate governance. There simply exists no fundamental need for Japanese firms faddishly to imitate the West. The same underlying mechanisms and relationship which offered a good basis for understanding Japan triumphant are still sufficient for understanding this post-triumphal Japan.

For Abegglen, despite superficial changes (especially among the younger generation) Japan remains a highly conservative society more focused on continuity than on change. Saving patterns, for instance, seem unaffected by the opening up of the financial system via the Japanese version of a 'Big Bang'. The fundamentals that have governed post-war Japan (including labour relations and corporate governance) are not ideas that have reached their 'used by dates'. Yes, the economic environment has been rapidly changing, but corporate Japan has been adept at shifting resources into dynamic growth areas and continues to do so today without kowtowing to short-term, shareholder interests and fixations. Proof of this is obvious in the way that the Japanese economy is rapidly shifting to a more service orientation without deserting its fundamental values or modes of operation. The current clamour for reform would then be yet another instance of a long history of the West, led by Western commentators and theorists, largely misreading all things Japanese. As Abegglen sums up the issue in this volume:

> Japan presents an economy that has changed in industrial structure and techno-logical level to a truly exceptional degree. That change shows every sign of continuing at a very rapid rate. Yet the systems of governance and personnel management of the Japanese company change slowly and only at the margin. The resulting tensions are real and difficult – and can be taken, mistakenly, to indicate a reversion to Western, especially Anglo-American, systems (p. 186).

When Abegglen looks at present day Japan he can only discern more of the same while someone like Mikio Wakatsuki sees more radical departures. It does make a reader wonder exactly what country is being put under the microscope. (How many Japans are there to observe?)

We are, though, talking only about differences of degree. Neither Hamada nor Abegglen would subscribe to a strict application of economic liberal principles.[25] Hamada even offers an alternative to the simple J versus A dichotomy of corporate structure. An intermediate option lying somewhere between these more drastic choices might better suit Japan's cooperative strengths while being more attuned to current economic environmental demands. Given market constraints, such an alternative equilibrium might not be achievable without an alteration of those constraints by government intervention (partially modifying basic contractual terms).

Still, it is clear that Hamada, unlike Abegglen, sees the necessity for deep-rooted change. If, for instance, bureaucratic regulation makes the transition to a more appropriate organizational structure prohibitively difficult, needed economic growth will falter. (A potentially fatal outcome given Japan's rapidly shifting demographics and its continued desire to obstruct immigration.) Past success can be an unreliable indication of where future economic trajectories may lie. As Hamada concludes (in this volume):

> Nobody doubts that the Japanese management style was effective during the high growth era. To exaggerate its past effectiveness and minimize the difficulty of continuing to employ it as a component of the current social system may involve, I am afraid, a danger of encouraging the 'unwarranted success syndrome' that revels in past glories (p. 155).

The argument for change extends not only domestically but internationally as well. Japan in the post-war years displayed a remarkable adeptness at configuring itself to meet the economic realities of the day. Noland argues that Japan was in fact a prime beneficiary of the new post-war order.[26] He makes this claim despite the fact that Japan has continued to punch below its weight on the international stage. Certainly, saving pure national vanity, there has been little reason for Japan to aspire to punch any higher. It seemed quite capable of achieving its limited menu of international objectives without dominating the relevant international organizations or agencies. Great Britain, which prided itself on punching above its weight, saw very little economic return from such a hard-won position. In fact, it can be argued that too many of its very limited resources were squandered in gaining an objective that lacked any quantifiable pay-off. The question would now be whether continuing Japan's very low-profile approach will handicap the country's attempt to achieve and maintain a sustainable and desirable long-run level of economic growth.

The answer is far from self-evident even after reading Noland's informative chapter. To be more aggressive, in something like the US sense, could only be justified if doing so created an environment more conducive to Japanese objectives. Though one can argue that this behaviour on the part of the US has been to some extent successful, the cost of such a strategy has been substantial. It is far from a simple task to say that this strategy has been an unequivocal success (though the US is not thought to punch above its weight but simply not to pull its punches).

Anointing Japanese nationals as heads of major international agencies (the IMF, WTO, World Bank) would seem to have no discernible or definite pay-off. Capturing the top position at UNESCO (by the tried and true method of greasing the right palms) has seemingly made no difference to Japan's international status (or, more importantly, had any effect on its domestic front). It is difficult to see how the Japanese have been in any sense victimized by these same agencies. In the past, more often than not, their decisions have been favourable to Japanese interests. The WTO has certainly done Japan no harm in the rulings involving Japanese practices (either by government or private industry).

It is often pointed out that Japan will be isolated as trading blocs form with the Europeans on one side and North America on the other. Certainly in the immediate post-war era, the economic promise of integration (in Asia) was not sufficient to overcome the wounds inflicted during the war (unlike the case of France and Germany in Europe). In fact, there have been more recent attempts to move towards a European-type solution. Yet, as Noland points out, it is far from clear exactly how mutually beneficial such unions would be. The most likely candidate for a bilateral agreement would be Singapore, since the potential conflicts between the two countries remain minimal. Unfortunately, the Singaporean economy would be unlikely to make much of a difference to Japan's economic well being. The more obvious choice would be (South) Korea, but what evidence there is fails to predict a definitive advantage for either side. (All calculations would be off, should a reunification between North and South occur in the not so distant future.) It is common wisdom that Japan will not be able to 'go it alone' (economically) for much longer. But like most common wisdom, it is uncertain that this particular insight is built upon any solid foundation. In some ways it is yet again another instance of the convergence theorem. Economists and other commentators seem to abhor substantial differences. As the volume demonstrates (if it demonstrates anything), change is inevitable but convergence is not. The jury is still out on this particular issue, and a conclusive verdict is not expected in the near future.

If we then return once more to our sad tale recounting the confused confrontation between elephant and sage, there is yet another moral (a particularly vital one) to be drawn when thinking about economic reform in Japan. While each separate description by itself is misleading, taken as a whole, a composite made up of each individual viewpoint is not without value. The mistake then is to read this volume with the idea that one particular author has somehow put together a correct appraisal. No individual piece has a monopoly on insight or truth, especially when we are traversing such ambiguous territory. It is rather the volume, when taken as a whole, that sheds some light on these rather shadowy regions of the Japanese economy.

NOTES

1. We must remember the limitations of a poem, let alone one designed for children. To attempt to examine an entire elephant would be a project more appropriate for a weekend's outing than a few stanzas. Besides, the propensity for self-styled sages to jump to conclusions based on partial and insufficient evidence is too well known to need any further comment.
2. Taking polar positions has long been a favourite pastime enjoyed by academic disciplines. In economics, the nineteenth century debates between the German Historical

School (see the works of Schmoller) and the rising neo-classical approach (Pareto, Walras and others on the European continent) played out a pantomime battle between specifics and generalities. Taken to the extreme, one side could only point out historical instances while the other felt free to cavalierly dismiss institutional differences.

3. 'Those to whom the King had entrusted me, observing how ill I was clad, ordered a Taylor to come next morning, and take my Measure for a Suit of Cloths. This Operater did his Office after a different Manner from those of his Trade in Europe. He first took my Altitude by a Quadrant, and then with Rule and Compasses described the Dimensions and Out-Lines of my whole Body; all which he entered upon Paper. And in six Days brought my Cloths very ill made, and quite out of Shape, by happening to mistake a Figure in the Calculations' (Swift, 1999: 126–127).

4. It is difficult to forget the Japan of the 1980s ('The Japan that Could Say "No"') lecturing the US on economic as well as moral issues. Nor should we fail to remember the thriving cottage industry of Japan experts rolling out books and articles, all of which purported to unravel the secret of those inscrutable Japanese. Meanwhile, the traditional Western approach was deftly relegated to the (Trotsky/Reagan) dustbin of history.

5. Dictatorships of whatever hue often attempt to hold back change (somehow getting the King Canute story upside down). It becomes increasingly difficult to keep control of a rapidly changing society. Predictability (and the secret police) are the chief allies of such regimes. Quite understandably information flows are severely impeded. This sets up an implicit trade-off. Information is suppressed at the cost of economic growth (fax machines, mobile phones, e-mail, the Internet remain limited). Growth, though, is required if the ruling regime is to pay off its set of key constituents that keep any generic line of dictators thriving. The inevitable collision of objectives would tend to limit the lifetime of such governments.

6. Change as necessity underlies the writing of the pre-socratic philosopher, Heraclitus. Two of his fragments adroitly encapsulate this idea. (Obviously, writing in fragments was not some fad that swept through the intelligentsia of Ancient Greece, but rather only fragments of the work of Heraclitus remain.) 'Everything flows and nothing stays' (Heraclitus quoted in Partington 1996: 333). 'You can't step twice into the same river' (Heraclitus quoted in Partington 1996: 333).

7. The feudal Japanese society stressed mutual obligations and relations between superiors and inferiors. Japan as a nation (an organism) was far more important than any individual, much in the same way that the family dominates its discrete components. Economic growth remained important, but not at the cost of any distinct disruption to the status quo. When forced, the Japanese absorbed outside influences (modernization) but then regrouped, creating updated institutions not unlike those defining the previous status quo. 'Institutions appeared to [the mercantilists] then to be everything, the free play of individuals to be but little. It is the business of the rulers to prevent there being too many producers or too few, to resist polypoly and monopoly' (Schmoller quoted in Marshall 1923: 721).

8. To be accurate, the flourishing of something resembling economic and social liberalism did not survive either the economic crises of the 1920s or the determination of the military. In addition, during the post-war period, the confrontational union movement was heavily leftist (when not starkly communistic) in its orientation. Still, this did represent an attempt to put forward a quite separate agenda (by a subgroup) that was not simply another version of the will of Japan as a nation.

9. Risk avoidance has always been one of the defining characteristics of the Japanese, moulded by Japan's own geography and demography. Though generalizations are far from perfect, different societies do seem to have different attitudes to risk taking (though it is unclear whether anyone has done serious empirical analysis of this issue).

> . . . much depends on the characters of nations, according as they partake more or less of the adventurousness, or as it is called when the intention is to blame it, the gambling spirit. This spirit is much stronger in the United States than in Great Britain, and in Great Britain than in any country of the continent. In some Continental countries the tendency is so much the reverse, that safe and quiet employment

probably yield a less average profit to the capital engaged in them than those which offer greater gains at the price of greater hazards. (Mill 1967: 414)

10. The puzzle is always how an economy will adapt to a largely unanticipated shock. Instead of experimenting with departures from tried and proven approaches, a serious shock may simply lead a nation to retreat to familiar and seemingly safer options. A clear illustration occurred in the Japanese and American reactions to the Great Depression. The US (see Wiebe 1967 and Weinstein 1968) in the first three decades of the twentieth century had seen a rise in what can best be described as corporate welfare (a privatized and often paternalistic version of the social safety net). The economic shocks of the 1930s reinforced more traditional arm's length, market contractual arrangements and shifted the welfare onus on to government. In contrast, the Japan of the 1920s was rapidly becoming more Westernized, both economically and socially. In a parallel fashion the same economic shocks moved Japan back towards a more conservative and traditional institutional structure.

11. Countries such as Russia have been less than an unqualified success. The case of China is much more ambiguous.

12. Clearly the restoration of the 1940 system did not happen by itself or even at the behest of the conservative elements still strongly entrenched after the war. It took a particular confluence of geo-political events for the US to recognize Japan's importance as an Asian surrogate (see Okimoto 1998). As just one striking instance of this transformation, Palace officials essentially reinvented the Japanese emperor with the concurrence of the US occupation forces. See the recent volume by Herbert Bix (2000) to understand the difference between the Emperor Hirohito and the post-war conservative invention.

13. At this point Noguchi and I part company. Noguchi is at pains to demonstrate the ability of the Japanese to change in sync with their economic environment. Given this objective, Noguchi is forced to conclude that there is nothing particularly Japanese about the 1940 system. Japan was in fact headed on a more Western trajectory in the 1920s. The force of circumstances created the conditions that made the 1930s military regime a more attractive alternative. For Noguchi, this represents an inherent degree of flexibility rather than a type of cultural fixity. In the absence of these cultural sunk costs, there is then no reason to assume that faced with another crisis Japan cannot once more shift gears by adopting an institutional structure more conducive to the existing economic environment.

14. The reality of a mass middle class was fading just as most of the Japanese had convincingly bought into the belief.

> Even though the shortcomings of such surveys are well known [reference is to a 1985 EPA study], their results are quoted extensively because they confirm that social and class divisions are not significant in Japan . . . The post-war economic boom was a period in which incomes rose rapidly, farmers became owner occupiers and lengthier education was made available to all, so few people in the 1980s want to be stigmatized as lower class. As the backbone of Japan is said to be its middling groups, not the parasitic rich nor the subordinate poor, the majority choose to label themselves among the safe, secure and normal middle class. (Eccleston 1989: 175–176)

The asset inflation of the late 1980s would begin to fracture this consensus, subsequently aggravated by the prolonged catatonic economy of the 1990s. In a society where the social safety net was largely privatized (a corporate responsibility), more of the population would automatically fall below the average standard of living if growth faltered and the employment machine ground to a halt. The basis for constructing an all-inclusive, middle-class society was guaranteed economic growth. Without that sustenance, the objective lost a good deal of its feasibility.

Table 1.1 Perceptions about own standard of living

	1965 (%)	1971 (%)	1977 (%)	Employed persons 1977 (%)	Farmers 1977 (%)
Lower than average	. 3.0	3.5	3.2	2.8	1.3
Slightly lower than average	17.8	16.5	14.6	13.8	9.9
Average	47.0	49.0	40.5	41.0	48.2
Slightly higher than average	27.0	27.1	36.1	37.2	36.0
Above average	5.3	3.2	5.5	5.2	4.6

Source: Ministry of Health and Welfare (1965–78).

15. There is something almost Prufrockian about many Japanese these days. At moments the country seems to be collectively despairing, to represent an ageing population much given to hand wringing.

> Though I have seen my head (grown slightly bald)
> brought in upon a platter,
> I am no prophet and here's no great matter;
> I have seen the moment of my greatness flicker,
> I have seen the eternal Footman hold my coat, and snicker,
> And in short, I was afraid.
> (Elliot 1963: 16)

16. Traditionally, Japan has been much closer to Continental Europe, particularly Germany. But those countries, as well, have felt pressure to change given what is perceived to be the new international challenge.

17. Dore has stressed the social glue of cooperation based on a system of mutual trust. The resulting saving in transaction costs has made the Japanese (in the past at least) internationally competitive. What for Dore is perhaps more important is the moral implication of labour relations and shop floor activity built upon this base. Dore was pleased to demonstrate that the search for economic efficiency need not be built upon a lessening of human civility:

> But the self-interest of best policy is not the way they naturally talk about the emphasis on quality and honestly delivering the goods on time. One hears much more about serving society . . . At any rate the Japanese economic system works on the assumption that the 'serving society' sentiments are for real. That is why the large Japanese firms where export products have become household words abroad founded their employment system on a belief in original virtue, not original sin. They base their work systems on the assumption that their workers can be trusted to be just as concerned as the managers are about conscientious testing procedures, about making sure that no faulty car is allowed to pass and damage the company's reputation for reliability abroad. (Dore 1986: 2)

18. For Dore, Japanese cooperation is predicated on a degree of trust not seen in the West. But in Dore's sense this would provide these economies with their own version of a flexible rigidity. In a parallel fashion, the individual entrepreneurial model would arise from the recognition that Western economies lack this vital element of trust. This state of imposed

19. self-reliance, ironically, might provide a greater willingness to trust outside the womb of habitual institutional comfort and thus represent greater flexibility to respond to un-anticipated events. 'The close co-operation relations between government and business have a quality apt to be missing in countries where individualistic versions of "free enter-prise" actually constitute an article of faith as well as rhetoric' (Dore 1986: 147).

19. Readers should keep in mind the importance for the Japanese of distinguishing between *tatemae* and *honne* (outside and inside face). One represents what the Japanese feel obliged to display, the other what they really feel and believe. At the present moment, most Japanese leaders feel called upon at least to talk about the need for economic reform.

20. There is a whiff of Dore wanting to protect the Japanese from their own worst (west-ernized?) instincts. This is often the problem presented by those commentators who take a strict 'Japan is different' cultural approach. Choices are attributed to culture, yet many of those same choices seem to be heavily buttressed by an intricate series of government restrictions and subsidies. At times it has been claimed that the Japanese won't eat foreign rice or shop in large discount stores. Nor supposedly would Japanese workers accept anything but long-term, secure employment. However, if such choices were purely the case, it is difficult to understand why government agencies need to erect bulwarks against potential desertion by Japanese consumers or workers. A strong argument can be made for allowing the Japanese public much more choice than they have enjoyed in the past.

21. This is strangely reminiscent of the previous financial consolidation movement in the 1930s and 40s. That programme was mandated. Although government officials are not plotting the current merger activity, it is being given more than simple official encour-agement.

22. As Ikeo points out (and Itoh agrees), this pattern of consolidation may lead to the estab-lishment of banks that are 'too big to fail'. Such a strategy would simply reprise the old convoy system while upping the ante in terms of underlying moral hazard.

23. Noel Gaston (in his discussion of Hamada's chapter) is willing to question this widely accepted characterization of the two systems. In re-examining accepted models, adopt-ing more sceptical attitudes can only be applauded. Much of what Gaston says about the two models is not without validity. But this approach still does seem to capture some vital difference between firms as they have existed in Japan and the US. In so far as this approach does pinpoint something essential, it makes an appropriate starting point for talking about the ways in which the two quite distinguishable organizations might be tending to converge.

24. One of the long-established management gurus, Rosabeth Moss Kanter (Harvard Business School), has the following analysis of the strengths that women bring to cor-porate management: 'Women get high ratings on exactly those skills needed to succeed in the global Information Age, where teamwork and partnering are so important' (quoted in Sharpe 2000: 104A4). Substituting 'Japanese' for 'women' in this quote would hardly raise even an eyebrow or two.

25. In its extreme version, government intervention is seen as inevitably dissipating market efficiency. There seems an almost ongoing tournament to justify a still lower minimum level for government activity. (Though it is wise to keep in mind the reasons for caution in advocating governmental action, precaution when taken too far can turn into pure prejudice.) There is a tendency for people to imagine their own success rests on boot-strapping skills while pointedly ignoring the government-financed hoist dragging them upwards.

26. In his comments, Colin McKenzie takes issue with this designation. No one argues that Japan did not find the post-war climate conducive to its own economic development and growth. In the decades immediately following the war, many other countries also benefited. Economic growth is not by necessity a zero sum game played between com-peting economies in some purely mercantilist manner. Whether Japan was the primary beneficiary (its rank in the league table) is another matter. Certainly post-war Japan was

rescued by the fortuitous occurrence (at least from the Japanese viewpoint) of the Korean, Cold and Vietnam Wars. Japan's position as America's Asian surrogate assisted its record of growth and prosperity.

REFERENCES

Abegglen, James C. and Geoffrey G. Stalk (1982), *Kaisha, the Japanese Corporation*, New York: Basic Books.
Aoki, Masahiko (1990), 'Toward an Economic Model of the Japanese Firm', *Journal of Economic Literature*, **28**(1): 1–27.
Bix, Herbert P. (2000), *Hirohito and the Making of Modern Japan*, New York: HarperCollins.
Dore, Ronald (1986), *Flexible Rigidities*, London: Athlone Press.
Eccleston, Bernard (1989), *State and Society in Post-War Japan*, Oxford: Polity Press.
Elliot, Thomas S. (1963), *Collected Poems 1909–1962*, London: Faber and Faber.
Marshall, Alfred (1923), *Industry and Trade*, London: Macmillan and Co.
Mill, John Stuart (1967), *Principles of Political Economy*, New York: Augustus M. Kelley.
Noguchi, Yukio (1998), 'The 1940 System: Japan under the Wartime Economy', *American Economic Review Papers and Proceedings*, **88**(2): 404–8.
Okimoto, Daniel I. (1998), 'Theoretical Approaches to the Japan–America Security Alliance', in Craig Freedman (ed.), *Japanese Economic Policy Reconsidered*, Cheltenham UK: Edward Elgar, pp. 46–81.
Partington, Angela (1996), 'Heraclitus', *The Oxford Dictionary of Quotations*, Oxford: Oxford University Press, p. 333.
Saxe, John Godfrey (1961), 'The Blind Men and the Elephant', in Louis Untermeyer (ed.), *The Golden Treasury of Poetry*, Glasgow: Collins.
Sharpe, Rochelle (2000), 'As Leaders, Women Rule', *Business Week*, 27 November, pp. 104A2–104A11.
Swift, Jonathan (1999), *Gulliver's Travels*, London: Longman.
Weinstein, James (1968), *The Corporate Ideal in the Liberal State 1900–1918*, Boston: Beacon Press.
Wiebe, Robert H. (1967), *The Search for Order 1877–1920*, New York: Hill and Wang.

PART I

Necessary Change or Shameless Surrender? Economic Reform in Japan

Will you, won't you, will you, won't you, won't you join the dance?
Alice's Adventures in Wonderland, Lewis Carroll

2. Japan's new dawn approaches

Mikio Wakatsuki

JAPAN'S LOST DECADE

Thirty-five years after opening its doors to the world, Japan entered the 20th century with high hopes of joining the ranks of the world's great powers. Both the aspirations and the dedication of Japan's elite in those days were described as 'Looking up at white clouds over the hill'. This is also the title of a best-selling book by the well-known author, the late Ryotaro Shiba. Despite a disastrous stumble along the way due to imperialistic ambitions, most of the 20th century was, at least for Japan, a time of brilliant success and prosperity. The last ten years of that century, however, became a period of disillusionment and despondency, now dubbed Japan's 'lost decade'. Much like a classical Greek tragedy, national hubris inevitably brought about its own devastation.

The protracted slump, which followed the bursting of the 'bubble economy' of the late 1980s, had two main causes. The first was a complacent belief that Japan's economy was inherently so strong, that it was in effect self-healing. No matter how accurately inflicted, even the sharpest wound could not seriously impede economic progress. The second was a failure to recognise the implications of a global paradigm shift, which coincided, approximately, with the economic bubble bursting. Since the fall of the Berlin Wall, the process of globalisation has accelerated, driven by the information revolution. Japan, however, was slow to recognise this groundswell of change in the global economy. It had become a prisoner of the past success of its own economic model.

Of course, Japan has not sat idly by during the past decade. The government initiated several fiscal packages amounting to ¥120 trillion in total, larger than the nominal GDP of Canada. The Bank of Japan, for its part, lowered its official discount rate from 6 to 0.5 per cent over the decade and has been pursuing a 'zero interest rate policy' for the past 18 months. Thanks to these efforts, the economy showed signs of recovery from time to time, but each recovery was short-lived. The reason why these extraordinarily large doses were not effective is rather obvious in retrospect: they were based on gradualism or, more bluntly, they were implemented for the sake of procrastination rather than revitalisation.

Money was spent largely on public works, to bolster sagging demand and employment. This basically cushioned the adverse impact of the bursting of the bubble economy. Increased public works expenditure absorbed some of the excess workers in manufacturing industries and moderated the decline in real estate prices. Extremely low interest rates kept many virtually bankrupt firms alive. These policies made it possible to avoid drastic measures such as the swift writing off of bad loans, an intensive restructuring of firms, sweeping de-regulation or a massive lay-off of workers. Arguably, they had one positive side effect: gradualism meant no sharp increase in unemployment and hence little social unrest and resentment; no widening of income inequality and no increase in crime. But it was too costly a trade-off. In short, policies have been too focused on maintaining economic and political stability and insufficiently reform minded.

JAPANESE POLITICS IN TRANSITION

Once Japan realised that globalisation is an irreversible process, it began belated efforts to adapt itself to this new paradigm. An internal sense of crisis drove the reform process. Without appreciable change, Japan would be left behind by global progress, which meant being lumbered with an economy gradually losing its vigour. Among other factors, the future continues to generate grave concern because of rising job insecurity, a huge fiscal deficit created by spending on the preservation of outdated industries, and an ageing Japanese society.

The challenge Japan faced in the 1990s was daunting, requiring strong political leadership. Unfortunately, at this juncture Japanese politics was itself in transition. Strong leaders were hard to find. When the Liberal Democratic Party lost control of the Diet in 1993 and relinquished its reign of 38 years, hopes rose that the new Prime Minister, Hosokawa, and his coalition government would overhaul the old regime. But those hopes quickly faded as he resigned because of an old scandal.

Mr Hosokawa was succeeded by a strange coalition government of socialists and conservatives under the socialist Prime Minister Murayama, which served only to symbolise the confusion of this transitory period in Japanese politics. Such an obvious marriage of convenience could not last long. Inevitably, it arrived at a stalemate. The fall of the Murayama government clearly underscored the fact that makeshift politics were not adequate to the complex task of reforming Japan.

Mr Hashimoto came to power in 1996 and announced that his govern-ment would undertake six reform programmes which included fiscal restructuring, financial reform, and an overhaul of the administrative system, as well as other pressing issues. His attempt to take a more radical approach, requiring Japan quickly to adapt to new global standards, was in itself quite legitimate and appropriate. Unfortunately it was overly ambi-tious and ill conceived, having been thrown together far too hastily.

His fiscal reform programme focused on drastically reducing the fiscal deficit. This involved raising the consumption tax from 3 to 5 per cent, abolishing a special income tax cut, increasing medical insurance contri-butions and curtailing investment in public works. Such a strong dose of fiscal rectitude was more than the still fragile and convalescent economy could swallow. By making the means an end in itself, what was meant merely to be fiscal dieting turned into a particularly virulent form of fiscal anorexia.

The Prime Minister's other initiative, a financial reform plan, dubbed 'Japan's big bang', was intended to liberalise the financial industry by lifting the existing barriers between banks, securities houses and insurance com-panies. Mr Hashimoto engineered sweeping changes involving the modern-isation of tax codes, legal procedures and accounting systems under the slogan 'free, fair, global'. The same spirit of reform made a stricter appli-cation of the capital adequacy criteria, one that would trigger a 'prompt corrective action' scheme, seem momentarily feasible. But the weak banking system, saddled as it was with mounting bad loans, reacted defen-sively to these measures, cutting lending to such an extent that it precipi-tated a severe credit crunch.

The Asian currency crisis, which originated in Thailand in May 1997, further exacerbated an already fragile situation. An unprecedented series of bankruptcies involving several major financial institutions created a sense of deep anxiety, compounded by a well-grounded fear of an imminent deflationary economic spiral. Mr Hashimoto was forced to abandon his fiscal reform plan towards the end of FY 1998 and, soon afterward, his pre-miership.

The mission of Mr Obuchi, who relieved Mr Hashimoto, was quite clear: pull the economy out of its downward deflationary spiral. Pragmatism characterised the way in which the new Prime Minister dealt with this problem. His priority was clearly economic recovery, which meant shelving other objectives for the time being. He encapsulated his intention by using the slogan, 'You can't chase two rabbits at once.' Mr Obuchi suspended the newly enacted 'Fiscal Reform and Consolidation Law'. Instead, he pro-duced another large fiscal package consisting of ¥18 trillion in expenditure and ¥9 trillion in tax cuts, the largest fiscal stimulus ever formulated. Plans to resuscitate and reform the financial system, backed by an infusion of ¥60 trillion, were quickly put in place. This flow of public money strengthened the capital base of the banking sector. In accordance with this policy, several ailing banks were 'nationalised' and subsequently sold to private entrepreneurs, including an expatriate consortium. An additional ¥20 trillion in government credit guarantees to small and medium-sized companies served to ease the credit crunch.

Mr Obuchi's all-out efforts to cope with the crisis were effective: apprehension subsided and confidence was restored. By the beginning of the year 2000, the economy was on a gradual recovery path, thanks to a considerable increase in public works and a surge in exports. Mr Obuchi's unexpected demise on the verge of this economic upturn left a great deal of sorrow. It also left a great deal of necessary reform work undone. The current government must follow up Mr Obuchi's policy line if it is to solidify Japan's still wobbly recovery. The main priority should be to resume the suspended efforts at reform. This and any future government must usher a Japan filled with vigour and dynamism into the new century. This involves reconstructing its currently debt-ridden public finances before Japan's demographics deteriorate much further.

Mr Obuchi's passing away also coincided with the retirement of his mentor, Mr Takeshita, as well as several other famous old-timers. In a way, this should symbolise the end of an era of fiscal pork barrelling, an acknowledged hallmark of the high growth days. All of this augurs a forthcoming major overhaul of Japanese politics.

What Japan has come to perceive, during the slow process of reform, is an increased blurring of the distinction between domestic and international problems. What until now have been regarded as domestic issues can no longer be dealt with from a purely domestic standpoint. In this new era of globalisation, there are few purely domestic issues any more. This means that Japan needs a different type of politician, one with the ability to see and understand matters from a global viewpoint. A group of prime ministerial advisers described this ability as 'global literacy', which includes a mastery of IT tools (such as the Internet) and of English, as the prevailing lingua franca.

Fortunately, a host of young politicians, who are internationally well exposed and who are proficient in this lingua franca, have risen to important political posts. This new breed, with their 'global literacy', have already played an active role in designing and implementing financial reconstruction programmes. Though they are still relatively few in number, this younger generation of politicians will make increasingly important contributions emphasising the need for more articulate communication with the rest of the world.

ECONOMIC REFORM IN PROGRESS

In the economic arena, the need for change is even more acute. Japan's once proud and dominant manufacturing sector now faces competition both from a reinvigorated industrial America and from the rest of Asia, which is beginning to gain a technological edge. The IT and financial industries of America are currently far more advanced and enjoy a comfortable lead over their rivals. If Japan is to catch up, the need for liberalisation and deregulation is quite apparent. Heavily protected and regulated industries such as banking and agriculture have turned out to be a burden on those industries exposed to fierce international competition. The out-dated regulation of the telecom industry, for instance, has been a serious handicap in expanding the new frontier of Japan's IT-related business.

In the 1980s, Japan was proud to say, 'There are three ways of doing things: the right way, the wrong way and the Japanese way.' Now in the 1990s, Japan is being told 'There are only two ways of doing things: the American way and the wrong way.'

American triumphalism apart, there is no doubt that Japan should adapt itself to the new paradigm defined by the principles of free markets, deregulation and privatisation. These principles are essentially American. Japanese businesses also have to accept the need for more transparency, more self-responsibility and an increased emphasis on profitability and corporate governance, all of which are part of the 'American way'.

But the memory of past success is persistent and the resistance to change is ingrained. Successful reform requires more than the force of internal necessity driven by a sense of crisis. To achieve a breakthrough, change must stem from some external force, which would call on Japan to meet a more globally acceptable code of conduct. The result would be similar to what Thomas Friedman of the *New York Times* recently termed 'globalution' (a portmanteau word combining 'globalisation' and 'revolution') or a revolutionary process generated by outside pressure. In essence, when internal forces are lacking, only external shocks can effectively initiate change as well as supplying the requisite discipline to regulate domestic market practices.

Foreign holdings of shares currently traded on the Tokyo Stock Exchange increased from 4 per cent of the total to roughly 10 per cent during the 1990s, forming a vanguard movement in the Japanese version of 'globalution'. By 1999, 46 per cent of Sony's stock was in foreign hands. Likewise, 30 per cent of Hitachi, 25 per cent of Nomura Securities and 19 per cent of Honda belonged to overseas investors. Responding to this change, Japanese firms are placing an increasing emphasis on ROE ('Return on Equity'). Today, the business community accepts the concept of shareholder value as an embedded principle.

Before the 1990s, the concept of corporate governance was barely recognised in Japan. 'Main banks' used to oversee corporate discipline. With
banks having largely relinquished this role, some alternative form of corporate governance is now a necessity for many Japanese firms. Some have
co-opted their outside board members into management roles. Others have
strengthened the roles played by auditors and CPAs. Credit worthiness, previously distorted by the so-called 'Japan premium', is now determined to
an increasing degree by more stringent disclosure standards. Japanese firms
now regard transparency, not with suspicion, but as something that
enhances confidence and trust in management.

The dismantling of Japan Inc. is even more profound. The ties of *keiretsu*
groups are loosening or even disappearing. As part of this trend, there has
been a reduction in cross-shareholdings. The recent merger of the
Sumitomo and Sakura banks, for instance, surprised many analysts.
Previously, each bank had been the mainstay of very prestigious, and quite
distinct, *keiretsu* groups. It brought home the fact that given globalised
competition, the subsequent race for survival ruthlessly eliminates taboos
and intrudes upon heretofore sacrosanct areas. The merger of these rival
'main banks' subsequently triggered further mergers both across and
within their associated groups.

The Japanese employment system is also undergoing far-reaching
change. In the face of a protracted slump and a heightened level of competition, lifetime employment and the seniority system cannot be kept
intact. As might be expected, firms are encouraging greater flexibility in
employment choices and adopting incentive/merit-oriented systems.
Companies are still mindful of the advantages of long-term employment
policies, such as the ability to invest more in training workers who maintain a long-term perspective. The current corporate challenge is to find an
appropriate compromise between increasing the use of incentive contracts
to create an added source of flexibility and relying on the more traditional
advantages that flow from a system of job security. Among current
workers, younger employees tend to prefer flexibility and mobility to being
tied to life-long jobs. Some would voluntarily opt for term-contract
employment augmented by incentive bonuses. In recent years, an increasing number of graduates from top-rated universities have been applying
for jobs in foreign firms, attracted by their more merit-cratic systems,
which promise greater rewards in exchange for greater risks. A lack of job
security used to cause Japanese graduates to shy away from working for
foreign firms. Today, staying with one company for a long time is no
longer regarded as a virtue. 'Headhunting' is finally becoming commonplace.

THE SEARCH FOR A NEW JAPANESE MODEL

Most of these changes were unthinkable a decade ago. People realise now that such changes are necessary, even inevitable. They still cannot help but feel uneasy that the evolving changes represent a blunt replacement by American practices of more accustomed Japanese methods. Such uneasiness is, in part, a reflection of the type of apprehension that attaches to any sudden change in the social order. More profoundly, it is rooted in the angst reflected by a loss of national identity and equally a fundamental discomfort with the triumphant and unfettered capitalism characteristic of the US system. Somehow, people feel that Japan's traditional values should not be dismissed out of hand.

To find a fair balance between a society based on efficient incentives and one that is more focused on equity is a crucial and contentious issue. Many people recognise the need for more incentives and competition in the Japanese system, but not to the extent that these incentives also foster greed. They support the principle of self-responsibility, but also the necessity of an appropriate safety net for the weaker members of society.

Business leaders are searching for a middle ground. Japan's Association of Corporate Executives has consistently been an ardent supporter of reform and deregulation. It has championed a system of corporate governance that would match global standards. More recently, the Association has been willing to consider the interests of longer-term stakeholders, seeking a fair balance of these concerns with the exigencies of the shorter-term returns that markets prize most. An increasingly urgent search for an appropriate model that suits Japanese culture and society underlies these tensions.

In 1999, a quality Japanese magazine carried an interesting polemic between Mr Okuda of Toyota Co. and Mr Miyauchi of Orix Corp. Both are well-known, articulate and outspoken business leaders in Japan. Mr Okuda's article was somewhat sensationally titled, by the editor, 'Managers Who Sack Workers Should Commit Harakiri'. By contrast, Mr Miyauchi's defiantly captioned his article 'Companies that Stick to a No-Lay-Off Policy Will Sink Like the Titanic'. Though the two titles may appear provocative, readers find that in spite of Mr Miyauchi's strong words, Orix has never actually had to lay off any workers, thanks to deft and flexible management combined with very loyal, hard-working employees. Toyota, on the other hand, tightly secures the employment of its regular workforce by the versatile use of seasonal and term-contract workers.

Notwithstanding these seemingly contrasting management philosophies, the end results do not seem very far apart. This suggests that a successful new Japanese management style would aim to combine a consideration for job security with management flexibility. Such an approach would have more respect for human values than the profit-oriented American model, but still be in touch with the reality of global competition.

PROBLEMS AWAITING THE NEW CENTURY

As we have seen, the 1990s were a period of muddling through, one of trial and error, hesitant reform and confused back-pedalling. Still, despite lacking any clear direction, Japan today bears little resemblance to the Japan of ten years ago. It has been a painful metamorphosis and something of a pathetic retreat from the successful past. Unlike 100 years ago, Japan is entering the new century, not with high hopes and innocent optimism, but only with a brave spirit that is ready to take on a new challenge. What awaits Japan in the new century is not a white cloud rising over the hill, but difficult problems of its own making: an ageing society and a huge government debt.

One of the crucial questions in considering Japan's future course is its growth potential. According to a survey conducted by the Economic Planning Agency, the expected rate of growth that Japanese business projects over a five-year period declined from 3.6 per cent in 1990 to 1.5 per cent in 2000. This can be linked to the loss of confidence that naturally follows any prolonged slump. However, it also reflects the uncertainty surrounding the clear possibility that Japan will have to cope with a shrinking labour force in the future.

Japan's current birth rate is 1.39 per woman (of child-bearing age), among the lowest in the world. Its population will reach its peak around 2005 and will then start to decrease. If the present birth rate is maintained, the population will halve by the end of the 21st century. The labour force will then inexorably shrink. For another decade or so, an extension of the retirement age combined with increased female participation in the labour market will keep the total labour force growing. But during the period 2000–2025, the annual average contribution of labour to growth potential is estimated to become slightly negative. The discussion of a new immigration policy is scheduled, but the probable implementation of any new plan will occur only at a very gradual pace.

The increase in total factor productivity (TFP), promoted by IT and other technological advances, is expected to more than offset the predicted negative contribution by labour. This should maintain the growth potential at around 2.5–3.0 per cent for the next 25 years. The *Keidanren* (Japan's business federation) projects that the TFP economic growth contribution for the next quarter century will average 1.5 per cent. Together with a capital contribution of 1.5 per cent and a labour contribution of -0.3 per cent, growth potential will be limited to 2.7 per cent.

Unfortunately, Japan's fiscal situation is very bleak. The deficit in FY 1999 reached 10 per cent in terms of nominal GDP, the worst of any of the G-7 nations. Government debt totalled ¥600 trillion, equivalent to 120 per cent of nominal GDP. One relief is that domestic savings finance these deficits. Nevertheless, the restoration of fiscal balance over the medium to long term is of crucial importance if Japan is to prepare adequately for the ageing of its population. Economic recovery will provide a good opportunity to redress this fiscal imbalance. Such an opportunity must not be ignored.

The problem requires administrative reform, which can make Japan's government smaller and more efficient. Privatisation balanced with the outsourcing of government functions should be promoted. Measures to contain public works expenditure, such as using private finance initiatives, need to be encouraged. The social security system has to be reformed by balancing benefits against contributions. Such reformation needs to be supplemented by some type of limited private pension scheme. The revenue base also needs to be strengthened; an increase in the consumption tax is the most likely candidate. Any comprehensive fiscal overhaul has to be phased in to avoid serious damage to economic growth.

For all of these difficult problems that lie ahead, the best prescription must be the resumption of healthy growth. The restoration of confidence will make people more bullish, encouraging them to start investing again. This in turn will raise Japan's growth potential. Keeping this in mind, let me now turn to the more immediate outlook.

THE NEW DAWN APPROACHES

The economy is headed, at last, towards a self-sustaining recovery. Besides the continued growth of exports and public works expenditure, private fixed investment has come out of the doldrums and is slowly contributing to the economic upturn. Private consumption still lags, but with unemployment no longer growing, consumer confidence is likely to improve, bringing with it the resumption of steady spending. With considerable progress in overhauling the old regime and adapting a more global paradigm, Japan approaches a new economic dawn.

The first ray of hope lies in ongoing technological breakthroughs. In Japan, as in many other countries including Australia, the IT revolution is generating a significant amount of change. Already, its impact has extended to many sectors of the economy. One-third of Japan's households had PCs and 11 per cent of them were Internet connected, as of 1999. The e-commerce market is expected to reach ¥20 trillion this year starting from nearly zero only three years ago. IT-related industries are becoming the major driving force of economic activity. Their contribution amounted to about 80 per cent of total growth in 1999. IT-related investment accounted for 34.4 per cent of total private fixed investment and reached ¥24.2 trillion in 1999.

Following the US example, IT fever is generating a new wave of entrepreneurial activity. Success stories of the new 'cyber-rich' are encouraging a rush of start-ups. Though the US has built a formidable lead in this newly created frontier, Japan hopes to catch up quickly in many areas by developing more products and applications tailored to the needs of the IT-related mass market. The striking success of 'iMode' digital mobile phones, which provide direct access to the Internet without the need for a PC, has encouraged Japanese scientists and engineers to expand their applied research programmes. They are now confident that more and better products will soon be in the pipeline.

The IT revolution is expediting the shift of economic resources from outdated sectors to more dynamic ones. Inevitably, some outdated sectors will be forced to the wall, but others through a judicious application of IT are trying hard to rejuvenate themselves. The government is belatedly making efforts to facilitate the IT revolution, stepping up deregulation and encouraging more efficient high speed bands.

Another silver lining is the positive role played by foreign capital and management. The Japanese economy has long been known for its homogeneity (if not absolute closedness) and the presence of foreign business has been relatively small. There was a marked imbalance between outgoing and incoming direct investments. The former was roughly 15–20 times greater than the latter. The enhanced visibility and influence of foreign firms in a growing number of sectors is starting to change the landscape of the Japanese economy. In 1999, FDI reached ¥1.4 trillion, 3.4 times more than the previous year. Such conspicuous foreign inroads are partly due to the relative weakness of Japanese firms. They are forced, out of necessity, to accept foreign participation in their management. Some are taken over by foreign companies in the form of a bail-out. In addition, with bureaucrats being criticised for their interventionist policy stance, political and administrative resistance has receded considerably. Foreign investors are now enticed to Japan by tax and other incentives. There is hardly any chauvinistic resistance to acquisitions by and alliances with foreign companies, which are no longer considered to be something extra-ordinary.

Areas of foreign inroads range from the financial sector to car manufacturing. Very few foresaw that the day would come when foreign CEOs would head major carmakers such as Mazda and Nissan. Although as of yet without foreign leadership, Mitsubishi Motors has also surrendered control of its shares to overseas investors, namely the Daimler/Chrysler group. More noteworthy is the fact that people generally accept this creeping infiltration of heterogeneity into the Japanese business community as something positive, providing new stimuli and competition, as well as job opportunities.

The third element bringing dynamism to Japan is a new Asia that has emerged since the Asian currency crisis. Through its superior IT and financial industries, the US managed to strengthen its economic hegemony. This allowed the US to dominate the new global paradigm that emerged, following the end of the Cold War. Forming a European Union with a single market and currency was the European response to this new American challenge. In a parallel fashion, Japan chose to strengthen its ties with Asia, which starting in the early 1990s had become a major world growth centre. It was fortunate for Japan that in 1989 Mr Hawke, the then Australian Prime Minister, took the initiative of establishing APEC. Seizing this opportunity, Japan cooperated closely with Australia to promote this regional economic forum. The aim has been to foster free trade in the Asian-Pacific area.

With the outbreak of the Asian currency and economic crisis, Japan's assumption that it would somehow float effortlessly on a river of Asian growth appeared shaken. The crisis confirmed that Japan and many other Asian countries are already deeply interdependent. Japan's economic weakness affects Asian economies, and weakness in the region must have a serious negative impact on Japan. Recognising the need to restore Asian economic vitality, Japan provided substantial economic and financial assistance.

In the aftermath of the currency crisis, solidarity and cooperation between Japan and other Asian countries appear to have strengthened. Recently, major Asian countries agreed to currency swap arrangements, with further monetary cooperation under discussion. The feasibility of free trade and investment agreements is being studied. Potential mutual benefits are leading Japan and its neighbours to make wider use of the yen in intra-regional trade and investment. Since the crisis, economic ties have strengthened. There are now more horizontal trade relations, especially in the telecommunications industry and in IT-related industries, including the manufacturing of PCs, mobile phones and other electronic products.

The trend of 'Asian fusion' is not confined to economic interdependence. In spite of being frowned upon in some quarters, Japanese pop-culture is widely accepted (even loved) throughout the Asia-Pacific region. Pokemon and Hello Kitty fascinate kids. Japanese fashion, pop music, comics, animation-movies and the new Play Station captivate teenagers. This cultural phenomenon is not one-way: Japan's art world has woken up to the rest of Asia. Contemporary art collections from Korea and China attract large crowds in Japan. Australian and Korean movies have a large and enthusiastic following. This cultural confluence will further enhance a growing sense of solidarity in the region and lead to greater Asian integration.

The strong recovery of the Asian economies will infuse a new vigour into the Japanese economy that, in turn, will make the Asian recovery more secure and sustainable. With the coming of a new global paradigm, Japan can no longer compete alone against a more united Europe and even less so against the mighty US. Only enhanced regional cooperation will make the whole Asia-Pacific region, including Japan, respected as one of the three pillars of the 21st century's global economy.

3.   Reform? The dubious benefits of marketisation

Ronald Dore

REFORM OR SURRENDER?

'Can the Japanese change?', the title of our Conference asks. There is a prior question. *Should* the Japanese change and, if so, is it, as the title seems to suggest, *themselves* that they should change (getting 'born again' perhaps). Or is 'change' meant to be a transitive verb, in which case what is it about their society that they should change?

I heard from an American friend the other day that he had recently met a leading light among Japanese reformers and mentioned me. 'Oh, yes, we know Dore,' said his friend. 'He's pro-Japanese.' By which he apparently meant that Dore's views of Japan were so coloured with sentiment rather than with hard analytical rationality that they were to be automatically discounted. The trouble with most of such reformers is that they rarely make explicit what *their* sentiments are (the values, the political objectives) to which *their* rationality is directed. Usually the implicit goals, the purposes for which they want to change Japan, are something like enhancing national competitiveness or maximising GNP growth without, usually, much concern for the distribution of the benefits of that growth. They advance these goals often (even) without much understanding of how their slogan-formulated demands to deregulate this and *ristora* that will actually contribute to growth. For my part, I suppose, the yardstick I would apply to potential change is whether it will make Japan a better society for the Japanese (more especially the sort of Japanese who are my friends) to live in. Of course I recognise that that includes having a rate of growth which makes its citizens feel satisfied, as well as social and economic systems which produce more cooperation than conflict and which allow people to lead fulfilled, not anxious, lives.

The simple point I want to make is that one's view of what aspects of Japanese society and economy ought to be changed will vary according to one's political and social values. So let me start by making my own wish list. The sort of changes I would like to see include:

- More frank and open debate and less timidity in the mainline press (though I would not break the price cartel among the major newspapers that allows them to be so employment-creatively inefficient by, say, British standards). Habits of cooperation, and social devices intended to avoid conflict and confrontation, may help keep the peace and spare people's feelings. They are useful in generating compromises between conflicting interests which all parties, even those with less bargaining power, can consider fair and reasonable. But, as our jokes about 'political correctness' acknowledge, they can also produce a lot of hypocrisy, dishonesty and obfuscation. Japan could do with a bit more plain speaking.
- Less corrupt use of public power for private purposes on the part of politicians (though I am not convinced that more democracy, Britishstyle, with politicians having more and bureaucrats less power, would help very much to bring this about).
- A more determined attempt to eradicate, rather than to tolerate and contain, the fringe gangster forces in Japanese society (*sokaiya*, *yakuza*, etc.).
- More arm's-length relations and less cosy collusion in areas where it is necessary (between professional auditors and the firms whose accounts they audit, for example).
- Deregulation, not across the board, but in those cases where it is necessary to attack the privileges of 'fat cats' who might quite reasonably be expected to exert themselves more on behalf of consumers and expose themselves to competition from newcomers.
- Less of the wrong kind of nationalism. The sense of belonging to a national community, which sustains cooperation within industries, makes possible inclusive and redistributive educational and social welfare systems, which almost by definition, entails xenophobia. That xenophobia, while quite harmlessly defensive when employed by what is conventionally defined as the political left, can become nastily aggressive and take the form of military fantasies on the right (the Ishiwara Shintaro right, for example). It can also become pretty despicable when it involves the passionate, or just irritable, defence of everything in Japan's past (the people who insist that Japan has nothing much to apologise for, even over Nanking, for example). However, I find almost equally unsympathetic their opponents who insist on apologising at every turn. These apologists are so full of self-righteousness that they cannot admit to themselves even the possibility that if they were adult Japanese in November 1941, they too, like 97? 98? per cent of their countrymen, would have thought that Japan no longer had any honourable course except to

go to war with the United States (however doom-laden such a course might be).

- More explicit recognition of how the egalitarian, 'straitjacketing' uniformity of the traditional educational system really helped the bottom half of the ability range to gain self-respect and to play a useful role in society. The clear danger is that the individuality-promoting reforms (greater curricular freedom, parental choice of school, etc.) are likely to be at the expense of that concern with the bottom half of the learning-ability spectrum.

Who knows what the new Prime Minister, Mr Mori, had in mind when he said, in his acceptance speech (April 2000), 'the system and the ways of thinking which for fifty years have supported Japan's astonishing development have now become inappropriate for the world we live in'.[1] Like his predecessor, who used to say much the same thing, especially and most forcefully when he was in America telling Americans about Japan's earnest desire to become just like them, Mr Mori is above average for Japanese politicians in his capacity for sticking to vague generalities. If pressed, he might well have included education in his agenda, but in the sense of pressing on ever faster with the individualising tendencies about which I have just been expressing cautious doubts. It would almost certainly have included the whole complex of the so-called *Nihonteki Keiei* (Japanese-style management), the trading patterns and other related features of the Japanese economic system.

Let me start by giving you my version of the nature of that system. My characterisation of it derives from my own experience of living under Anglo-Saxon capitalism (if I can use Michel Albert's term for the system in Britain, the US, Canada, Australia and New Zealand) over the last 20 years of its transition from a mixed economy to a fully marketised economy. By mixed economy I mean not only, as in the conventional definition, an economy with a mixture of public and private ownership. I also extend the definition to include an economy in which it is generally recognised that people work for mixed motives, including wanting to do something socially useful as well as make private gains. This approach has been increasingly overwhelmed by a strict embrace of market incentives, the belief that cash, and the fear of being deprived of cash, are the only reliable means of stopping people from, to use the economists' jargon phrase, shirking (from becoming lazy time-servers). Both the main British parties now share the belief that only competition for private profits can bring us an efficient train service, cheap electricity or safe nuclear fuel. Performance-related pay has been spread throughout the public service. The academic marketplace gets more like a prize-bull or a footballer market every day. And, in industry, there is an ever-heavier reliance on stock options, rather than fixed salaries, to remunerate senior executives.

JAPAN AS A LESS MARKETISED SOCIETY

So my simple, encapsulated characterisation of Japan is that it is a less marketised society (less marketised than Britain ever was in the corporatist 1970s, or indeed has ever been in the whole of the 19th century). What do I mean by this statement?

Let us start with labour markets. For executive talent there just is no labour market in Japan (no headhunters luring managerial supermen with attractive packages of options, pensions and bonuses). Only a growing number of foreign firms provide an exception to this rule (in the financial sector this has become by no means an insignificant exception). Top managers constitute the boards of major Japanese corporations, mostly appointed after a lifetime of working for the firm. The president, appointed from among these board members, receives a salary that represents the highest rank of an incremental pay structure. He would have started his way up this ladder 40 years earlier when he was recruited as a raw graduate (just as used to be the case in the British civil service before it started recruiting permanent secretaries from the market). After four years, the president will have the major say in appointing his successor. He will then move on to become the chairman and four years later a senior adviser.

Lower down the occupational scale, and especially in the service sector, there is more movement from firm to firm, and somewhat more direct influence of market forces (the supply and demand for skills) on pay levels. But even in small firms there remains a strong propensity towards long tenures, with wage adjustments depending primarily on the firm's ability to pay. In larger firms with enterprise unions, even manual workers have an employment system similar to that of their managers (an unwritten but effective guarantee of employment to retirement, a guarantee only broken by generous early retirement packages). They also have a similar internal promotion system which mixes seniority and performance criteria. Economists, who are uncomfortable if they don't see markets everywhere, like to say that Japan has internal labour markets. But an internal labour *market* usually implies that although the competition for vacancies is confined to existing employees, there is still competition, followed, when an appointment is made, by a process of recontracting (bargaining over the appropriate wage for the job). But that is not what happens in Japan. People are 'posted' by the personnel department from one job to another, in almost exactly the same way as people are posted to jobs in the British army or diplomatic corps. If the posting changes their salary, it does so according to the rules of the pay system. The so-called internal labour market is internal all right, but not really a market.

All this tends to give the employees of a Matsushita or a Sharp a sense of their relation to their firm as being a bit like regimental loyalty in the British army. The board members (typically there are a lot of them) represent some 15 per cent of all Japan's male employees between the ages of 50 and 54. They are more likely to see themselves as the elders of an enterprise community, rather than as the agents of shareholder principals. Though employees at the top of the employment hierarchy, they are still employees (of the company seen as a kind of transcendental entity). This is a long way from the notion of the company as a network of contracts. One indicator of the difference this makes: in annual (the so-called spring offensive) wage negotiations, a manager who talks down the union's demand from 4 to 2 per cent knows that this is likely to mean that his own pay will go up by only 2 per cent as well. Again, this is much like civil service pay negotiations in Britain.

How can it be that managers have so little sense of being the agents of shareholder principals, despite Japanese law giving shareholders not such very different powers over the firm than does English law? The answer lies in the cross-shareholding system, which gives most large firms 'stable shareholders' who can provide a safe guarantee against the possibility of a hostile takeover.

The trading of a relatively small proportion of outstanding shares sets share prices (by securities companies, by individual speculators and, increasingly in recent years, by foreign pension and mutual funds which now have some 14 per cent of the market). More than half the equity is locked up in what one might call relational as opposed to arm's-length shareholding patterns. Japanese firms have up to 60 or 70 per cent of their shares in the hands of either:

- the banks with whom they do their loan business;
- the insurance companies with whom they do their insurance business; or
- other industrial and commercial companies with whom they do a lot of their trading or have joint ventures.

With these last mentioned, as with their banks, a good deal of their shareholding is on a reciprocal basis (Hitachi owns several million Nissan shares and vice versa). Once again, there is less dependence on market exchange, more emphasis on relations. The stock market does not act as a market for corporate control. Agreed mergers do take place, but the cultural antipathy towards the idea of buying and selling what are seen as communities is reinforced by the assurance that stable shareholders will rally to the defence of a given corporation should anyone attempt a takeover.

RELATIONAL TRADING

So that is one, and the most crucial, way in which Japan distinguishes itself as less marketist than, say, Britain; the nature of the firm and the self-perceptions and objectives of managers. I shall skip lightly over the other salient characteristics of Japan as an economy, by just picking out three:

- the pattern of relational trading, that is to say, long-term patterns of inter-firm cooperation that can survive considerable changes in market conditions (main banks and the firms that they have a special relationship with, for instance, or the case of automobile firms and their suppliers);
- the balance between cooperation and competition which everywhere characterises market competitors (a greater tilt than elsewhere towards cooperation, largely through strong industry associations);
- a strong role for government, partly in a developmental role (all the winner picking, selective subsidies, promotion of research clubs and so on of industrial policy), but just as importantly in a sort of umpire role (resolving distributional conflicts of interest, largely in negotiation with the industry associations), in much the same spirit as the army of industry regulators which has grown up in Britain, but with much of the regulating being done in Japan by informal administrative guidance.

I used the term 'relational trading' as opposed to 'arm's length contractual trading'. 'Relational banking' is another familiar term. One could talk of employment patterns as relational as opposed to arm's length contractual employment. In the same sense, one can talk of Japan as having relational regulation.

This wide applicability of the term 'relational' gives a clue to the *systemness* of the economy. One thing that holds it stably together is what one might call 'motivational consistency'. Similar behavioural dispositions are called for in a variety of situations:

- primarily the acceptance of certain basic obligations imposed on one as a member of Japanese society;

- secondarily, the willingness to take on further obligations by entering into long-term commitments which seriously limit one's options (to shift to another employer, another supplier, another bank).

Another mechanism that makes it a system is, of course, institutional inter-lock, i.e. institutional complementarity. You couldn't expect to maintain a lifetime employment system, for instance, if you did not have the cross-shareholding system suppressing takeovers.

THE SOURING OF THE SYSTEM

So much for the nature of the system, the system which until the 1990s received so much praise, so much discussion in America's business schools, as the secret behind Japan's success. Its capacity for long-term investment and cooperative synergies were said to be responsible for growth rates, at 4–5 per cent in the 1980s, which were double what the short-termist, ruth-lessly competitive Anglo-Saxon economies could manage. 'Every American weakness,' wrote an American banker, was seen to mirror a Japanese strength: the twelve-year-old schoolboy in necktie and short pants doing college-level maths; the modestly-paid company executive pouring funds into research and development; clean, crime and pothole free city streets; gleaming bullet trains and world-class factories; high savings rates and the sober brilliance of MOF bureaucrats.[2]

That same banker addressed a Japanese business lunch more recently:

> Only when we see less well-performing Japanese companies taken over by real owners can we expect to see a thorough purging of excess capacity. Only when the Tokyo Stock Market becomes a genuine stock market, with shares that represent real ownership of corporate assets changing hands, can we find out what Japanese companies are actually worth. And only when owners capture the residual returns of business can we expect them to shoulder the full risks of bankruptcy.[3]

Such talk has gone down well in Japan in the late 1990s. Mr Mori's Diet speech, which I quoted previously, is a reflection of how much it has become part of a dominant consensus. Later, I will come to the reality content of the slogans that have dominated the debate:

- deregulation;
- greater disclosure and transparency;
- better returns on equity;
- global standards;
- rethinking lifetime employment (rethinking, not abandoning).

But a prior question is why, in the second half of the 1990s, there should *be* such a broad consensus that reform is necessary. There is one overwhelming reason. While the United States, whose deficiencies the Japanese used to be so patronising about, is booming ahead, Japan is stagnating.

And why is it stagnating? My potted economic history of the 1990s goes like this. The asset bubble of the late 1980s, whose bursting brought a collapse of both real estate and stock market prices, left the banks with a debt overhang of massive proportions and this, together with a strong negative wealth effect on consumers, brought an initial severe recession. The banks' strategy was to trade through, and conceal the fact that rigorous accounting would show them to be technically insolvent. They need only continue until the economy began to pick up and they could write off their bad debts against profits (the Credit Lyonnais strategy, collusion in which has been getting M. Trichet in trouble).

Thanks to some heavy Keynesian reflation packages, by the middle of the decade the economy was indeed beginning to pick up. 1996 showed a growth rate of 5 and a half per cent. But then the Ministry of Finance, in a premature burst of fiscal prudence, tried to wind down what was already thought to be an alarming level of public debt by raising the sales tax and social security charges in 1997. The dampening of consumer spending which resulted coincided with the blow delivered by the Asian crisis to exports and to the banks. A couple of major financial institutions were allowed to fail. The sense of gloom, and insecurity, brought a major fall in investment and consumer spending. Still, today, even though the banking crisis has more or less been solved with public money, Japan's problem is one of confidence, a demand deficiency problem. Its exporters continue to do well in spite of an overvalued exchange rate. Its second-biggest car-maker, so badly managed financially that it had to sell a controlling stake to Renault, continues to run Europe's most efficient auto plant in Sunderland, England. Japan's industrial research flourishes. The number of patents registered annually in the United States by Japanese firms grew by over 50 per cent during the 1990s. It is domestic demand that is the problem. At first it was a matter of consumers saving too much and spending too little. Now, as spending is further hit by a rise in unemployment and reduced purchasing power, it is hard to see how the underlying productive strength of the economy is ever going to be translated into respectable growth rates.

Meanwhile, the American boom goes from strength to strength. Buoyant Americans consume 4–5 per cent more than they produce. Anxious Japanese consume 2–3 per cent less than they produce and send their savings across the Pacific to help support the consumer debt that, together with the paper wealth of the Nasdaq bubble, sustains the American boom. It's a funny old world.

THE REFORM MOVEMENT

That gloom and loss of self-confidence is the central factor in the general consensus that Japan must fundamentally change seems beyond doubt. Japanese opinion has reverted, after the self-congratulatory mood of the late 1980s, to what has been a consistent stance since 1870, namely acknowledgment of the need to catch up with what are still often called, in a five-character cliché phrase, the 'advanced countries of Europe and America'. Today, though, it is almost exclusively America that people have in mind. Much is known and written in Japan about the dangerous horrors of American society, about its inequalities, about the excesses of American boardroom salaries. But for all that, in all things to do with competitiveness, America remains the model:

- the exemplars of self-reliant entrepreneurship are to be found in Silicon Valley;
- the exemplars of bold and effective risk taking are to be found in American venture capitalists;
- the exemplars of effective and honest corporate governance are to be found in American corporations;
- the exemplars of 'transparency' in financial transactions are to be found in the American stock exchange;
- the exemplars of consumer protection in American courts.

Once, Japanese businessmen used to be sent for 'know thine enemy' purposes to get their MBAs at American business schools. They came back to their firms to serve as loyal participants in a consciously different Japanese system. Nowadays more of them either go under their own steam or desert their sponsoring firm, to come back as 'consultants' offering to teach Japanese corporations how to maximise shareholder value. And it is economists with PhDs from Chicago and MIT who nowadays make the running on government committees.

The reformers' targets have concentrated on two main objectives. One consists of deregulation, more competition, consumer sovereignty, a reduction of the power of the industry associations that are in cahoots with bureaucrats (the end of what was called the convoy system of mutual support in banking), and the opening up of sectors such as insurance to foreign firms.

The second has been the transformation of Japanese corporations into proper capitalist firms. This means, on the one hand, raising profit levels and heightening managers' concern with shareholder value through changes in corporate governance. On the other hand it requires (as a means

to that all-encompassing end of greater efficiency) much more flexible
labour market practices, an end to lifetime employment, and a revolution
in pay systems that gives more reward to performance and less to seniority.

There have been clear phases in these two reform movements.
Deregulation was the 1994–95 hot topic. One could not open a newspaper
without finding some headline relating to what came to be known as the
'great chorus' of voices calling for *kisei kanwa* (deregulation). Then, after
the 1996 recovery, the centre of attention shifted to (as everybody is now so
ashamed to admit because the consequences were so disastrous) *zaisei
kaikaku* (fiscal reform). That produced the tax increases of 1997 and a fiscal
reform law which held up resolution of the banking crisis for something
like six months. Then the great topic became corporate governance. Every
economic organisation in the business set up a committee to produce a
report on the reform of corporate governance, including one ad hoc newly
created Corporate Governance Forum with close links to the major
American pension fund, the California Public Employees Retirement
Scheme (CalPERS). All the reports said much the same thing. There
should be:

- more concern for shareholders;
- management capable of raising return on equity;
- transparency, greater disclosure (not greater disclosure to employees
  or to their enterprise union, but to investors, you understand);
- the end of the insider board system;
- stronger auditing.

Lastly, all the numerous studies agreed on the importance of preventing
fushoji, a curious code word mainly representing two common practices.
The first was paying bribes to the *sokaiya* (the blackmailing thugs who
threaten to make trouble at shareholder AGMs). A firm's most respected
executives often had the unenviable task of dealing with these criminals. If
found out, they subsequently had the honour of being hounded by the
press and eventually sent to jail. The second practice was a certain amount
of illegal, but often personally honourable, creative accounting. The objective was to conceal technical insolvency, or impending insolvency, and
allow a firm to trade through to better times. This particular form of non-
transparency is seen as a great betrayal of the innocent investor, who ought
to have the chance of getting his or her money out and thereby absolutely
ensuring the collapse of the firm (perhaps with the result of bringing the
whole financial system collapsing about his or her ears).

So far I have explained this reform movement solely in terms of the
gloom induced by the fact that Japan was doing so miserably growth-wise

while the Americans were doing so well. Were there no good economic arguments to support reform? Were there no other changes in Japanese society which could explain this concern with reform?

The answer is 'yes' to both questions. Let me deal with the social changes first. There are two trends of long-term change in Japanese society which lend support to the reformers. The first is a change towards greater heterogeneity and greater individualism. A symptomatic quote comes from a lawyer writing about the cross-shareholding system. He is criticising a 1980s book praising the Japanese system as being not plain capitalism but 'human-capitalism'

> Is human-capitalism really so good for humans? In the truly modern labour contract a worker sells his work; he doesn't sell his soul, his commitment. The employee-sovereign firm requires Japanese to spend their whole lives, from birth to retirement, in enforced competition, first to enter the firm, then for advancement within it. For that they have to sacrifice freedom and individuality, human feeling and creativity. They have no time for cultural pursuits, for playing a useful role in the family or community. They are offered spiritual poverty in return for material riches.[4]

The second major change: managers and the chattering classes of the media and the universities in the 1960s were as poor as church mice, saving to get out of employer-owned housing and into their own home before they were 50. Today, a much larger proportion has sizeable financial assets. The 'more power to the shareholder' slogan of the corporate governance reformers clearly has greater appeal than ever before. It particularly enchants those in universities and in MITI who are not private sector employees. Managers who envy the yachts and ranches of their American counterparts (earned by being loyal agents of shareholder principals rather than the most responsible among a firm's employees) also find such slogans especially appealing.

As for the economic arguments, the following seem to me to have most force. First, the globalisation of financial markets means that Japanese firms will be starved of capital if they do not offer rates of return comparable with those in countries that use capital more efficiently. This argument is, however, weakened, as far as long-term capital is concerned, by the remarkable volatility of yen exchange rates. The second argument is that demographic change has two consequences. On the one hand, in an ageing society, people are going to want their savings to be profitable; on the other, the growth in population which for 40 years drove a steady increase in land prices was a major factor in four decades of steady asset inflation. Capital gains in the stock market, as much asset inflation as real-asset accumulation, provided respectable rates of return to capital in spite of dividend yields which rarely exceeded 1 per cent (the abysmal level which America is only just reaching at the peak of its stock exchange bubble). Absent these capital gains (ultimately sustained until now by population growth), profits and dividend levels must rise or nobody will save and the life insurance companies will all go bust.

ACTUAL CHANGE?

I have gone, at some length (some might think excessive length), into the background and motives of reform proposals. What has actually happened? The answer: not a great deal. And, as you will gather from the foregoing, reasonably so, I would say. Deplorably so, as all the visiting American dignitaries say, and as the speech-writer for the OECD's Director General told me he was going to have him say when he visits Japan in May 2000.

Among the marginal changes have been the following. Some firms have sliced their boards in two and brought in one or two outside directors to their strategy board, but not with any clear role of representing shareholder interests. Whereas six years ago only a handful of company presidents or chairmen made the rounds of fund managers in London and New York, now they go in droves. But the number of Japanese firms with as much as 40 per cent of their capital in foreign hands is still tiny, much less than the 60 per cent represented by the German firm Mannesmann, which fell victim to Vodafone's takeover bid recently. Almost every firm has gone over to what it calls a merit pay and promotion system less geared to seniority. But even in Nissan, under vigorous Renault management, the age of the latest board appointments dropped from the traditional 51–52, only to 46 and 47. The pay spread for managers in their 40s used to range between approximately 30 per cent above and 20 per cent below median levels (the median for lifetime employees of the same age on the same career track, that is). In most firms, this spread has widened by only a few percentage points. There is much talk of the cross-shareholding system unwinding, but it does not yet show up appreciably in the available statistics. A change in the law allows firms to pay their directors and senior managers with stock options. But the two hundred or so companies which have adopted the scheme have done so more as a means of making a symbolic gesture than as an attempt to use options to supply a substantial part of directors' emoluments. Deregulation has broken up a number of cosy arrangements, which gave producers a comfortable life at the consumer's expense. But, except in a few industries such as domestic airlines and petrol distribution, its impact has been limited. Lifetime employment has been, as they say, 're-thought', but still it is voluntary early retirement and bankruptcies that are adding to the unemployment rolls, not redundancy dismissals. Labour legislation has enlarged the scope of agency despatch and other non-standard forms of employment, but the numbers involved are still small. There is much talk (standard OECD talk) about rolling back the welfare state. But the pay-as-you-go pension scheme, which provides pensions by redistributing labour income (rather than relying like most pensions in the typical Anglo-Saxon economy on the capital share of GNP), is still alive and well. Recently revamped, it should see its way through the worst period of ageing effects. At the same time, a new old people's long-term-care insurance scheme has been launched and should have beneficial employment side effects. When Sasebo Shipbuilding applied for restructuring (June 2000), the list of diversification start-ups it was planning (to absorb its former workers) included a long-term-care provider agency. The banks are finally going to get a tax-privileged equity saving scheme modelled on the American 401(K) plans, but 87 per cent of the great pool of ten-year-deposit post office savings which came due last month went back into post office accounts.

Moreover, since the ending of the banking crisis, and with everyone holding their breath as they watch the apparently unsustainable course of the American economy, the reformers' control over the ideological airspace seems to have weakened. A straw in the wind was a symposium held by a major newspaper a month ago. The President of the financial lease firm Orix, Yoshihiko Miyauchi, is well known as a leading shareholder value man. Two years ago he was Chairman of the businessmen's committee on corporate governance, which I mentioned, whose report was greeted with great enthusiasm by CalPERS. In the symposium, Miyauchi spoke of coming

> to have doubts about shareholder capitalism. I'm forever sending out the message that the kinds of shareholders we want are those interested in medium and long-term growth. And if it's medium and long-term growth you are interested in, then what you are talking about is what is often spoken about as the Japanese vice, namely concern for stakeholders.[5]

So you see that I still have considerable hopes that Japan will remain, by my lights, a decent society. What it takes to make it also a society with a reasonable, steady (2 per cent, say) growth rate, I just don't know. I suspect it depends on the long-awaited arrival of the American bear market and the depressing consequences thereof. I would guess that, as factors affecting economic vitality, the chance of that prompting a return of national self-confidence would outweigh the severe blow it would give to Japanese exports. But who knows? I am less confident about my economic forecasting than I am about my moral judgements.

NOTES

1. *Nihon Keizai Shimbun*, 20 April 2000.
2. R. Taggart Murphy, *The Weight of the Yen,* New York, Norton, 1996.
3. R. Taggart Murphy, 'Tinkering or reform? The deregulation of Japan's financial system', Hotel Okura, The Tokyo Report, June 1997.
4. Nakajima Shuzo, *Kabushiki no mochiai to kaishaho* (*Cross-shareholding and Company Law*), Tokyo, Shoji Homu Kenkyukai, 1990, p. 87. The book is a printing, with after-thought comments, of a 1977 Masters thesis. The foil for his arguments is Itami Hiroyuki, *Jimpon-shugi kigyo* (*The Human-capitalist Enterprise*), Tokyo, Chikuma Shobo, 1987.
5. *Asahi Shimbun*, 12 April 2000.

COMMENT ON 'REFORM? THE DUBIOUS BENEFITS OF MARKETISATION'

Aiko Ikeo

Can the Japanese change? Dore's answer seems to be as follows: 'I do not think that they can. It is all right though. There is no need for them to strain themselves to change.' It seems that Dore likes to talk to practical Japanese and recently has taken many opportunities to speak to business leaders. However, in doing this he seems to have talked only to those with very negative views of Japan. In his paper, he lists not only written evidence, but also refers to evidence from these discussions. We should not over-generalize from that latter type of argument here. Therefore, I would rather comment on Dore's chapter by referring to his earlier writings from a more historical perspective. This may help us consider our main question, which this conference is trying to address.

Dore has been studying Japanese society for half a century. His command of Japanese is so proficient that he has published several books in Japanese, including a number written by him exclusively for a Japanese audience. His works on Japanese society are mostly the result of his fieldwork rather than the application of a theory or hypothesis. As we head towards the 21st century, several Japanese magazines have invited Dore to present his views on the future of Japan. I will take up four of his points.

Dore first came to Japan in 1951, when Japan was still occupied by the Allies. The occupation ended in April 1952, and Dore lived in a community in Tokyo for a year and a half. He lived in the same type of small abode as a Japanese university student of the day, usually one or two rooms with a *tatami* mat. He closely observed the people living in the neighborhood, while learning how a young Japanese man in Tokyo was supposed to live. He picked a random sample of 100 households, interviewed these families, and analyzed their answers to his questions. The results were published in

1958 as *City Life in Japan*. This is an important record of the life of a community in Tokyo almost 50 years ago, one that was close knit and lacking in privacy, but surely safer than its modern day counterpart. Dore's description of their lives and conversations are so vivid that I can imagine Dore sitting quietly in order not to intrude on the lives of these people.

Since then, Dore has published a number of scholarly books and papers on Japanese society, as well as admirable articles for Japanese newspapers and magazines. He has also attended many conferences on contemporary Japan. I assume he witnessed the change in Japan and the Japanese during these 50 years. I believe that the Japanese have changed more than the British since he first arrived in Japan.

Among scholarly books, I was amazed from the viewpoint of methodology by his *British Factory–Japanese Factory: The Origins of National Diversity in Industrial Relations* (1973). When I picked up the Japanese version, I thought the original English title was *British Factories–Japanese Factories*, because the Japanese language usually does not distinguish the single or plural number. Dore made a close and detailed examination of two factories in each country's electronic appliance industry with careful reference to the national data. He produced a very detailed report on the differences in industrial relations, the recruitment and training of laborers, wages, unions, contracts, power, function and status in British factories and in Japanese factories. He concluded that British companies performed better than Japanese with regard to individual independence, freedom to choose a way of life, and the power to demand fairness in contracts and self-fulfilment. Japanese companies had the advantage of providing better incentives, an ethos of mutual help and industrial stability based on business groups.

Dore's collection of excellent writings, originally in Japanese, includes the titles (translated into English):

- *A Japan That Can Say What To Do* (1993; the English version is included in Dore, 1997a);
- *A Dialogue with Japan: Aspects of Dissatisfaction* (collection of interviews, 1994);
- *The Enigmatic Country, Japan* (1994);
- *Asking about Japan, Asking to Japan* (collection of interviews, 1997);
- *Don't Mix 'Public' with 'Private': Still the Enigmatic Country, Japan* (1997).

Dore has interviewed many Japanese activists who he believed were dissatisfied with the conditions of Japanese society. His wish list in the conference paper reflects the complaints heard in those interviews and his own

observations of events in Japan. I have virtually no objections to make
against his wish list. I agree with him.

I also agree with Koichi Hamada, who pointed out the problems in the
Japanese system of education at the conference (see Chapter 6). I've sum-
marized 'Japanese feelings' based on one of my assignments in the classes
I presented on the modern history of economics at Kokugakuin University.
It still seems worth repeating. Ikeo (1990: 115) wrote as follows:

> Many Japanese are not good at expressing themselves and live in ambiguity.
> They do not use clear cut yes and no answers partially because they think that
> the band between the two answers is so important that it should be read 'between
> the lines' – the equivalent Japanese expression is 'through the atmosphere'.
> Another reason is that they do not want to take responsibility for what they say.
> Japanese are taught not to assert themselves, and to avoid making themselves
> appear selfish. They prefer tacit communication or mutual-understanding to
> articulated expression with words.

I plan to use Dore's *Japan, Internationalism and the UN* (1997a) as the textbook for one of the classes I will teach in the autumn of 2000. I hope that
such a book will provoke my Japanese students and make them say something (in response to Dore). Still, it will take time to change educational
structure in Japan.

Until the mid 1960s in Japan, the study of the Japanese economy was
mostly conducted either by an idiosyncratic type of developmental economist or by Marxian economists. Yet the number of economists trained in
mainstream economics, that common international economic language
which includes neoclassical microeconomics and Keynesian macroeco-
nomics, was increasing during the 1960s, a period of rapid growth in Japan.
The number of mainstream economists finally exceeded the number of
Marxian economists in Japan in the late 1960s (see Ikeo, 1996). Dore helped
these Japanese mainstream economists publish the English (1994) edition
of *Business Enterprise in Japan* (Imai and Komiya, 1989). It was probably
his idea to add the subtitle '*Views of Leading Japanese Economists*'. The
subjects include the firm, intercorporate relations, enterprise behavior,
human resources, and public and cooperative enterprises. As far as I know,
most of the Japanese authors in the book had been trained in the United
States. Following this, Dore organized the project on the Japanese firm with
economist Masahiko Aoki, a professor at Stanford University.

Although Japanese society changed as the Japanese economy grew
rapidly, the changes were not sufficient to produce a mature state.
Economics and other social sciences also changed during this period. The
language used by (mainstream) economists had become international.
There were now economists who had been trained to speak that common
language. We learned that standard economic tools are able to explain the

characteristics of the Japanese economy and to clarify these differences with those other countries (see Coats (ed.) 1996; Ikeo (ed.) 1999). Or at least I thought so.

However, Dore criticizes the Japanese usage of the concept of *market* in his discussion of internal labor markets. Most likely, I learned this theory when I was a graduate student in the 1970s. I was not the only person who found such a theory strange because these internal labor markets could exist even though they were devoid of any competition. We (including some of my classmates) simply memorized it and tried to understand that markets do not always generate competition. I did not think the concept of a market without competition (as presented in the theory of internal labor markets) stranger than the neoclassical convention of perfect competition, under which competition ceases to operate altogether. The internal labor market is not a description of real markets but a theoretical concept of the type that is commonly found in neoclassical economics. This is one of the reasons why the so-called Austrian economists, who are quite active in the United States, are so critical of neoclassical economics. For example, Donald Lavoie has advocated the use of the term *rivalry* instead of competition in his discussion of the function of markets (Lavoie 1985). I think that this is a more accurate term, especially when contrasted with the neoclassical model of a market operating under perfect competition.

As we can see from Wakatsuki's paper (Chapter 2), the Information Technology Revolution has been a buzzword in Japan since around 1998. Advanced information technology has been introduced not only into the workplace but living rooms as well, given the expanding electronic network. The increasing number of Internet and personal computer users has been changing both business practices and the form that communications takes in the world. This trend has been far more important in Japan than in those countries where the 26 or more characters of the Western alphabet are used. The Japanese language uses *Kanji*, *Hiragana* and *Katakana* characters, which are totally different from Western alphabets. About 3,000 Japanese (complicated) characters are used in everyday life and more are needed in writing an academic paper. Until the mid 1980s, the existing typewriters were too expensive for ordinary Japanese to own and very difficult to operate. Yet thanks to the spread of less expensive Japanese word processors and/or software, Japanese people (since the mid 1980s) have begun to operate keyboards much like Westerners. They transform the typed words into Japanese by selecting the words suitable for the context out of a group of homophones. Japan has been developing domestic e-mail networks based in Japanese since the early 1990s. In writing e-mail it is a rule to use straightforward expressions and avoid exercising euphemistic phrases. As Japanese people have more and more opportunities to correspond using e-mail, they have begun to use articulated expressions with words instead of traditional tacit communication and mutual understanding. I think this is a big change for the Japanese. Honestly speaking, I hope to see the Japanese continue to change.

Note

I wish to thank Phillipa Brennan and Paul Pecorino for editing my comments.

References

Coats, A.W. (ed.) (1996), *The Post-1945 Internationalization of Economics*, Annual Supplement to Volume 28 of the *History of Political Economy*, Durham and London: Duke University Press.

Dore, R. (1958), *City Life in Japan: A Study of a Tokyo Ward*, London: Routledge & Kegan Paul Ltd.

Dore, R. (1973), *British Factory–Japanese Factory: The Origins of National Diversity in Industrial Relations*, London: Allen & Unwin.

Dore, R. (1993), *'Koshiyo' to ieru Nihon* (*A Japan That Can Say What To Do*), Tokyo: Asahi Shimbun. The English version is included in Dore (ed.) (1997a).

Dore, R. (ed.) (1994a), *Nihon tono Taiwa* (*A Dialogue with Japan: Aspects of Dissatisfaction*), Tokyo: Iwanami Shoten.

Dore, R. (1994b), *Fushigina Kuni, Nihon* (*The Enigmatic Country, Japan*), Tokyo: Chikuma Shobo.

Dore, R. (ed.) (1997a), *Japan, Internationalism and the UN*, London: Routledge.

Dore, R. (ed.) (1997b), *Nihon wo tou, Nihon ni tou* (*Asking about Japan, Asking to Japan*), Tokyo: Iwanami Shoten.

Dore, R. (ed.) (1997c), *'Ooyake' wo 'Watakushi' subekarazu* (*Don't Mix 'Public' with 'Private': Still the Enigmatic Country, Japan*), Tokyo: Chikuma Shobo.

Ikeo, A. (1990), 'Japanese economics from another sociological perspective', *Kokugakuin Keizaigaku* (Kokugakuin University), **39**: 112–128.

Ikeo, A. (1996), 'The internationalization of economics in Japan', in Coats (ed.) (1996), 123–141.

Ikeo, A. (ed.) (1999), *Nihon no Keizaigaku to Keizaigakusha*, Tokyo: Nihon Keizai Hyoronsha. The English edition appeared as *Japanese Economics and Economists since 1945*, London: Routledge, 2000.

Imai, K. and R. Komiya (1989), *Nihon no Kigyo*, Tokyo: Tokyo University Press. The abridged English edition was published as *Business Enterprise in Japan*. Translation edited and introduced by R. Dore and H. Whittaker, Cambridge, Massachusetts: MIT Press, 1994.

Lavoie, D. (1985), *Rivalry and Central Planning*, Cambridge: Cambridge University Press.

PART II

The Fine Art of Financial Incompetence

In the past we have had irresponsible borrowers, and in the past we have had irresponsible lenders, but what we had here, and are having to witness the consequences of in profusion, is the meeting, for the first time, of the irresponsible lender and the irresponsible borrower.
Funny Money, Mark Singer

4. The financial system of post-1945 Japan: its formation, development and deterioration

Kazuhito Ikeo

1 INTRODUCTION

This study analyzes the formation and development of the Japanese financial system after World War II. Examining the process by which it deteriorated in recent years extends the analysis. The chapter concludes with a brief discussion of the current state of financial reform, what has become known as the Japanese 'Big Bang'. The 'system that soured' paradigm inspired this chapter. It is a paradigm which has tried to explain the course of Japanese economic development. However, I think that this particular paradigm has two intrinsic defects, which are mentioned initially below and are expanded upon later in the chapter.

In the past, US academics pursued research on the Japanese economy by employing either a 'traditionalist' or 'revisionist' approach. However, according to Katz (1998), these frameworks have rapidly lost their influence because neither one can explain adequately the long-lasting stagnation of the Japanese economy in the 1990s. This theoretical vacuum provided an opportunity for a new framework, the 'system that soured', to gain greater credence. The origins of this paradigm can be traced to a paper entitled 'Success That Soured' by Professor Kozo Yamamura (1982).

While Japan was striving to catch up to Western advanced countries, the Japanese system seemed to be efficient at accelerating economic development. However, in the 1970s, when the catch-up process was fundamentally complete, the Japanese-style economic system turned into a hindrance. By protecting inefficient industrial sectors, it ended up depressing economic growth. The system persisted even after the necessary conditions for its success had vanished. This type of analysis tries to explain why the Japanese economy first fell into a slump and then why policy makers allowed that initial slump to grow progressively more serious during the

1990s. Such an understanding of the Japanese economy forms the gist of the 'system that soured' paradigm.

I substantially agree with this paradigm. However, I would insist that two essential problems undermine the approach. The first question is, 'Why was the system not reformed despite the remarkable changes in the surrounding environment?' The second question is, 'Did the system stay the same?', although this second question seems to contradict the first. In light of these two questions, the story provided by the 'system that soured' paradigm fails to be fully persuasive.

This chapter provides the following hypothesis in response to these two questions. Japan actually made some modifications that reflected its changing environment. However, these alterations focused so entirely on sustaining the *status quo* that they failed adequately to change the Japanese economic system. As a consequence, it substantially lost the crucial ability to adapt to change. At present, the Japanese economic system is not identical to the system that supported Japan's period of high economic growth. The current system is only a distorted version of the original.

In this chapter, I refer to the Japanese economic system that supported industrial catch-up after World War II as 'the 1940 system' (after Noguchi (1995)). The distorted version of the Japanese-style economic system that evolved out of the changed economic environment, I refer to as 'the 1970 system' (after Harada (1998)[1]). I choose these titles to emphasize an ease of understanding rather than any attempt to concentrate on precision in expression. Many elements of the post-war economy have their origin in the building blocks of Japan's wartime regime, largely in place before 1940. Hence the label 'the 1940 system'. On the other hand, Japan's more recent economic structure, a distortion in response to environmental changes, is called 'the 1970 system' or 'the 1975 system' since these key distortions had largely occurred by the mid-1970s.

As Okuno-Fujiwara (1999) recently emphasized, the 1973 Oil Crisis initiated a series of modifications resulting in economic distortions. When the Oil Crisis broke out, Japan had become justifiably proud of its economic success. The economic shock created by the Crisis caused the Japanese people to fear that the fruit of their hard won success would be completely lost. The Japanese felt compelled to adopt an extremely defensive stance. Japan's attempt to defend its economic success by any means possible resulted in the direct opposite of its goal: a hardening of its already outdated system.

Until the Crisis, Japan maintained its progress through checks and balances between relevant interest groups. This not only disciplined Japanese society but also supported a relatively high level of adaptive efficiency. However since the 1970s, the notion has been promoted that all of Japan's various groups should close ranks, be they government, private firms, labor unions or consumers, in order to confront periodic difficulties. This obligation to stand together, no matter what, weakened any mutual checking built into the system. The consequences could only be a lowering of both social discipline and adaptive efficiency.

As previously argued, it is not true that the Japanese economic system has remained unchanged despite confronting significant environmental changes. The system has changed, but in the wrong direction by modifying itself in order to maintain the *status quo*. This only hardened the system. The dynamism and flexibility that previously characterized the Japanese economic system were lost. In this sense, the current Japanese economic system should not be called the 'system that soured', but the 'system that dried up'.

In this chapter, my analysis focuses on the financial system as one of the core sub-systems of the Japanese economy after the war. By examining the financial system of post-war Japan, the chapter aims to prove the appropriateness of my hypothesis. The chapter is organized as follows:

- Section 2 discusses the formation of the Japanese financial system after the war. I investigate the role played by the 'artificially low interest rate policy' instituted under the 1940 system.
- Section 3 examines the distortion to the Japanese financial system which resulted from a failure to respond adequately to change. The setback to financial reform in the 1980s typifies such a failure. After the setback in the 1980s, the system continued to deteriorate, which resulted in the banking crisis of the 1990s.
- Finally in Section 4, in place of concluding remarks, I briefly consider the prospects of the Japanese 'Big Bang'.

2 THE 1940 SYSTEM AND ECONOMIC DEVELOPMENT

2.1 Formation of the Japanese Financial System after World War II

The Japanese-style economic system, which produced a high level of economic growth after World War II, was shaped by three major historical events.

The first was the banking crisis in the second half of the 1920s. In 1927, Japan had experienced a severe banking crisis, which from 1930 further degenerated into an overall economic panic (the *Showa* Crisis[2]). The failure of the gold-export embargo policy coupled with the worldwide ripple effect of the Great Depression was the primary cause. The second key event was

the impact on Japanese society of a wartime regime, especially its implementation of economic controls. Despite being modified, many of the
incremental changes introduced to achieve a controlled economy persisted
after the war. The third contributing factor was the experience of post-war
reforms, in particular the consequences of an immediate and widespread
number of labor disputes. Japanese-style labor relations were born out of
a series of severe labor disputes that occurred from the second half of the
1940s up to the beginning of the 1950s.

These events, and the responses by which the government and private
firms hoped to accommodate them, strongly influenced the Japanese economic system. However, the influence of the third event is the least
significant when considering the formation of the Japanese financial system
as a sub-system of the post-war Japanese economy. While post-war reforms
included the break-up of big business combines (*zaibatsu*), with nonfinancial major firms being divided into smaller entities, banks alone were
immune,[3] though the reason for this is unclear. The financial system was
almost free from the influence of post-war reforms.

On the other hand, the first two events considerably influenced the
financial system. It is safe to say that the post-war financial system is in fact
a reincarnation or even a continuation of the 1940 system. Nonetheless,
one can hardly ignore the post-war influence on other aspects of the economic system such as labor–management relationships. Therefore, whether
it is appropriate to call this whole structure 'the 1940 system' is arguable.
However, along with the bureaucratic system, the post-war financial system
shows the greatest continuity between the pre- and post-war periods. It is a
typical example of the 1940 system.

I will clarify later (in much greater detail) the influence that the first two
events exercised on the formation of the post-war Japanese financial
system. Then I will review the formation of that financial system.

2.1.1   Banking crisis and bank merger policy

Before the 1927 crisis, the structure of the Japanese banking industry was
similar to that of the United States, both then and now. That is, there were
many small-sized financial institutions. The Japanese consensus at that
time pinpointed the existing banking structure as a key cause of its own vul-
nerability. A widespread belief placed the responsibility for the banking
crisis on the number of financial institutions and the weakness of each
one's capital base. This perception formed the basis of the government's
policy response.

As a consequence, Japan actively promoted mergers and acquisitions, in
the hope that relatively large-scale financial institutions with adequate
capital bases could more vigorously resist periodic crises. This approach

was labeled the 'bank merger policy'. The Banking Law of 1927 set the minimum required capital at 1,000,000 yen. For those times, this was not a negligible sum.[4] Banks incapable of meeting this required minimum were forced out of business. In addition, banks were *not* permitted to issue new stock to increase their capital base. To stay in business, merger was virtually the only method available to small banks.

Japan's policy contrasted strongly with that of the United States in the 1930s. The United States also faced a banking crisis at that time. However, with a tradition of opposing economic power in the form of concentrated finance capital, the US viewed the existence of small, regional financial institutions in each region as more desirable. For this reason, the goal became to restore stability to the financial system without changing its structure. In 1933, the US initiated a new system of banking regulation with deposit insurance as a safety net.

In contrast to this US stance, Japan believed that concentration would promote stability in the banking industry. The objective of the bank merger policy was 'one bank per prefecture'. For example, banks located in the northern part of a prefecture were merged into a single large bank. Likewise, banks located in the southern part were also merged. These two banks were further merged into an even larger single bank. The Japanese orchestrated a process of bank concentration incrementally to accomplish this target. Many bankers strongly resisted this mandated bank merger policy, fearing a loss of their management independence. This prevented either the smooth or the timely implementation of government objectives.

As a result, the goal of 'one bank per prefecture' was not attained until Japanese society moved onto a wartime footing. This provided the government with the legal power required to institute forceful action against recalcitrant bankers. The current regional banks were born as a result of the bank merger policy. At the same time, people concerned for the safety of their money rushed into the 'big five' banks affiliated with the big business combines (*zaibatsu*) and the state-operated Postal Savings System. The 'big five' banks further increased in scale and became the predecessors of today's city banks. This policy gradually shaped the formation of the city-bank and regional-bank system, establishing a framework for the post-war banking industry in Japan.

In addition, we can consider this bank merger policy to be the starting point, after the war, for what would become a 'convoy' system of financial administration. 'Convoy' is used to describe an administrative system where the cruising speed of a fleet of vessels (banks) is determined by the speed of the slowest vessel (the least efficient bank). Strict adherence to such a system would produce necessarily a very inefficient result. It could be said that adopting the convoy method became possible only because, as a result of the previous bank merger policy, inefficient banks had already been weeded out. Only banks in a strong financial position remained.

The post-war Japanese financial system did not emerge spontaneously. Strong government intervention artificially created it, as demonstrated by the bank merger policy. It was not then surprising that the Japanese government wanted to protect its creation by using measures such as a convoy administrative system. That is, the Japanese government took a major part in the formation of the post-war financial system. As a result, it was strongly committed to maintaining that system.

2.1.2　Wartime financial controls

Needless to say, the Japanese wartime government not only wanted to preserve the existing financial system but also intended that it be subservient to a prescribed set of objectives. These included promoting economic development in general but, particularly after the 1930s, achieving military victories. Based on their World War I experience, the Japanese, like many others, believed that all wars would henceforth be all-out wars. These wars could not be won solely by military prowess, but would also necessitate the full force of a country's power, including its economic strength. Consequently, a national social system would have to be built, capable of conducting all-out wars.

Plans to build up such a system (the national mobilization system) were instituted intensively around 1940.[5] Noguchi (1995) has labeled this system 'the 1940 system' and discussed its formation and characteristics in detail. I will leave any detailed discussion of the whole system to Noguchi (1995) and others, limiting myself here to matters that directly concern the financial system.[6]

Securing the control of fund allocation was crucial to the 1940 system. The Japanese government's objectives were to:

- fund the munitions industry and a limited number of selected companies (established in line with national policy and engaged in colony management) in preference to all others;
- finance the budget deficit, which was the result of increased military expenditure, by smoothly issuing bonds.

At that time, private financial institutions regarded almost all of the companies associated with munitions and colony management as relatively high credit risks. It was very difficult for these firms to obtain funds on a commercial basis. The government was forced to devise a method for issuing large quantities of government bonds without producing an interest rate rise or igniting inflation.

The outbreak of the Japanese–Chinese War triggered full-scale fund control. The first step in 1937 was to implement the Temporary Fund Adjustment Act. The Act aimed at controlling the allocation of investment funds. It gave the government the power to determine the priority of bank loans. Lending when the amount was more than 100,000 yen required the government's permission. The government refused this permission when it judged that the borrower's industry did not have a high enough priority. In 1940 the 'Fund Allocation Ordinance for Banks and Other Financial Institutions' was issued. Based on the National Mobilization Act of 1938, this decree gave the Japanese government similar controls over operational funds.

The government concurrently organized loan syndication groups, awarding the Industrial Bank of Japan (IBJ) (a state-operated special bank) a central role. These syndicates were meant primarily to fund the munitions industry. The 'Company Profit, Dividend and Financial Policy Ordinance' of 1939 gave the government the right to direct the IBJ's lending operations. This ordinance also assisted the IBJ in procuring funds by either guaranteeing the IBJ's debentures or by buying them directly with postal savings funds. The IBJ played a crucial role in the wartime financial control system.

After 1941, as the Japanese economy grew increasingly harnessed to the needs of a wartime state, organizing the syndication of loans gradually shifted from being unregulated to being more controlled. Established in 1941, the 'Loan Syndication in the Wartime Situation' included only the IBJ and other major private banks. Then in 1942, the 'Financial Control Association Ordinance' was issued. This ordinance established the 'National Financial Control Association', which preempted the 'Loan Syndication in the Wartime Situation' by completely controlling bank loans. The final full year of the war (1944) introduced the 'System of Rationing Financial Institutions to Munitions-Associated Companies'. This system paired up munitions companies with banks.

The Postal Savings System (the Japanese government's own fund procurement vehicle) played a major role in purchasing government bonds. Depositors had shifted their funds to government-guaranteed postal savings after the banking crisis of 1927. The Japanese government used almost all of this increase to buy government bonds. In order to enhance the appeal of government bonds, the Bank of Japan (BOJ) made low interest loans available to local banks, subsidizing bond purchases whether or not these local banks required additional funds. However, as the war drew to an end, it became impossible for the government to issue bonds, except by having the BOJ purchase them directly.

Although Japanese capital markets were very active in the pre-war period, wartime controls gradually restricted their function. Since the

'Company Profit, Dividend and Financial Policy Ordinance' of 1939 restricted dividends on stocks and shareholders' rights, the stock market became less and less attractive and gradually was forced out of operation. The wartime financial control system superseded the corporate bond market, completely controlling corporate bond issues. The BOJ and the Ministry of Finance (MOF) stage-managed these issues, at least in part, by working closely with the IBJ.

2.1.3   The financial system of post-1945 Japan

By the end of World War II, Japan's financial system had been converted into a typical bank-based system. The number of ordinary banks was reduced to 61, with small financial institutions weeded out. Since the end of the war, except for limited periods, Japan has restricted new entry into the banking sector. Since 1954, except for foreign banks, mergers or conversions from other types of financial institution, Japan has granted no new licenses. As a result, no new entry by an ordinary bank has occurred. Instead we see quite a number of non-bank depository institutions (credit unions or associations) established after the war to ameliorate severe shortages of funds. Mutual companies became mutual savings and loan banks. Labor unions established labor credit associations for their members. Almost all of these financial institutions were small in size. In this sense only, it might be true that post-war policy partly destroyed the achievements of the bank merger strategy. However, and perhaps more importantly, the Japanese banking system (at least a basic part of it) retains its highly concentrated industrial structure.

On the other hand, post-war Japan did abolish the state-operated special bank system. The IBJ became, and remains, a private bank. In 1952, the Long Term Credit Bank Act transformed the IBJ, converting it into a private bank specializing in long-term financing with the right to issue bank debentures. At the same time, two other long-term credit banks, the Long Term Credit Bank of Japan and the Nippon Credit Bank, were established.[7] The Japan Development Bank (JDB), founded in 1951, was a new type of state-operated financial institution that took the place of the wartime special banks.

Although I stated earlier that post-war reforms exercised no great influence on the financial system, I must point out an exception. Replicating the aims of the US Glass–Steagall Act, the post-war reform measures introduced a separation between commercial and investment banking. The intention of this separation was to promote the development of Japanese capital markets. However, this may have produced a contradictory outcome. The separation ensured that securities houses, the new market intermediaries, lacked the banks' expertise or any significant security experience.[8]

Securities houses were newcomers that quite naturally would lack such expertise. Banks, on the other hand, had gained the necessary experience in the universal-banking environment that dominated pre-war Japan.

The highly distinguishable Japanese and US experiences ensured that at least two main differences would characterize how these two countries handled a mandated separation of banking roles. To begin with, Japanese banks are not prohibited from owning stock. Within a limited range of restrictions imposed by anti-trust laws, Japanese banks can freely hold other companies' stock. Second, the 'Trustee Bank System' allows banks to influence considerably the issuing of corporate bonds. Banks surreptitiously retained this option long after the war by substituting the term 'adjustment' for 'control'. The IBJ continued to control the way in which corporate bonds were issued.

Post-war reforms abolished *zaibatsu* holding companies, but banks, as mentioned earlier, escaped this penalty. Therefore, city banks came to play a pivotal role in the new industrial groupings. As a result, the official post-war termination of the *zaibatsu* saw the simultaneous birth of financial *keiretsu* (affiliations). Relationships developed through syndicated loans during the war years formed the basis for post-war financial affiliations, which had nothing to do with the old *zaibatsu*. Similarly, it might be said that the 'System of Rationing Financial Institutions to Munitions-Associated Companies' promoted close relationships between firms and banks that persisted after the war (the 'main bank' system). By the second half of the 1950s, the post-war Japanese financial system was largely complete.

2.2 Artificial Low Interest Rate Policy

Under the 1940 system, the approach taken in regulating the financial system is generally known as the 'artificially low interest rate policy'. Two pillars supported this policy: ceilings on deposit interest rates and credit rationing. Its result, intended or not, was to provide financial institutions with rent-seeking opportunities. Japan implemented the artificially low interest rate policy believing that its own interest rate at that time was higher than that of other countries. Policy makers assumed that the higher interest rate reduced the international competitiveness of Japanese industries. Lowering interest rates therefore became one of the most important political objectives.

An orthodox method for lowering interest rates is either to decrease the demand for funds or to increase the supply. Since corporate investment activities determine the demand for funds, reducing that demand is linked to decelerating economic growth. Therefore, reducing the demand for funds was not a viable option in Japan immediately after the war. On the other hand, it is almost impossible, at least in the short run, to markedly increase domestic savings. Introducing foreign capital was the only available measure that would rapidly increase the supply of funds.

However, in contrast to the recent experience of East-Asian countries, Japan at that time was exceedingly hesitant to allow foreign capital to enter. It feared that foreigners might take control of domestic companies. Instead, Japan continued to pursue a policy of foreign exchange controls that severely restricted capital imports. The hoped-for increase in the supply of funds was not realized. As a result, there was no decrease in the interest rate, as there was no easing of the existing balance between the supply and demand for funds.

In response, Japan adopted an alternative to more orthodox methods, namely an 'artificially low interest rate policy'. This policy tries to control the interest rate in order to force it lower. Placing a ceiling on the interest rate paid to depositors became one prong of the artificially low interest rate strategy. Setting the interest rate below an equilibrium level must necessarily generate an excess demand for funds. Under these conditions, allocating funds to particular groups or organizations was tantamount to providing them with a guaranteed rent. It was not capital markets, but financial institutions (city banks or long-term credit banks), that determined the allocation of funds and their associated rents. Credit rationing by banks was the other strategic policy prong.

In the following subsection, I examine more closely both aspects of the artificially low interest rate policy.[9] I argue that this policy can be interpreted as a variant of the 'financial restraint' policy, discussed by Hellmann, Murdock and Stiglitz (1996).

2.2.1   Interest regulation and branch restriction

Although other interest rates were officially regulated along with the interest rate on deposits, the effect of each of these regulations was not the same. While placing ceilings on the interest that could be offered for deposits had a major impact, it is doubtful whether the regulation of other interest rates was particularly effective.

Regulating the interest rate on deposits was based on the Temporary Interest Rate Adjustment Act of 1948. Since 1970, the guidelines of the BOJ have required it to set a ceiling on the interest rates on deposits. The height of this ceiling is revised when the BOJ's lending rate (discount rate) changes. Without viable financial alternatives available to Japanese households, regulating the interest rate on deposits was likely to prove effective.

The same Temporary Interest Rate Adjustment Act also provided the basis for regulating interest rates on loans of less than one year. However, even when the loan interest rate itself was low, banks were able to adjust the effective interest rate of the loan by forcing borrowers to hold compensating balances. This leads me to conclude that regulating interest rates on loans was not as effective as has been widely believed. There were no legal regulations on interest rates charged for long-term loans of one year or more. However, it was a well-established tradition to base the actual interest rate of both the long-term and short-term prime rates on changes in policy-determined interest rates, such as the BOJ's discount rate.

While none of these legal regulations affected the yield rates of public and corporate bonds, the government still managed to keep these substantially under its control. The Japanese government was eager to reduce its fiscal burden. To achieve this, the government sold its bonds directly to banks, setting their yield at a low level.[10]

Control over issuing corporate bonds continued as previously described. The issuers could not themselves determine the yield rate. This was set at a deliberately lower level than the prevailing secondary market rate. Purchasers of corporate bonds initially suffered a capital loss when they bought them. Only banks could invest, because only banks could obtain sufficient compensation by means of other transactions with the issuers. This prevented household savings from flowing directly to the bond market. Closing off this alternative helped to sustain the effectiveness of regulating the interest rate on deposits. However, while an artificially low interest rate policy was implemented, Japanese interest rates were not actually low when compared with those of other countries at that time. This interest rate on deposits was meant to be below the market rate that would have prevailed in the absence of regulation. It was still a bit higher than the US rate during the same period. Undoubtedly Japanese loan rates were considerably higher in effective terms, but only if we take into account the existence of compensating balances. In sum, regulated interest rate levels were not so low as to be completely out of step with actual market conditions.

Rates on the fund-raising side of banks (interest rates on deposits) were relatively (though not absolutely) regulated, at least at lower levels. On the lending side, interest rates were not directly constrained. The more banks could attract deposits, the more profit they generated. However, the only means the banks had of increasing deposits was by expanding their branch networks and increasing access to them. Banks were not allowed to provide non-pecuniary rewards, such as free gifts, to their customers. Needless to say, the government also regulated the opening of new branches.

Japanese banking law required the Finance Minister to approve the opening of a branch or an operating office. Under this law, the MOF established administrative guidelines, called branch restrictions, which determined new locations and any relocations of each bank's branches. Banks could not expand their branch networks as they chose. Controlling branch expansion became a powerful lever with which the MOF could influence the banks' management. The operation of these branch restrictions was exacting for ordinary banks but relatively lenient for small financial institutions.

2.2.2 Credit rationing mechanism

As previously stated, the attempt to regulate the interest rates of loans was not effective. Logically, this suggests that the loan market was regulated by market interest rates, leaving no excess demand for funds. However, careful observation of the balance of power between banks and debtor firms during the high growth era reveals that a shortage of funds was the norm. The availability of funds was substantially restricted. In other words, the effective interest rate on loans was still lower than the market-clearing level. As a result, some part of the rents created by the regulating interest rates on deposits spilled over from the banking sector to the corporate sector.

The loan market cannot adequately be viewed as a Walrasian auction market that balances supply and demand exclusively by price (interest rate) adjustment. Since the management and/or financial constraints of each firm are so dissimilar, a costly exercise of gathering sufficient corporate information is the only way of learning the true situation of each borrower. Those banks able to obtain such information could safely lend. Necessarily, banks that had previously provided loans to specific corporations (those that had conducted this investigation in the past) would be better placed to offer loans to those firms than banks lacking this background.

Viewed from the other side of the equation, a borrower can obtain a loan more easily from a bank where they already have a track record than from another bank where they do not. This is because of the initial set-up costs involved. Lending conditions have to be sufficiently favorable so that a bank can cover the cost of the initial information gathering. The system strongly favors an incumbent lender. This can decisively influence fund allocation and the client relationship between banks and firms. Those firms with existing relationships receive a priority when funds are allocated.

The relationships between banks and firms during the high growth era can be roughly summarized as follows. Every city bank established its own financial affiliations with major companies and maintained a close relationship with them. On the other hand, the specialized financial institutional system restricted small financial institutions to accepting only small firms and/or firms in a specific region as their customers. Small financial institutions were prohibited from any direct dealings with major companies. However, they were able to lend their excess funds to big banks, such as city banks and long-term credit banks, by using inter-bank markets.

Taking the monitoring costs and credit risks of lending to small firms into account, the profitability of inter-bank lending was relatively high. Therefore, a considerable portion of deposits collected by regional banks and small financial institutions flowed into city banks through inter-bank lending. On the other hand, long-term credit banks raised funds by issuing financial debentures. Regional banks and small financial institutions were a major market for these debentures. In this way, big banks such as city banks or long-term credit banks became the recipients of the major portion of all deposits gathered throughout the nation. City banks lent most of their available funds to companies belonging to their respective financial groupings. These companies, so grouped, especially firms engaged in heavy manufacturing and in the chemical industry, increased their levels of investment in order to compete more effectively with one another. Japan's postwar financial system assisted the rapid, equipment-investment-oriented economic growth that occurred between 1955 and 1970. Syndicated loans, organized by city banks, provided the funds required for such huge investments. The long-term credit banks, which are 'independent' of any financial affiliations, also coordinated syndicated loans and provided funds to growing industries.

Private banks could determine independently the allocation of funds to corporations. On a micro level they decided how credit should be rationed. However, the government also allocated funds directly to industry by using state-operated financial institutions such as the Japan Development Bank (JDB), newly established after World War II. This created something of a demonstration effect by prompting private banks to provide funds to these same companies. Although such state financing certainly had a limited positive effect, the companies the government chose were seldom in growing sectors. The government did not allocate funds strategically. Certainly the main consideration was never solely to promote economic growth. If anything, private banks, especially the IBJ, allocated funds in a more strategic manner.[11]

2.2.3 Financial restraint

In discussing what types of state financial intervention might effectively promote economic development, Hellmann, Murdock and Stiglitz (1996) labeled a version similar to the Japanese system as an example of 'financial restraint'. While financial restraint appears, at a glance, to be similar to 'financial repression', the two should be clearly distinguished. Governments design financial restraint policies to create rent-seeking opportunities for the private sector. The intention behind financial repression is to allow the state to extract rent from the private sector.

Interest rate controls accompany either one of these policies. However, in the case of financial restraint, the regulated interest rate is slightly lower than the actual market rate. The real interest rate remains positive. With a policy of financial repression, the regulated interest rate is set at such an exceedingly low level, when compared with the market rate, that the real interest rate becomes negative. Except in the rare (and utterly unexpected) case when the government can make more effective use of funds than the private sector (efficiently allocate all of those funds), a financial repression policy will not promote economic development. Instead, the policy will tend to obstruct economic development.

A financial restraint policy creates rent-seeking opportunities for the private sector. These are thought actually to promote economic development. Rent-seeking opportunities change the incentive structure faced by private financial institutions in the following ways:

- First, there is a substantially equal provision of 'franchise value' between financial institutions. This allows equal access to rent-seeking opportunities. Financial institutions can enjoy their franchise value only as long as their business continues to be successful. Therefore, the very existence of franchise value forces financial institutions to make business success a priority. This not only makes them more prudent, but also increases their willingness to invest in new skill acquisition.
- Secondly, the rents created by a mild regulation of interest rates are not lump sum transfers, but increase proportionally as the volume of deposits controlled by financial institutions grows. Given this incentive, gaining additional deposits must necessarily become the strategic focus of the banking sector. Under financial restraint, as compared with a policy of inaction, financial institutions are willing to invest more in the construction of branch networks in order to bring in new deposits.

During a period of economic development, this process delivers positive external benefits (efficient mobilization of savings, for example) that are greater than the private profit accruing to financial institutions that construct branch networks. In other words, if network construction depended solely on private judgment, without any policy intervention, then the actual amount of investment would be less than the social optimum. A financial restraint policy produces value for financial institutions while at the same time achieving positive external effects (preventing under-investment). In this sense, financial restraint beneficially promotes economic development.

Perhaps a typical example of using a financial restraint policy is the artificially low interest rate policy that prevailed during the Japanese high growth era. To re-emphasize a point made previously, contrary to the impression conveyed by the name artificially 'low' interest rate policy, the actual interest rate was not so low as to make the real interest rate negative. Consequently, interest rate regulation did not seriously discourage saving. Instead, individual financial institutions intensified their efforts to collect deposits, seeking to acquire at least some of the available rents. Mobilized savings seemed actually to increase. In this regard, the second (increased savings) effect described by Hellmann, Murdock and Stiglitz (1996) was a consequence of this policy.

However, the first effect was significantly different from what Hellmann, Murdock and Stiglitz (1996) anticipated. Japanese financial institutions did make great efforts to survive in order to maintain their franchise value. This effort was not channeled automatically into socially desirable profit seeking, such as the 'rigorous monitoring of its portfolio of loans'. More often it flowed into socially undesirable rent seeking that could strengthen connections to those in charge of regulation. Capturing officials in this manner was positively harmful to economic development.

Although Hellmann, Murdock and Stiglitz (1996: 173) clearly claim that '[B]y contrast, the franchise value created by financial restraint does not undermine the commercial profit-maximization orientation of banks', their insistence may be wrong, if we judge from the Japanese experience. In the next section, I focus on the deterioration of the Japanese financial system since the 1970s.

3   THE 1970 SYSTEM AND ECONOMIC STAGNATION

3.1   Setback in the Financial System Reform

The high growth era came to an end at the beginning of the 1970s. The standard explanation attributes this to the Oil Crisis of 1973. However, had the reduction in economic growth primarily been the result of the sudden rise in oil prices, the fall in oil prices in the 1980s should have produced a corresponding increase in growth in the Japanese economy. It is necessary to look elsewhere for a cause, other than the Oil Crisis, that can explain the demise of high economic growth.

Yoshikawa (1992:88) provides a persuasive explanation. His hypothesis, based on economic theory, employs an 'exhaustion of excess population' explanation. The Japanese high growth era ended when the absorption of excess population previously engaged in agriculture in the country was no longer viable. This excess population had produced large-scale migration from rural to urban areas, enabling the industrial sector to increase labor inputs. It had also contributed to an expansion of demand. However, by the beginning of the 1970s this population had been completely absorbed. As a result, the economy could no longer grow faster than its natural rate. Domestic causes rather than any external shock caused the high growth era to end.

The end of the period of high economic growth was not caused by the Oil Crisis, but by full employment. The Oil Crisis, nevertheless, had a significant influence on the economy and on Japanese society. It occurred suddenly, just as Japan reached a level of sound economic prosperity. Most Japanese reacted to the Oil Crisis as if it might wipe away their success at a single stroke. Policy reflected an excessively defensive response. This climate gave birth to modifications that succeeded in changing the Japanese economy. Japanese efforts aimed at maintaining the economic system, which had delivered success and prosperity, produced a hardening of that system.

In the following subsections, I intend to identify the process that brought about the deterioration of the financial system. This stemmed from a series of persistent attempts to withstand change, which in turn prevented any successful adaptation. I then discuss the way in which policies continued to disregard changes in the economic environment.

3.1.1 Changes in the financial environment

Since 1975, the ratio of private investments to GDP has rapidly decreased, reducing the Japanese economy to a low state of growth. In contrast, the decrease in the ratio of private savings to GDP has been relatively mild. As a result, private savings have tended substantially to exceed investment. While much of the excess savings of the private sector went towards financing the increasing budget deficits produced by central and local governments, a significant portion still remained. Since the mid-1970s, the Japanese economy has moved suddenly from one characterized by excess investment to one characterized by excess savings.

Disturbances, such as the second Oil Crisis in 1978, ensured that most Japanese did not immediately perceive the structural changes taking place. Widespread recognition of the change to an excess savings type of economic structure occurred only in the early 1980s. Rising inflation further confused the general perception of the economy. Although real GDP growth rate had dropped to around 5 per cent during the second half of the 1970s, nominal GDP growth rate remained high because of increased inflation. Only when inflation fell at the start of the 1980s did the growth rate fall in nominal terms as well.

This point is very important, especially if we are to evaluate correctly the behavior of financial institutions. Since financial contracts are usually expressed in nominal terms, it is easy for financial institutions to increase their outstanding loans as long as nominal GDP continues to grow rapidly. However, if growth begins to falter in nominal terms, banks should face a greater degree of difficulty in increasing their lending levels. Ignoring this, in the 1980s Japanese financial institutions continued to increase their outstanding loans at the same rate as previously.

As a result, since 1981 the ratio of bank loans to GDP has risen steadily. Loans outstanding (held by the domestic branches of all banks) as a percentage of nominal GDP (previously stable at approximately 70 per cent in the 1970s) rapidly increased to nearly 110 per cent by the end of the 1980s. This credit expansion became instrumental in generating and maintaining the 'bubble economy' that characterized the second half of the 1980s.

Major companies, long viewed by Japanese financial institutions as their best customers, lowered their demand for bank funds during this period. We can explain the sizeable increase in lending that did occur by the fact that banks successfully spread their nets wider to 'find' a new class of unconventional borrower.

Though this explains how lending continued to grow, it doesn't explain why Japanese financial institutions were unwilling to slow down their lending activity. One answer is that the artificially low interest rate policy still existed in the 1980s. The opportunity for rent seeking provided by this policy created a powerful incentive for financial institutions to continue expanding their balance sheets. The pursuit of rents drove every financial institution to seek new clients.

In Japan's development stage, referred to earlier, this had positive external effects. It encouraged outcomes beyond simply generating private profit for financial institutions: the efficient mobilization of savings, the construction of branch banking networks. The financial restraint policy played a significant role, providing incentives that convinced financial institutions to make adequate investments. However, once the development process was complete, this policy no longer produced a desirable outcome. Traditional policy, sustained beyond its usefulness and cavalierly ignoring changed circumstances, began to have negative effects.

Rents no longer produced subsidies that could successfully internalize positive external effects. Instead, they created distortions more conducive to producing additional private than social benefits. Distortions of this type induce financial institutions to over-invest. Inevitably this leads to a banking industry obsessed with growth and growing excessively (the so-called 'over-banking' phenomenon). Just such a phenomenon seems to have existed in Japan since 1975. Even when the catch-up phase of economic development was clearly finished, the artificially low interest rate policy continued. Credit expansion and the enlargement of the financial sector were an unavoidable result.

The financial restraint policy became a car without brakes. While the car continued to run, its defects remained hidden. But once the car needed to stop, these defects made this impossible. Although Hellmann, Murdock and Stiglitz (1996: 198) do state that '[I]n fact, it will most likely become the vested interest of the bureaucrats running the system to uphold it long beyond its economic justification', this point is too important to minimize when evaluating the pros and cons of the policy. A car without brakes must be regarded as defective, no matter how good its performance might be in other respects.[12]

3.1.2   Financial liberalization at a gradual pace

Despite great changes in the financial environment, almost none of the parties concerned with the Japanese financial system proposed abolishing the artificially low interest rate policy. All incumbent parties and politicians believed that those with a vested interest in continuing this policy would withdraw their support given any attempt to change it. Nevertheless, starting in the mid-1980s financial liberalization commenced. Reform ultimately aimed at abandoning any and all regulations on interest rates and all restrictions and limitations on the range of business activity permitted to financial institutions. 'Outside pressure' had played a decisive background role, in a sense giving birth to financial liberalization.

During the 1980s, the current account imbalance between Japan and the United States expanded, resulting in frequent trade frictions. To help resolve such friction, the Japan–US Yen–Dollar Committee was formed and held meetings during the period 1983 to 1984. The problem, from the US standpoint, lay in the closed nature of Japanese capital markets, which severely restricted overseas entities by forcing them to hold yen balances. This, according to the US, caused the yen–dollar misalignment. Responding to outside criticism, the Japanese government agreed to liberalize euro–yen transactions and to deregulate interest rates incrementally.

The liberalization of euro–yen transactions provided major corporations with a loophole, which enabled them to avoid a variety of Japanese financial regulations. This initial reform acted as the thin end of the wedge pushing for major changes to the *status quo*. Despite these early steps, the path to financial liberalization proceeded with more than its fair share of obstacles. For example, it took a long time to deregulate interest rates, despite being unambiguously agreed to by the Yen–Dollar Committee. Japan rationalized its delaying tactics by discovering a persistent need to avoid 'drastic changes'. Complete deregulation became a reality only in 1994.

The year after the Yen–Dollar Committee closed its operations, the Meeting Group on Systemic Problems took its place. This new group operated under the umbrella of the Financial Systems Council, a board advising the Finance Minister. Ostensibly set up to enlarge the range of business that financial institutions could undertake, the board quickly became bogged down. For substance and substantial reform, it substituted increasingly sterile debate, accompanied by endless and rather pointless conferences. Each vested business interest vigorously resisted any deregulation. Restructuring was very difficult to negotiate. Laying out a blueprint that would define new ranges of business for financial institutions became almost unthinkable. When the discussions finally concluded, participants found that the 1980s had also run their course.

The actual agreed upon draft of June 1991 and the implementation of the reform system flowing from that agreement (April 1993) were incomplete and far from radical. For instance, the reform supposedly ended the long-lived prohibition preventing banks and security houses from mutually entering the same business. However, entry could only be via a subsidiary. If, for instance, a bank proposed to enter the security business, it had to establish a new security house as a subsidiary. The same applied in reverse. This paradoxically strengthened the 'walls between business activities' because banks still could do only banking business and security houses only security business.

Drastic changes in the environment further delayed interest rate deregulation (already about 20 years behind the UK and 10 years behind the US). Coupled with a completely inadequate attempt to redefine the range of financial businesses, these attempted reforms only led to the Japanese system hardening. Performance deteriorated further. Since the 1980s were noteworthy as years of financial innovation and radical change worldwide, this left Japan at a distinct disadvantage. By being so eager and preoccupied with protecting their vested interests, Japanese financial institutions ended up neglecting the almost categorical requirement to adapt to a changed economic environment.

While the Japanese slumbered, financial innovation was making rapid progress, with information technology (processing and networking) achieving epoch-making advances. To take advantage of such technology, business processes needed to be revamped if they were to yield corporate structures conducive to network-oriented specialization. Unfortunately, Japanese financial institutions, coddled and chronically idle behind the protective walls artificially separating business activities, neglected corporate restructuring. The express bus to the IT revolution pulled out of the station, leaving the Japanese behind.

3.1.3 Policy persistence
The story behind the Japanese artificially low interest rate policy is not unique. In general, a policy, once implemented, is not abolished easily.

Policies are preserved even after their original purpose has been accomplished or when the environment that gave birth to them has changed substantially. According to Coaste and Morris (1995), there are at least three reasons for such policy persistence:

- 'Uncertainty about the distribution of gains and losses from a policy reform can lead to the reform not being undertaken, even if it would be supported once introduced' (1995: 3). Not knowing what the effect of a policy change might be makes people hesitate in accepting the change.
- 'Agreement is required to change a policy, but no agreement is required to sustain it' (1995: 4). Since negotiation is required for agreement to be reached and the cost of negotiation is not negligible, this produces a bias towards policy persistence.
- When a policy is introduced, agents (corporate or otherwise) respond by making investments that enable them to benefit by its continued application. Given the quasi-rents at stake, they are now more willing to make additional payments to defend and retain their policy benefits. The pressure exerted to protect the value of these investments produces policy persistence. This third reason forms the analytic basis of the work by Coaste and Morris (1995).

In addition, a psychological consideration is at work. Those responsible for introducing a policy find its abolition a strikingly unpleasant prospect. They respond by resisting any such attempts at reform or change. Be that as it may, an economic perspective finds that the previous three reasons carry the most, if not all of the determinative weight.

What is the most significant explanation for the persistence of the Japanese artificially low interest rate policy? While all three reasons have some relevance, in my opinion, the third is the most significant. Although the effect of changing this policy was not entirely clear, the actual uncertainty attached was slight. However, all parties directly affected by the Japanese financial system recognized that the abolition of the artificially low interest rate policy would threaten their interests. While acknowledging that the negotiations required to reach agreement are difficult, the real difficulty still had more to do with pressure exerted by those wishing to retain the policy.

Japanese financial institutions responded to the artificially low interest rate policy by forming corporate structures and accumulating human capital, which could best squeeze the most profit out of this policy. For example, the planning department in charge of negotiating with regulatory authorities came to assume an important place in organizations. The best staff were assigned to this department. Adaptation and investment of this sort represented a sunk cost whose usefulness would almost certainly be lost if any radical policy change was made. To protect the value of their investment, these institutions lobbied vigorously to retain such an advantageous policy.

As part of their strategy, Japanese financial institutions attempted to capture the personnel of the relevant regulatory authorities. Favorable re-employment opportunities proliferated to benefit retired (*amakudari*) high ranking government officials. These positions preserved corporate rents. The practice of *amakudari* effectively shared a portion of the sought-after rents with key personnel of regulatory authorities. As Aoki (1988) has pointed out, the secretary bureau of each Ministry handled re-employment opportunities. Rarely could individual officials directly be bought off. Nevertheless, under this system, Ministry policy tended towards maintaining the *status quo*.

Policy makers placed primary emphasis on any negative impact (especially on existing financial institutions) when judging whether a policy should be changed. Harmful outcomes that might result if changes were not made were likely to be ignored. But even a single group of financial institutions opposing a policy was often sufficient to cause postponement. Once introduced (artificially low interest rates), the policy, even if beneficial at the time of its introduction, persisted long after it had ceased to generate any public advantage due to changes in both economic circumstances and technological conditions.

A lingering persistence of these outdated policies prevented the Japanese financial system from adjusting to environmental changes. This inability substantially contributed to its own deterioration. The inherently individualistic approach adopted by interest groups generated a stubborn degree of policy persistence. The larger the vested interest, the greater the effort and the more determined the approaches made to regulatory authorities could be in protecting that interest. Withstanding such an all-out attack could succeed only if regulatory authorities were able and willing to take the public interest solely into account in making appropriate policy changes. It was clearly unrealistic to suppose that these officials would always be able to ignore their own interests.[13]

For an optimal result (an outcome which maximized social welfare), policy makers should have implemented a financial restraint strategy during the catch-up phase and abolished it once that phase was complete. The Japanese experience shows that once introduced it became almost impossible to abolish the policy at the appropriate time. If a best option cannot be attained, if the government cannot ensure policy abolition at the appropriate time, then the second best option may be to avoid undertaking a financial restraint policy in the first place. The rejection of such a policy is preferable to its persistence.

3.2   Banking Crisis in the 1990s

The economic euphoria in the second half of the 1980s, later called the 'bubble economy', seemingly ended the economic deadlock faced by Japan. An illusion that high economic growth was possible without needed reform gained credibility. Investment became based upon excessively bullish expectations of future growth. The widespread belief that rises in asset prices would continue indefinitely fueled speculation. The Japanese banking sector willfully supplied the funds that supported excess investment and speculative action. Credit expansion reflected the guiding compulsion of Japanese financial institutions, the drive to increase their size.

The bill for this unwarranted credit expansion proved very expensive. When the economic euphoria of the previous decade disappeared in the 1990s, the price of assets, such as corporate stocks and real estate, declined sharply. In Japan, bank loans are not based so much on the future cash flows of investment projects, but on the value of the collateral behind the loans. Discounted cash flows yielded by these projects were often insufficient even to service interest payments. The decline in the value of those assets, acting as collateral, automatically reclassified these loans into the non-performing category.

By the summer of 1992, as declining land prices became a reality, concern about the Japanese banking sector spread. It appeared to be in a bad way, laden with many non-performing loans. The first signs of financial instability emerged in the Japanese system. Since then, Japan has found itself in the throes of a large-scale, long-lasting banking crisis. Even now, after so many years, Japan is only beginning to escape from that crisis. Nor can anyone seriously claim that the banking system is completely out of danger. During this banking crisis, the 1970 Japanese financial system proved to be a major casualty, as did the artificially low interest rate policy.

A car without brakes cannot stop until it collides with an object or runs out of fuel. This metaphor can be applied to the bumbling Japanese financial sector in the 1990s. Colliding with a huge mountain of bad loans gradually consumed the rents previously accumulated by Japanese banks. In the next subsection, I will review the course taken by this banking crisis. The incompetence exposed when confronted with difficult problems, as well as a critical incapacity by the existing system to solve those problems, made the need to reform the 1970 system obvious.

3.2.1 Bad loan problem

Although I wrote earlier that 'Japan has found itself in the throes of a large-scale, long-lasting banking crisis', most Japanese were still unaware that there was a crisis. In the first half of the 1990s, not only ordinary people, but even bankers and banking regulators, had underestimated the extent of the problem. Underpinning this underestimation was a deep-rooted belief that the decline in asset prices was a temporary phenomenon. Asset prices would bounce back in due course. There was an expectation that the problem would cure itself when this asset price revival arrived.

This belief, based on the experience of the catch-up period, took no account of the changed external conditions facing Japan. Domestically, the Japanese economy had completed the catch-up phase and was maturing. The high economic growth which once characterized Japan would not come again. Internationally, the Cold War ended as the 1990s began. Linked to this was a worldwide increase in supply capacities, which had a deflationary impact on the entire world. Given these changes, asset prices were unlikely to revive.

Far from bouncing back, the decline in asset prices accelerated as people gradually realized that no bounce was left. The demand for assets based on prior inflationary expectations decreased. Even then, asset prices in Japan were probably still higher than justified by the assets' discounted cash flows. This downward price spiral meant that the prevailing strategy of 'waiting', based on the belief in an imminent upsurge in asset prices, was now revealed as a complete failure.

From 1992 to 1994, neither financial institutions nor regulatory authorities took anything vaguely resembling a drastic measure to solve or even to head off the bad loan problem. Most Japanese financial institutions not only indulged in window-dressing their profits, by realizing previously accumulated off-record gains, but also resisted disclosing their own financial condition including the amount of bad loans they held. Camouflaging the surface rather than improving the substance of the problem seemed the object of all the efforts banks exerted. With hindsight, it is clear that this attitude subsequently made the bad loan problem more difficult to solve.

Among the measures taken by the government during this period, the only one of note was the establishment of the Cooperative Credit Purchasing Company (CCPC), which began operations in January 1993. Financial institutions had to lend the funds required by the CCPC to purchase the institutions' own bad loans. The only advantage financial institutions could gain by making use of the CCPC was in the form of a tax break, writing off the loss due to the bad loans purchased, even though they had failed to find final buyers for these same bad loans. Needless to say, using such a minor incentive could not solve the critical bad loan problem in Japan.

In the first half of the 1990s, the Japanese government shifted the responsibility for bad loan problems to individual financial institutions. A failure to recognize the serious difficulties faced by the banks formed the basis of this policy stance. Prime Minister Kiichi Miyazawa's suggestion, in August 1992, of an 'injection of public funds into the banking sector' met with public hostility. This reaction helped to shape the government's subsequent position. Neither the Japanese people nor the mass media really understood how serious the problem was at the time.

On the contrary, to Japanese households the bad loan problem was something that only concerned financial institutions. It could have nothing even indirectly to do with them or their lives. Instead, public antagonism to financial institutions, which had enjoyed substantial rents until that time, was the dominant popular concern. This attitude was partially a response to the existing financial structure in Japan. For the most part, households secure their assets exclusively in the form of deposits that have their principals guaranteed. Even if the value of assets held by financial institutions, or other companies, fluctuated enormously, the value of Japanese household assets would neither be marked to market nor changed. Consequently, Japanese households regarded financial fluctuations as simply being an institutional concern rather than a problem that could affect them.

3.2.2 Delay in the settlement of bank failures

The policy stance of the Japanese government during the period 1992 to 1994 was one which Mitchell (1999) has called a 'policy of self-reliance'.

Drawing on the experience of East European countries in transition-economies, which faced a banking crisis, Mitchell (1999) classified policies available to governments that try to deal with large amounts of non-performing loans into three categories: self-reliance, debt transfer and debt cancellation. Of the three, self-reliance is the most *laissez-faire* policy. The problem remains essentially the banks' responsibility, leaving the bad loans to the banks' own ministrations. In contrast, debt transfer involves a government-sanctioned transfer of bad loans from the banks' balance sheets to that of a professional 'bad debt' bank.[14]

Given that the interests of bank managers differ from those of bank owners (shareholders), the responses of managers to an excessive number of bad loans are not necessarily going to be in the best interests of shareholders. When managers find themselves in this difficulty, they tend to hide the true position of their bank by renewing bad loans or making additional loans rather than making efforts to collect the bad loans. According to Mitchell's analysis, such behavior is more likely to occur under the self-reliance policy. The bank managers' behavior produces a soft-budget problem for debtor firms. The result is a strong likelihood of further depreciation in the value of the problem loans.

This predictable phenomenon was just becoming manifest in Japan in the first half of the 1990s. Japanese policy, supposedly based on self-reliance, simply put off solving the problem until some future period. Financial institutions took a tolerant attitude to their troubled clients by eagerly shoving non-performing loans under the rug instead of aggressively trying to deal with them. This tolerance meant that managers of heavily indebted firms pursued their own private interests at the cost of their companies' well being. Not surprisingly, the result was a further decline in the value of these loans.

This outcome is an inevitable consequence of the mechanism previously described. It is for this reason that I have argued against loan deferral, or a tolerant attitude, because it makes the problem eventually more difficult to address. Rational self-interest dictates that under a self-reliance policy individual bank managers will leave the problem for future consideration. Without the abolition of this policy, ethical considerations will have little impact in shaping their attitudes. Consequently, given the dominance of this approach, non-performing loans held by Japanese financial institutions became much worse over time. In December 1994 the *Tokyo Kyowa* and *Anzen* credit unions failed, the first time something like that had happened since World War II.

Needless to say, financial institutions had fallen into deep financial trouble prior to the 1990s. However, troubled banks or financial organizations had been rescued routinely by merger with other sound institutions. This strategy prevented outcomes, such as bankruptcy, from coming to light. Rents accumulated over the years by Japanese financial institutions paid all the necessary rescue costs.[15] The situation had so degenerated by the end of 1994 that a conventional response could no longer prevent bankruptcy.

After the failure of the two Tokyo credit unions (*Cosmo* Credit Union), *Kidu* Credit Union, *Hyogo* Bank and others followed in 1995. It now became clear that neither the existing laws nor organizations could deal adequately with bank failure. The 'convoy' system of financial administration gave institutions a guarantee of future survival. Consequently, legal procedures failed to anticipate this potential, nor did organizations structure their operations to respond to such a possible situation. While it was fortunate that a deposit insurance system had been established in 1971, compared with the US version its scale and function were limited and inadequate.

From 1995, laws and organizational structures to address bank failures were promoted in a desperate attempt to respond to a worsening situation. However, bank failures could not wait for such schemes to reach completion. Since the groundwork was incomplete, the result was a patchwork of settlements based on individual cases. It was hard to find consistency or any underlying principle at work in the *ad hoc* responses to this series of bank failures. In particular, between 1995 and 1996 people were given no persuasive explanation for the injection of public funds into housing finance companies (*jusen*). Thus the Japanese people became increasingly suspicious of bank regulatory authorities, making it more difficult later on to resolve the bad loan problem.

3.2.3   State control of the financial system

To the Japanese, their government's response to bank failures seemed driven by neither consistent nor impartial principles. A series of scandals, exposed at this time, further persuaded the public that regulatory authorities were under the sway of those very same financial institutions they supposedly were regulating. As a consequence, people entirely lost faith in the *ancién régime* of the Japanese financial system (the 1970 variety). The government's response was to restructure the regulatory authorities. A June 1998 decision established the Financial Supervisory Agency (FSA). Authority to supervise banks would be vested in this agency alone and kept apart from the powerful Ministry of Finance.

However, a scheduled restructuring of regulatory authorities was not sufficient to correct the bad loan problem plaguing Japanese financial institutions. The banking crisis continued to deteriorate. By the autumn of 1997, the crisis had managed to penetrate the central system of the Japanese financial sector. Successive failures by very large financial institutions now occurred. Immediately following the failure of *Sanyo* Securities, *Yamaichi* Securities and then the *Hokkaido Takushoku* Bank each went bankrupt in turn. *Sanyo* Securities defaulted in the call money market. Although the amount on which *Sanyo* Securities defaulted was small, it was the first default in the Japanese inter-bank markets since World War II. Out of all proportion to its size, this failure triggered a sharp contraction in inter-bank credit.

The contraction of inter-bank credit induced an overall squeeze. Suddenly, it became significantly more difficult for the corporate sector to procure funds, despite an ostensibly super-easy monetary policy. The public at last began to realize that the delay in resolving the non-performing loan problem would have a serious impact on the economy as a whole. Japanese households could now understand that the banking crisis was not other people's business, but something directly linked to their own employment prospects and standard of living. This change in public perception made a bailout involving large sums of public money acceptable and thus much more feasible.

Thirty trillion yen underwrote a rescue plan cobbled together at the beginning of 1998. Of that sum, 1,815,600 million yen flowed into the 21 major banks. However, this was still only a stopgap measure and not sufficient to deal completely with the bad loan problem. The limitation of this approach became painfully obvious when the Long Term Credit Bank fell into financial disrepair almost immediately after receiving an injection of public money. Confronted by this critical situation in the autumn of 1998, the Diet hotly discussed ways to settle the bad loan problem and stabilize the financial system. As a result, yet another rescue plan budgeted at 60 trillion yen made its debut.

The new rescue plan rested on two pillars:

- the Law Concerning Emergency Measures for Reconstructing the Functions of the Financial System (commonly referred to as the Financial Reconstruction Law);
- the Financial Early Restoration Law.

The Financial Reconstruction Law empowered authorities temporarily to nationalize a failed bank (a system of special public administration) and to designate a Financial Reorganization Administrator to deal with the insolvent institution. The Financial Early Restoration Law established a framework for new capital injection. The authorities could inject public money into a bank with a weak capital base by purchasing its preferred stock. The Long Term Credit Bank and the *Nippon* Credit Bank, both in deep financial trouble, were nationalized under the Financial Reconstruction Law. In March 1999, the 18 major banks received an injection of public money totaling 7,459,200 million yen under the Financial Early Restoration Law.

The organizational structure of the Financial Reconstruction Commission (FRC) was established. The FRC operated as the parent organization of the FSA. In addition, merging the Resolution and Collection Bank and the Housing Loan Administration Corporation created the Resolution and Collection Corporation (the RCC, the Japanese version of the American Resolution Trust Corporation). It now became possible to purchase bad loans from sound financial institutions as well. The creation of the RCC and the capital injection framework already mentioned signaled a policy which marked a clear turning away from simple self-reliance towards a debt transfer approach.

This latest rescue plan[16] appears to have stabilized, to a degree, the Japanese financial system. However, stability has mainly reflected a heightened degree of government control. It is unlikely that this newly won stability can be maintained without continued government aid. As a result of these capital injections, almost all of the major Japanese banks are partially nationalized. More importantly, the government has guaranteed not only deposits, but also the entire value of debts held (since 1996) in excess of the limit set by the deposit insurance law (initially scheduled to go into effect in 2001).

In this sense, the stability of the Japanese financial system at present is the result of state control. Until this state control of the financial system ends, the Japanese banking crisis will not be over.

3.3   A Supplement

In this subsection, I consider a simple model[17] that helps to explicate the structure of capturing. The model assumes informational asymmetry in regard to bank revenue.

For the sake of simplicity, assume that all banks are identical. The average revenue (= marginal revenue) from a loan after deducting the costs, other than the funding cost (the deposit interest rate), R, is constant. Suppose that only banks know the true value of R, although the value of R could be either R_H or R_L ($R_H > R_L$). Let the probability that $R = R_H$ be denoted by p (so that the probability that $R = R_L$ is $1 - p$). Assume that these probabilities are common knowledge. On the other hand, suppose that the government (regulatory authority) has imperfect monitoring ability. It can find the true value of the banks' average revenue with the probability of q (or fails to find the true value and remains uncertain about it with the probability of $[1 - q]$) if it spends the monitoring cost of e.

Suppose that the demand for deposit (supply of fund) function is D in Figure 4.1. Let the surplus when the deposit interest rate is R_L be denoted by X and divide the additional surplus when the deposit interest rate is R_H into two parts as illustrated in the figure. Let the sizes of those parts be Y and Z. In addition, assume that all agents are risk neutral.

Even in the situation assumed above (the true value of the marginal revenue is known solely by banks),[18] the standard expectation is that the deposit interest rate will coincide with the true value of the marginal revenue. This equivalence will occur since banks more eager to attract deposits than their rival banks will bid up the deposit interest rate. In this way, the (assumed) competitive environment will substantially reveal the information possessed by banks. However, if the government (regulatory authority) controls the deposit interest rate then information will not be sufficiently revealed. This approach creates an opportunity for seeking rents based on hidden information.

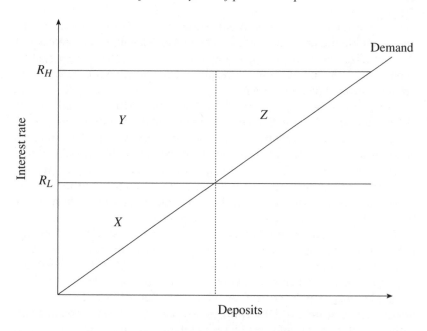

Figure 4.1 Deposit demand (supply of funds) function

Keeping such a situation in mind, consider first that the deposit interest rate (the banks' funding cost), r_D, is perfectly controlled by the regulatory authority. Without monitoring the banks' average revenue, the regulatory authority is unable to set the deposit interest rate ceiling at any level other than R_L. If the deposit interest rate is determined such that $r_D > R_L$, no deposits will be offered to banks when R actually equals R_L. I assume that the cost of losing deposits is prohibitively high.[19] The consumer surplus at $r_D = R_L$ will be X and the banks' expected profit (supplier surplus) would be pY.

When monitoring the banks' average revenue, the regulatory authority can determine if $R = R_H$ and it can determine that $r_D = R_H$ with the probability of qp (or in other cases, $r_D = R_L$). Therefore, with monitoring, the consumer surplus is $X + qp(Y + Z)$, whereas the banks' expected profits are $(1 - q)pY$. Compared with the no-monitoring case, although the banks' expected profit decreases by qpY, the consumer surplus increases by $qp(Y + Z)$. Total surplus increases by qpZ. However, net surplus does not increase unless $qpZ > e$ because a cost of e is required for monitoring.

On the other hand, if the interest rate on deposits is no longer regulated and a required level of competition eventuates, then the consumer surplus is $X + p(Y + Z)$ and the banks' expected profit is 0. This implies that regulating the interest rate on deposits without monitoring makes it possible for the banks to obtain rents as high as pY. The banks' franchise value consists of the capitalized value of its rents. Similarly, regulating the interest rate on deposits and also monitoring the result make it possible for the banks to obtain rents as high as $(1-q)pY$.

There is a possibility, described by Hellmann, Murdock and Stiglitz (1996), that the existence of such rents will tempt banks into trying to shift the deposit demand function D to the right (see Figure 4.1). If such attempts are made, then a fruitful outcome, exceeding the deadweight loss in a static sense $[pZ$ or $(1-q)pZ+e]$, may occur next period. However, the same rents might be used as a bribe given to regulatory authorities. As stated earlier, there is no guarantee that the banks' efforts will automatically be directed towards a socially desirable outcome.

Now assume that the regulatory authority is willing not only to pursue public benefit but also to consider its own private benefit. This seems a very plausible assumption. Let the marginal rate of substitution[20] between public and private benefits be denoted by λ. The benefits transferred (from the banks to the regulatory authority) are represented by t. Then, regardless of a decrease in the total surplus, regulating the interest rate on deposits without monitoring is adopted by the regulatory authority if:

$$\lambda t - pZ > 0. \tag{4.1}$$

On the other hand, the amount of benefits that banks permit to be transferred should satisfy the next condition:

$$t < pY. \tag{4.2}$$

If there exists a t that concurrently satisfies inequalities (4.1) and (4.2), an authority that is captured by banking interests will regulate the interest rate on deposits so that the public does not benefit. It should be easy to understand that a larger λ (the more a regulatory authority regards its private benefit as important) and a larger pY (the larger the rents the banks enjoy are) means a greater possibility that we will find a t that satisfies both inequalities. On the other hand, if the regulatory authority hardly takes its own private interest into account (λ is close to zero), then equation (4.1) is never satisfied.

Furthermore, even in the case that $qpZ > e$ and it is desirable to monitor the banks' average revenue, if the inequality

$$\lambda(1-q)pY > qpZ - e \tag{4.3}$$

holds, then bribery might not bring about monitoring. The larger λ is (the more the regulatory authority regards its private benefit as important) and the smaller q is (the lower the regulatory authority's monitoring ability is), the more inequality is likely to result.

Relatively low administration costs have too often formed the basis for evaluating the effectiveness of Japanese banking regulation. This may mean that socially desirable but costly monitoring will not be carried out. Although regulating the interest rate on deposits without simultaneously monitoring is less expensive, this strategy reduces social welfare if $qpZ > e$.

4 RECENT REFORM OF THE FINANCIAL SYSTEM

While the *ancién régime* (the 1970 system) of the Japanese financial structure was collapsing, attempts to reformulate the system have been undertaken since the second half of the 1990s. Something of a transformation began in earnest when the then Prime Minister Ryutaro Hashimoto issued instructions for 'financial system reform' in November 1996. Three principles, best described as 'free, fair and global', aimed at challenging the dominance of New York and London in the international money markets by bringing Tokyo up to speed by 2001. This 1996 reform package became commonly known as the 'Japanese Big Bang'.

The principle of 'free' implies that deregulation leads to Japanese financial markets operating *free* of regulatory burdens. The principle of 'fair' means those marketplace transactions should be *fair* in terms of transparency and reliability. Lastly, the principle of 'global' suggests that rules and regulations governing the Japanese financial markets should match and be compatible with *global* standards. Propagating these three principles required a 'big bang' method employing simultaneous deregulation (based on a predetermined short-term plan). The conventional method of reform implies only a gradual liberalization. A proper evaluation of each previous step preceded any new step to be taken.

Gradual financial liberalization (the conventional way) had not accomplished the bulk of Japan's financial objectives. A widespread agreement that this was indeed true led the Japanese to believe that their financial system was doomed to deteriorate. By this time, any competitive ability Japanese major banks may have possessed in the international marketplace had vanished quite spectacularly. This proved to be a decisive spur accelerating the switchover from a reform approach defined by gradualism to a more 'big bang' approach. However, it must be pointed out that even though current financial reform is known as the 'Japanese Big Bang', it is not literally a *big bang*. Compared with the more gradual liberalization of the past, reform has accelerated considerably. But clearly, reform is still proceeding in stages.

The first step of the Japanese Big Bang abolished foreign exchange controls. A revised Foreign Exchange Law has been in force since April 1998. By removing the previous approval and reporting system characterizing foreign exchange transactions, cross-border capital movements were liberalized. Eliminating any and all restrictions on foreign exchange business made possible such activities as providing network service across domestic and foreign markets. Reform dramatically increased the openness of the Japanese financial markets.

The Financial System Reform Law, enacted in June 1998, represented the next step. This was a package that revised laws concerning the financial system. By December 1998, implementation of almost all these measures was in place. A full liberalization of brokerage commissions remained a major exception. Japan did not manage to complete this piece of the package until October 1999. At that time, deregulation that aimed to ensure the basic principle of 'free' was nearly complete. This accomplishment loses some of its luster when we remember that Europe and America had introduced almost all of these financial market measures in the 1980s. Japan was more than 10 years behind in deregulating financial markets. For example, the US fully liberalized brokerage commissions in 1975 and the UK in 1986. Japan lagged behind these countries by 24 years and 13 years in achieving the exact same objective.

More important than simply being a laggard, deregulation alone is not sufficient to build a new system. Constructive effort is essential to establishing something significantly different. In particular, at least some legislation is required to achieve the principle of 'fair'. Specifically, laws have to establish comprehensive cross-business rules and regulations, which go beyond those that are merely conventional and specific. If this is not done, along with mechanisms to enforce such regulatory intentions, there is little hope of keeping financial transactions fair.

Despite this, there has not yet been enough effort made to accomplish completely satisfactory outcomes. The Financial Council (the successor of the Financial System Council), serving as an advisory board to the Finance Ministry, has discussed new rules and regulations, even taking the Financial Services Law in the UK as a model. Still, the Japanese have failed to produce any strategy that would result in the passage of such a fully fledged law. At present the Japanese financial system is forced to fly on only one engine because even after liberalizing its structure, it still lacks the other engine of a comprehensive set of rules and regulations that would also outline the permissible ranges of cross-business activities.

Japan also suffers from a conspicuous delay in constructing infrastructures that facilitate financial transactions. For example, Japan has no unified securities settlement system. The current system is divided into sub-systems according to each financial instrument (government bonds corporate bonds and stocks, among others). Some of these sub-systems cannot yet effectively differentiate DVP (delivery versus payment). This example shows that the Japanese securities market trails both the European and American markets in the efficiency and safety of transactions. Constructing and enhancing such physical infrastructure is an urgent undertaking, one that is necessary to revitalize the Japanese financial system.

The role of financial institutions in the system is also advancing in line with the progress of reform. At least two tasks remain:

- to reduce overcapacity and improve the efficiency of commercial banking;
- to facilitate the growth of investment banking by boosting the capacity to handle the necessary financial technology.

Japan aims to reduce excess capacity by promoting mergers and consolidations. However, this strategy seems insufficient to produce a large and speedy downsizing of the Japanese commercial banking sector. Similarly, it is still not certain how Japanese financial institutions will overcome delays in developing financial engineering skills and making IT investments.

Recently, plans for a series of mega-mergers or consolidations were officially announced in Japan:

- the consolidation of the IBJ, the *Dai'ich Kangyo* Bank and the *Fuji* Bank (August 1999);
- the merger of the *Sumitomo* Bank and the *Sakura* Bank (October 1999);
- the participation of the *Sanwa* Bank in the consolidation of the *Asahi* Bank and the *Tokai* Bank (March 2000).

It is doubtful that any of these mega-mergers or consolidations will have positive economic effects beyond bringing into existence banks that are 'too big to fail'.

Japanese financial institutions find it difficult to map out a clear strategy that will lead to the recovery of their competitive power and profitability. Considering the opaqueness of its recovery strategy and the continued overhang created by non-performing loans, the Japanese financial system still has some major restructuring to do. This will take time. However, some hope still remains.

Between 2001 and 2003, Japan will introduce significant changes in corporate accounting rules, from separated and historical-cost accounting to consolidated and market value accounting. During the same period, the

Japanese will phase out government guarantees on all debts held by Japanese financial institutions beyond the limit set by the deposit insurance system. These changes are anticipated to have a great managerial impact, forcing banks (and their managers) to undertake extensive reform. Given the impetus created by such changes, I expect that the Japanese financial system will surely and steadily be restructured.

NOTES

1. Professor Okuno-Fujiwara of the University of Tokyo refers to the same system as 'the 1975 system'.
2. *Showa* is the name applied to the imperial period that lasted from 1926 to 1989.
3. As an exception, the Imperial Bank was divided into two, the *Mitsui* Bank and the *Dai'ich* (First) Bank. However, this might be regarded more as the dissolution of a forcible merger conducted during wartime.
4. Strictly speaking, the minimum required differed according to the population of the bank's location. The minimum amount for banks having their headquarters in Tokyo or Osaka was more than 2,000,000 yen. If headquartered in regions with populations under 10,000, banks needed no more than 500,000 yen.
5. Japan rushed headlong into the war with the United States in December 1941. Before that war, Japan and China had been in a state of hostility since the Manchurian Incident of 1931.
6. In the following discussion, I am much indebted to Ueda (1993) and Teranishi (1993).
7. The *Nippon Kangyo* Bank (one of the wartime special banks) divested its long-term financing section when it converted into an ordinary bank. This became the Long Term Credit Bank of Japan. Japan in its role of colonial ruler established the *Nippon* Credit Bank as a special bank out of the Korean Bank's domestic account.
8. See Horiuchi (1999a:14).
9. I am much indebted to Iwata and Horiuchi (1985) and Teranishi (1982) for explaining the content of the low interest rate policy.
10. Being obliged to buy low yield government bonds would seem to saddle banks with big losses. In fact, until the second half of the 1970s, the volume of bonds issued was relatively small. Bonds purchased by banks were repurchased by the BOJ within one year. When the investment term was only a year, the banks did not sustain a loss. The yield on government bonds was still higher than that on regulated one-year deposits. However, from 1975 the Japanese deficit expanded rapidly. As a consequence, the volume of government bonds issued became much greater. The BOJ could not repurchase all of these bonds. Banks actually did incur great losses. This unsustainable situation created pressure for interest rate liberalization.
11. Calder (1993) has scrutinized the role of private banks during the high growth era.
12. Horiuchi (1999b:197) criticized Hellmann, Murdock and Stiglitz (1996) in much the same way.
13. With regard to this point, refer to the supplement (p. 82).
14. Debt cancellation seems to be a policy specific to countries in transition. It is not described in this chapter.
15. Opportunities for expanded rent seeking (either preferential treatment in branch restriction or access to BOJ lending at low interest) persuaded financial institutions to rescue those in trouble.
16. Refer to Nakaso (1999) for additional details of the new rescue plan.
17. The model in this subsection is a modified version of that in Hillier (1997, chapter 11, section 2). Coaste and Morris (1995) inspire the modification I make.

18. I assume that banks can compete strongly with each other and that price (deposit interest rate) competition is permitted.
19. That is, I suppose that $pZ < (1 - p)X$.
20. The amount of public benefit that the regulatory authority permits to be sacrificed in compensation for a one-unit increase in its private benefit.

REFERENCES

Aoki, M. (1988), *Information, Incentives, and Bargaining in the Japanese Economy*, Cambridge: Cambridge University Press.

Aoki, M., H.K. Kim and M. Okuno-Fujiwara (eds) (1997), *The Role of Government in East Asian Economic Development*, Oxford: Oxford University Press.

Calder, K.E. (1993), *Strategic Capitalism*, Princeton: Princeton University Press.

Coaste, S. and S. Morris (1995), 'Policy Persistence', *CARESS Working Paper No. 95–19*, University of Pennsylvania.

Harada, Y. (1998), *The End of the 1970 System* [in Japanese], Tokyo: Toyokeizaishinpo-sha.

Hellmann, T., K. Murdock, and J. Stiglitz (1997), 'Financial Restraint: Toward a New Paradigm', in Aoki, Kim and Okuno-Fujiwara, (eds) (1997), 163–207.

Hillier, B. (1997), *The Economics of Asymmetric Information*, New York: St. Martin's Press.

Horiuchi, A. (1999a), 'Fundamentals of Financial Structure in Japan: A Perspective' [in Japanese], *Coping with the Changes in Financial Structure*, The Report of Financial Study Group, **23**, pp. 1–36.

Horiuchi, A. (1999b), 'An Overview of the Financial Reforms in Japan' [in Japanese], *The Economic Review*, The Institute of Economic Research, Hitotsubashi University, **50**(3), pp. 193–205.

Iwata, K. and A. Horiuchi (1985), 'Banking Regulation in Japan' [in Japanese], *The Journal of Economics*, The Society of Economics, University of Tokyo, **51**(1), pp. 2–33.

Katz, R. (1998), *Japan: The System That Soured – The Rise and Fall of the Japanese Economic Miracle*, Armonk, New York: M. E. Sharpe.

Mitchell, J. (1999), 'Theories of Soft Budget Constraints and the Analysis of Banking Crises', downloaded from http://www.ssrn.com.

Nakaso, H. (1999), "Recent Banking Sector Reforms in Japan', *Economic Policy Review*, Federal Reserve Bank of New York, July, pp. 1–7.

Noguchi, Y. (1995), *The 1940 System* [in Japanese], Tokyo: Toyokeizai-shinpo-sha.

Okazaki and Okuno-Fujiwara (eds) (1993), *Origins of the Contemporary Japanese Economic System* [in Japanese], Tokyo: Nihon-Keizai-Sinbunsha.

Okuno-Fujiwara, M. (1999), 'The Contemporary Japanese State System and Its Reform' [in Japanese], *The Economic Review*, The Institute of Economic Research, Hitotsubashi University, **50**(3), pp. 206–17.

Teranishi, J. (1982), *Money, Banking, and Economic Development in Japan* [in Japanese], Tokyo: Iwanami-shoten.

Teranishi, J. (1993), 'Main-Bank System' [in Japanese], in Okazaki and Okuno-Fujiwara (eds) (1993).

Ueda, K. (1993), 'Financial System and Regulation' [in Japanese], in Okazaki and Okuno-Fujiwara (eds) (1993).

Yamamura, Kozo (1982), 'Success That Soured: Administrative Guidance and Cartels in Japan', in K. Yamamura (ed.) (1982), pp. 77–112.

Yamamura, K. (ed.) (1982), *Policy and Trade Issues of the Japanese Economy: American and Japanese Perspectives*, Tokyo: University of Tokyo Press.

Yoshikawa, H. (1992), *Japanese Economy and Macro-Economics* [in Japanese], Tokyo: Toyokeizai-shinpo-sha.

COMMENT ON 'THE FINANCIAL SYSTEM OF POST-1945 JAPAN: ITS FORMATION, DEVELOPMENT AND DETERIORATION'

Eileen Mauskopf[1]

Professor Ikeo has written an interesting and thought-provoking chapter, one that provides a very valuable historical perspective on why things are the way they are in the Japanese financial system, especially in the banking sector. He has described both the external influences on the financial sector (the effects of the Second World War, the high growth period that followed the war) as well as the equally, if not more, important cultural and national influences on this system. This chapter should be required reading for anyone who hopes to understand the crisis in the banking sector and the relatively limited extent of the sector's recovery over the past several years.

Professor Ikeo's analysis has left me less optimistic about the prospects both for a pickup in the pace of the banking sector recovery in the near term and for sustained health in the sector in the longer run. The roots of the current problems are deeper than I had thought. The response of the financial authorities to the problems, which I would characterize as tepid at best, is most likely viewed by the Japanese banking community as a fair, and even fairly aggressive, posture. Finally, this chapter (as well as several others written for the conference) reinforces my impression that significant reform to corporate governance may be a long way off for the banking sector. To many in Japan, 'American-style' corporate governance, with its emphasis on shareholders and share prices, represents too radical a departure from long-prevailing traditions of the workplace culture. My sense is that a major change to corporate governance, if it occurs, will owe at least as much to the pressures of globalization as to any internal support for such change.

The Financial System in the Past

Turning first to the *past* performance of the financial system, I would like to suggest that, however impressive the Japanese economy was in the 1950s,

60s and early 70s, it may have been successful not because of, but in spite of, the financial system. This suggestion is likely to be a bit controversial. It is somewhat at odds with Professor Ikeo's premise that the Japanese financial system was really quite good up until growth started slowing in the early to mid 1970s. I think a case can be made that the regulations that allowed the economy to mobilize capital to aid the munitions industry during the war would not necessarily have been the best system to maximize growth after the war and through the high growth period. Just because growth turned out to be very high, this does not mean that it could not have been even higher. Possibly this could have occurred by producing even greater savings and investment but, more likely, by ensuring that savings were allocated to those uses with the highest marginal product.

During the war, regulation of the financial system was colored by two imperatives: the need to finance a wartime budget and the desire to direct the allocation of savings to the munitions industry. In support of these goals, corporate bond issuance was controlled, the stock market was essentially closed, and the banks and government became the only players in the intermediation of savings. This makes sense when you are fighting a war: you don't worry about the allocative efficiency of capital in the economy as a whole – you maximize munitions output at the cost of allocating less capital to other industries. And that is what was done. But after a war, regulations such as these become less compelling. The bank control over corporate bond issuance continued, and the stock market was dormant so that, in addition to the Postal Savings System, the banks essentially were handed a monopoly in attracting savings. Moreover, under the 'artificial' low interest rate policy (a policy that, by keeping interest rates low, was supposed to raise the international competitiveness of Japanese industry) banks were virtually guaranteed profits regardless of their efficiency. And, under this system, the large banks did most of the credit allocation. Credit rationing itself employed non-price mechanisms, which were, in turn, heavily dependent upon the relationships between banks and nonfinancial corporations built up during the war.

It is hard to see how this system was the most efficient way to fund corporate investment – although it is very likely that the system was beneficial in many respects. For sure, continuing the relations between banks and firms built up over the war probably increased the stability and certainty needed to encourage immediate postwar investment. But, unless savings were perfectly interest inelastic, the ceilings on deposit rates likely held savings below the level that a more market-oriented system would have produced. Second, and still more questionable, credit rationing favored firms within a given bank *keiretsu*, apparently overlooking the principle that (absent some overriding concern such as war) capital should be allocated efficiently, first funding those projects with the highest marginal product. No doubt long-standing relationships between banks and firms in the same *keiretsu* reduced the information and monitoring costs a bank would ordinarily have in extending a loan. But, it isn't clear where the pros and cons netted out. Were these savings large enough to justify the bias in favor of lending to those firms that banks knew the longest?

Another aspect of the postwar system that necessarily would have diminished the overall efficiency of the system (increasingly so over time) is that banks competed for deposits, not through adjusting their deposit rates, but by opening more branches. This is a grossly inefficient way of increasing savings and down the road it appears to have led to overinvestment in bank branches and bank personnel. Worse still, it set the stage for a long-standing and ultimately very costly inefficiency: establishing additional branches required approval from government officials (especially those in the Ministry of Finance) and thus, in the process, these officials gained more sway over the banks. In fact, it is probably not a stretch to say that the weak governance structure in the banking industry today stems at least in part from the pattern of ties between bank managers and government regulators established during this earlier period.

Although I am suggesting that the carryover of the wartime financial system fostered various inefficiencies in the procurement and allocation of capital that only recently raised strong concerns, it is of course possible that the system did well enough during the high growth period – with banks doing a pretty good job of taking in deposits and making loans. It is certainly true that (despite a ceiling on deposit interest rates) an enormous amount (of savings) was mobilized. The savings rate may indeed be relatively interest inelastic in Japan and, even if it is not, perhaps additional savings would have pushed the economy past the 'golden rule point', thus reducing, rather than raising, the sustainable level of consumption.

Perhaps, too, firms that were given priority in loans by virtue of their connections to the banks achieved returns that were not substantially different from what would have occurred under a more arm's-length transaction. Certainly, after the war the capital base of the country was so very low that many productive alternative investments would have existed in any case. Thus the exact allocation of capital may have had only a marginal effect on aggregate growth. Moreover, in the immediate postwar period, the relational contracting between bank and firm was probably critical to encouraging some firms to undertake investment. And Professor Ikeo argues that the branching network established by the banks increased the efficiency with which savings were mobilized in the early years.[2]

Nevertheless, as time passed, and well before the slowing of growth in the early 1970s, it is conceivable that the financial system had a negative influence on the economy. However, growth remained high because of a very favorable endowment of human capital, combined with a strong work ethic and an impressive propensity to save. Equally important, output of, and capital in, nonmilitary-related industries were so low after the war that almost any system that generated savings and allocated resources could not fail to achieve high growth for some time.

I bring up this question because, whatever the truth about the past performance of the financial system, in looking forward, it is difficult to overstate the importance of a financial system and a banking system that allocate capital efficiently and, in so doing, maximize the return to savings and the aggregate capital stock.

The Future of the Banking and Financial System

A development that could complicate the current problems and ultimately require a more aggressive set of reforms in the banking system than is in the works is the projected slowing in the potential rate of growth of the Japanese economy. This is largely a consequence of the slowdown in the growth rate of the working age population (and an implicit assumption that productivity growth will not increase by enough to offset the decline in labor force growth). The aging of the population presents two major concerns. First, although it is too soon to say whether this is happening in Japan, a decline in the potential growth rate of an economy is consistent with a secular drop in investment demand relative to GDP, assuming that the capital intensity of production is unchanged.[3] Some countervailing factors occur when growth slows, such as a decline in the real interest rate, that would tend to raise the capital intensity of production and thus moderate a fall in the ratio of investment to output.[4] But, to the extent that such factors do not significantly raise the optimal capital intensity, expenditure on investment will decline as a share of GDP *and therefore the demand for investment financing will decline relative to GDP.* Consequently, even if the share of the banking system in meeting the credit needs of industry were not to change in the coming years, we would expect to see loans originating in the banking sector decline relative to GDP.

But, in fact, the relative importance of the banking industry as a financial creditor (particularly as a creditor to the large firms) has been *declining* since at least the mid 1980s, when deregulation increased the financing options of large corporations. Bond markets at home and abroad now flourish, a domestic commercial paper market operates, and profitable firms must have plenty of internal funds available for financing because they certainly have not been paying much in the way of dividends during the postwar period. Although initial public equity offerings are expensive relative to US standards, equity issuance has become more attractive as a source of finance. It would appear to be only a matter of time before the smaller firms also reduce their bank dependence.

The implications of these developments for the banking sector entail several possibilities. One is that future flows of household savings continue to favor banks (despite the Big Bang reforms that should make other savings vehicles more attractive to households). Therefore banks, as they make fewer loans to nonfinancial firms, will need to move into other lines of business and utilize other assets to make use of these savings. This does not seem too likely right now given their limited expertise (all but the foreign banks) outside of traditional banking. It could happen but, if it doesn't, the temptation to make risky loans to businesses or for real estate might increase. Repeating the mistakes of the late 1980s would become a distinct possibility, although this time the chance that bank regulators would encourage this behavior is probably nil. Another possibility is that households will more rapidly embrace some of the other savings options that have come on board (such as US-style mutual funds) and divert their savings away from the banks.

In either case, a decline in the *aggregate* need for investment financing relative to GDP and the diminishing share banks could retain of investment finance, casts some doubt on the advisability of the injection of public capital into problem banks. It would seem that a downsizing of the banking sector is inevitable if Japan is to avoid being saddled with an unwanted degree of excess capacity as the traditional banking business shrinks. Public injections into the banks, with little in the way of sanctions, appear inconsistent with this incontrovertible trend, particularly as some of the recipients of the funds are banks that likely will have to exit the industry. Nor are either the recent and/or proposed mergers of some banks likely to remove the excess capacity. Only a very small number of branches have been closed and few employees have lost their jobs. In fact, as Professor Ikeo has indicated, these mergers are probably doing little more than creating 'banks that are too big to fail'.

A second concern associated with the slowing of labor force growth and the aging of the population is that it becomes imperative to raise the overall rate of return on Japan's large stock of capital to minimize the negative effect on per capita income. I have mentioned that, at least in theory, the rate of interest should fall with a drop in the growth rate of potential output. Thus the marginal return to capital, including capital owned by the retired population, will be under *downward* pressure over the foreseeable future. Raising the average return on the capital stock will require that the existing stock be allocated efficiently and new investment be directed to the areas with the greatest returns. This is true in all industries but it is especially true in the banking sector. Over the past two decades, the average return on equity in Japan has been very low, significantly lower than on US equity. And while it has fallen sharply in recent years, it is hard to claim that the returns are purely a consequence of the Japanese recession.

This leads to the issue of corporate governance. Many observers have argued that the low rates of return on capital, both in the banking sector and elsewhere, and even the slow speed of recovery (again markedly in the banking sector but also reflected in the economy's aggregate growth rate) are due at least in part to shortcomings in the corporate governance system. This is a system that has failed to emphasize either efficiency or return to capital to the extent that it likely will need to as it goes forward.

From the perspective of the American corporate system (a system that many may fault for its own weaknesses and drawbacks), several bottlenecks stand in the way of maximizing the return on capital, including the return to shareholders. First is the sizable presence of inside stakeholders among the owners of a firm's equity. In the case of the banks, these include firms that borrow from the bank. Because these inside stakeholders earn a return on the totality of their relationship with the bank, which includes the return on their customer-type relationships with the bank in addition to the return on their holdings of bank equity, it is not necessarily in their interest to focus purely on bank profits. To do so might mean less favorable terms on a loan. Because these inside stakeholders monitor the firms' managers, it is also not in the managers' interest to focus exclusively on shareholder wealth. The share of financial firms' equity owned by inside stakeholders has been around 50 per cent in recent years, about twice as high as the shares owned by insiders in nonfinancial firms. The presence and the influence of inside shareholders are much less in the US and tough rules apply to bank–nonbank cross-ownership. For instance, in the US a nonfinancial firm can own only up to 5 per cent of a bank's shares before so-called 'commitment rules' apply in varying degrees. These rules include having no say in management decisions, no representation on the Board of Directors and, perhaps most importantly, not being allowed to borrow from, or conduct other business with, the bank. (Even with these rules applying, a firm cannot own more than 25 per cent of a bank.) I don't know of any specific changes in the 'Big Bang' that will have a significant impact in moving bank–nonbank transactions to a more 'arm's length' posture.

A second characteristic that appears to insulate managers from shareholder pressure for high returns is that, among outside shareholders, institutional investors are relatively small. They account for only about 15 per cent of household assets in Japan compared with about 35 per cent in the US. Institutional shareholders generally get more management attention because they are larger and better organized than individual shareholders.

But, in addition to their small size in Japan, there is little history of Japanese institutional investors pressuring firms to maximize shareholder return. Episodes of institutional shareholder pressure are well known in the US. It seems as if every year or so, a large pension fund is in the news for some concession it managed to get out of some company whose shares it owns. The 'Big Bang' does contain some measures that will encourage the growth of institutional investors:

- lifting restrictions on corporate pension funds' choices of investment;
- allowing investments in foreign mutual funds;
- changing the tax treatment of mutual funds.

However, it does not appear to contain measures to encourage institutional shareholder activism.

Among other factors that lead to a lack of emphasis on rates of return is a very limited market for corporate control in Japan. Takeovers have been perceived as incompatible with the system of long-term relationships between suppliers and customers and, anyhow, are difficult when a large fraction of the firm's shares is held by insider stakeholders. Additionally, it is not very common for Japanese managers' pay to be tied to share price through stock option plans.

The Banking System Today

Because corporate governance changes play only a distant secondary role in the 'Big Bang', and because the institutional reforms mentioned above can do little to solve the current problem, it is important to reexamine what, if anything, can be done in the short run to improve the situation in the banking sector. For this, it may be useful to highlight a few of the measures adopted to deal with the US banking and thrift crisis.

In contrast to Japanese regulators, US bank and thrift regulators were extremely aggressive. They liberally closed banks and Savings and Loans, liquidating some and merging others. In terms of the funds necessary to do this, the banking industry itself was forced to cover the costs of the bank failures, using Federal Deposit Insurance Corporation (FDIC) assets and insurance premiums collected by the FDIC from the banks until they ran out, and then sharply raising the required premiums after that. The banks were forced (both by the market and ultimately by the regulators) to write off bad loans and to hold adequate loan loss reserves, reducing *reported* earnings and shareholder capital dollar for dollar with the bad loans. And, most importantly, the banks themselves were forced to raise private equity capital. In the case of the problem thrift institutions, taxpayer money was used, a lot of it. But it was used to pay off depositors of the failed thrifts, not to bail out shareholders and managers. The problem Savings and Loans were closed and the assets were sold by the regulators. The federal government issued bonds to fund the liquidation of the Savings and Loans and required *both* the banks and the thrifts to pay the servicing costs of these bonds. In short, there was far less regulatory forbearance in the US than appears to be going on in Japan.

Finally, one additional outcome of the episode was much more diligence in assessing the credit riskiness of loans. (At one time, as in Japan, US financial institutions had relied on the nature of the collateral in assessing the risk associated with a loan. This is far less likely now.) In fact, immediately after the banking crisis, starting in the late 1980s, banks became so obsessed with the issue of risk that in many parts of the country a credit crunch materialized. But after eight years of a booming economy, the tide has turned and banks may be erring, once again, in the sense of becoming a bit too lax about risk standards. Nevertheless, the moral is that there has been an enormous effort to educate the banks' loan officers about evaluating risk. We do not see that happening yet in Japan but we do see a continued reliance on assessing the riskiness of a loan by looking at underlying collateral such as land and equity, rather than cash flow from a project.

Notes

1. Many thanks to my colleagues Sally Davies, Ed Ettin, Michael Gibson and Nathan Sheets at the Board of Governors of the Federal Reserve, and to Anil Kashyup at the University of Chicago. The views expressed in the chapter are my own and are not necessarily endorsed by them.
2. Professor Ikeo has told me that the choice of the postwar financial structure was also a response to the relative costs of setting up this system compared with a more market-oriented system. I fully agree with his point. My concern is that, over time, the initial savings in the set-up costs were diluted and ultimately outweighed by the inefficiencies that came with the system.
3. In the steady state, the ratio of investment to capital is the sum of the growth rate of output plus the depreciation rate of capital. So a decline in the growth rate of output lowers the ratios of investment to capital and investment to output for an unchanged capital intensity of production.
4. Another factor (although not related to the projected slowing in growth) that, at first glance, might be expected to work against a projected decline in the investment share of output is the increasing investment worldwide in computers, owing to an ongoing and dramatic decline in the relative price of computing power. However, unless the (relative) price elasticity of demand for computers (and capital goods in general) is greater than 1, the decline in the relative computer (or capital) price raises the capital–output ratio in real terms but leaves the nominal ratio and the nominal share of investment to GDP unchanged to a first approximation. Empirical evidence at the aggregate level generally favors a Cobb–Douglas production function so that the relative price elasticity for capital is 1. Thus a change in the relative price of capital (or investment) would not offset the tendency for the nominal investment share of output to decline as growth slows.

5. Japan's continuing financial difficulties and confused economic policies*

Makoto Itoh

Compared with the preceding decades, the Japanese economy changed greatly in the 1990s. The economy shifted from what was already a lowered growth level down to an extremely low growth trend. Internationally, its continued stagnation has caused concern among advanced economies. Clearly in the late 1980s, these difficulties were caused, to a large extent, first by the swelling of a speculative bubble in the share market and then by a parallel movement in real estate prices, followed by a subsequent bursting of these inflated values. This saddled Japanese financial institutions with an enormous number of bad loans, created a credit crunch, caused the value of assets owned by firms and households to deteriorate, precipitated uninterrupted business failures, and more generally produced a vicious circle of asset deflation.

The inherent ability of a credit system to expand has produced bubbles before. Throughout the economic history of capitalism, the destruction produced by the bursting of speculative bubbles has been seen repeatedly. In the nascent period of capitalism, during the 17th and 18th centuries, the tulip crisis in the Netherlands and the South Sea bubble in the UK destabilized these early economies. This pattern is again reflected in the cyclical crises of the 19th century and throughout the great crisis after 1929. Since the late 1980s, the tendency of capitalism first to create speculative bubbles and then to burst them has reappeared strongly. The Japanese economy failed to avoid falling into this very familiar trap. At an abstract level, Minsky's post-Keynesian financial instability hypothesis[1] attempts to explain why such speculative bubbles collapse. If we employ his hypothesis, then starting in the late 1980s, Japanese firms and individuals took what can best be described as a hedge financing position. Their cash inflow from assets they held was expected to exceed cash outflow arising from liabilities in every period. Soon, increasing numbers of these players shifted to using this type of speculative finance. Cash flow from assets in the near future were expected to fall short for near-term contracted payments, but cash receipts in the longer term were still expected to exceed outstanding cash payments. Unfortunately, at the very last stage of speculative development, an increasing number of economic agents turn to Ponzi finance. Net income from receipts now falls short of interest payments in both the short run and the long run. Only a future profit bonanza can cover the growing mountains of outstanding debt.

However, neither the distinct possibility that financial bubbles will emerge in capitalist economies, nor a description of a largely hypothetical course of events, can explain sufficiently the reasons for, or the magnitude of, the damage wrought by the continuing financial instability in the Japanese economy during this period. We urgently need to reconsider the role played by the government and the Bank of Japan in fiscal and monetary policy. Only then is it possible to comprehend the deepening fiscal crisis of the Japanese State.

1 THE SWELL OF THE BUBBLE

We begin by examining how and why the huge bubble swelled in Japan in the late 1980s. Speculative trading and rising prices in shares and real estate characterized the bubble economy. Asset values outstripped real economic growth. While Japanese nominal GDP grew by a factor of 1.35 between 1985 and 1990, average share prices on the Tokyo Stock Exchange tripled. Average land prices in Tokyo and the three other major metropolitan areas rose 2.5 times. What were the main factors that caused this asset price bubble?

1.1 The Triggering Role of Monetary and Fiscal Policy

The 1985 G7 meetings leading to the Plaza Accord triggered the Japanese 'bubble economy' by promoting expansionary fiscal and monetary policies. The Accord attempted to weaken the strong US dollar and ease US trade deficits.

After 1983, recovery of the Japanese economy had depended largely on export-led growth, especially exports to the US market. This strategy was greatly aided by favorable exchange rates. The high interest rates characteristic of the early years of 'Reaganomics' had attracted massive international capital flows into the US. An appreciating US dollar was the inevitable result. The dollar had risen on a flood of speculative capital, directly violating the logic underpinning actual trade flows. After the Plaza Accord, the dollar began to depreciate rapidly. In the eight months leading up to March 1986, the yen appreciated from 240 to 150 to the dollar. This was a serious shock to Japanese export industries and generated a distinct potential for depression.

However, in 1986 the Nikkei average of 225 share prices began to rise, starting from a value of 13,137 at the beginning of the year, ending the year at 18,701. Despite an apparent depression in the real economy, the market rose by some 42 per cent. This marked the beginning of the subsequent bubble in share prices. An abrupt fall in interest rates was the key causal factor. Following the Plaza Accord, the prime rate set by the US Federal Reserve Bank fell from 7.5 per cent at the beginning of 1986 to 5.5 per cent in August of that year. Correspondingly, the Bank of Japan dropped the official rate from 5 per cent at the end of 1985 to 3 per cent in November 1986. The rate dropped further to an unprecedented level of 2.5 per cent in February 1987. It then remained unchanged until the spring of 1989. In the post-Plaza Accord period, the expansion of domestic demand was partially intended to mitigate trade friction with the US. Only monetary policy could hope to sustain such expansionary objectives since fiscal operations were constrained by a worsening of the State budget crisis. At the same time, the floating exchange rate system, combined with increasing Japanese foreign reserves, provided justification for a significant lowering of interest rates.

Other things remaining equal, a fall in interest rates raises the prices of shares and land (or the value of fictitious capital) relative to alternative investment.[2] Indeed, share prices began to rise on both the New York Stock Exchange and Tokyo Exchange in 1986. Japanese land prices simultaneously began rising sharply, starting with the Tokyo area.

To augment this incipient domestic expansion, the Japanese government dramatically deviated from its previous tight fiscal policy, adopted as the 1980s began. In an about face, it substituted a large emergency-spending plan in the spring of 1987. By using a supplementary budget of 6 trillion yen it aimed to spur public investment. Boosting domestic demand could skirt any danger of depression and ease a growing history of chronic trade frictions with the US. The central government also strongly advised local governments to expand regional redevelopment projects. A typical plan would encourage the construction of a bay area business center in Tokyo. These policies provided clear incentives for developers, real estate agents and construction companies to expand their operations. These incentives also facilitated the subsequent rise in the price of land and in other real estate as well.

The Bank of Japan, like many other central banks, traditionally has been obsessed with maintaining the value (or purchasing power) of its bank note, mostly by avoiding general inflation. The general price level remained stable in the late 1980s as energy import prices and other basic material costs were relatively depressed due to the appreciation of the yen and an improved balance between demand and supply in world markets. The Bank of Japan continued to supply money funds, which allowed banks and other financial institutions to expand loans for speculative trading in shares and real estate. The Bank largely ignored the danger of asset inflation. As a result, the money supply (the aggregate of cash, deposits payable on demand, time deposits and negotiable certificates of deposit) registered double-digit annual growth rates from the second quarter of 1987 until the third quarter of 1990. The growth of these money aggregates clearly outstripped real economic expansion.

1.2   An Economic Recovery Based on Expanding Domestic Demand

Monetary and fiscal policies do not automatically produce a desired economic recovery. But at this particular conjuncture of events in the 1980s, expansionary policies did increase effective demand in a top-down fashion. Initially, increased capital gains from rising share and property prices boosted the purchasing power of those already wealthy as well as the market value of business firms.

Income elastic goods (such luxury commodities as large passenger cars, fur coats and jewels) saw the biggest initial boost in sales. Department stores and fashion shops expanded their range of high grade expensive goods, featuring more world-famous brands. Japanese firms were largely incapable of sustaining export sales due to the strong yen. They turned instead to the domestic market, offering ever multiplying new models, to generate additional consumer spending. At the time, commentators joked that Japanese firms were only now discovering the world's second biggest consumer market. Expanding consumer credit, lowering interest rates and increasing the use of credit cards all encouraged greater consumer spending.

When the general public became aware of the rising house and land prices, demand for residential units in condominiums and for houses actually expanded rather than declined. The postwar Japanese economy had been plagued by a continuous housing shortage, especially in the more populous urban areas. With the number of families rapidly growing, the prices of housing units and of residential land had never fallen. People believed that no other asset was as secure as residential units and land. Naturally, to purchase a family housing unit before retirement became a primary objective for a great number of working people. Starting from these pre-conditions, a dramatic rise in real estate prices created expectations of future increases. The earlier one then jumps into the market, the bigger the subsequent capital gain. Widely held beliefs of this type become self-fulfilling prophecies.

People started to enter and buy into the housing market, beginning with the wealthier classes and eventually working its way downward.

Rising prices of residential units and land fostered further demand for these assets. The allure of quick capital gains created an increasingly herd-like mentality. Banks had promoted housing loans since the late 1970s. They substantially stepped up their efforts in the late 1980s.[3] From the third quarter of 1986 until the first quarter of 1988, each quarter of private housing investment surpassed its level in the same quarter of the previous year. Real estate agencies and banks urged clients to realize large capital gains by selling their houses. This would then form the downpayment for a larger unit financed with a low interest loan from a willing bank. Many Japanese consumers not only followed this advice but also supplemented their new home purchases by buying cars, furniture, electrical appliances and apparel, using additional lines of credit.

At the same time, demand for office space also swelled, especially in the Tokyo metropolitan area. Firms with rapidly expanding international activities logically relocated their headquarters to the Tokyo metropolitan area to be nearer the country's international finance and business links. Many companies which traditionally had been based away from the metropolitan area, especially in Kansai (around Osaka), shifted their headquarters to Tokyo. As globalization proceeded, many foreign companies moved into the Tokyo area by opening up branch offices. Consequently, construction of office buildings boomed in these years, leading to a further rise in land prices, which once again began in the Tokyo area.

A feeling of economic recovery and even prosperity spread from the construction industry into the manufacturing sector, as a result of this deliberate expansion of domestic demand. Japanese firms relying upon growing domestic demand could take advantage of both lowered interest rates and lowered yen prices of imported raw materials to boost profitability. Since many companies within the same *keiretsu* (groups of business companies) held shares in each other (as well as land at book value), higher share prices and land values broadly increased the latent worth of corporate assets, which correspondingly strengthened their financial position. Many Japanese firms also held idle money balances, which were growing not only by an increase in retained profits but also due to expanded equity finance (using both domestic and international markets) taking the form of new share issues, convertible bonds and warrant bonds. A portion of these funds fostered plant, equipment and office expansion. But funds also flowed liberally into *zaitech* (financial technique) operations, speculative finance seeking capital gains through rising share prices and booming real estate markets. Such *zaitech* activity among capitalist firms greatly accelerated the growth of the bubble economy.

As domestic demand expanded, Japanese investment in plant and equipment revived, beginning in 1987 and extending for the next three years. The recovery and boom seemed to cover all sectors. Economic growth driven by domestic demand even spread to raw material suppliers for the first time since 1973. The panicky fall of share prices that followed Black Monday in October 1987 did not significantly curtail this expansive trend in the real economy. In Japan, it was considered to be no more than a temporary setback in the inexorable course of economic recovery. The average annual rate of economic growth reached 5.2 per cent between the fiscal years 1987 and 1990.

This appearance proved to be misleading, though the galloping price levels of shares and real estate were no illusion. The economic recovery, led and fostered by asset inflation, was actually quite fragile. The bubble economy ended up both causing and reflecting the real economy. By the end of the 1980s, the existing economic growth could no longer support what had become an out of control level of asset inflation. Domestic demand, based upon ever increasing capital gains and swelling asset values, lacked a solid, sustainable foundation. High rates of economic growth before 1973 depended on an expansion of domestic demand fueled by real wages keeping pace with increased labor productivity. The bubble economy did encourage plant and equipment investment in the manufacturing sector. For the most part, such investment only encouraged numerous variations of more sophisticated model lines for a newly affluent domestic consumer. But when the feverish and unsubstantiated domestic demand collapsed, the same industries were burdened with a dangerous and ineradicable level of excess capacity throughout the subsequent stagnation and recession of the 1990s.

Unlike the speculative boom at the beginning of the 1970s, inflation remained subdued during the boom of the late 1980s. An increasing supply of money and credit left the price level largely unchanged. The appreciating yen, the realignment of global commodity markets (especially oil), plus stagnating real wages conspired to dampen input prices. The annual wholesale price index fell continuously between 1985 and 1988. Instead, stock exchanges and real estate markets monopolized speculative trading, providing a convenient outlet for an ample and particularly cheap supply of money and credit.

1.3   The Role of the Financial System

The saving rate of Japanese households has been higher than other comparable advanced countries throughout the postwar period. This unarguable fact provides an essential foundation for comprehending how the

Japanese financial system functions. The average household in Japan saved at a rate approaching 15 per cent of disposable income during the high growth period. This rose to 23 per cent in the middle of the 1970s and then fell slowly, returning to the same 15 per cent as before.[4] No definitive theory explains why it has been so relatively high. However, the following historical and institutional factors when combined can yield a more than reasonable account.

Japanese working people worry about their life after retirement. Social welfare is inadequate while the average lifespan has been increasing. Saving alleviates such worry. Its feasibility stems from a series of economic policies, practices and perceptions. We can begin with a continuing increase in the level of disposable income. Income often comes in the form of a bonus system that supplements annual sums by up to 4–6 times monthly wages. This puts extra money into employees' pockets some two or three times a year. Retirement pay for full-time workers often runs 2–4 times yearly wages. Saving also provides the means of purchasing relatively expensive residential units prior to retirement.

In the period of high economic growth, banks and other financial institutions could attract these household savings by offering a nearly zero real rate of interest. Main banks for each *keiretsu* group, in cooperation with other financial institutions, transformed these funds into investment loans for plant and equipment required by big businesses. This dependable recycling of household saving by financial institutions into such types of investment developed into a tendency for banks to 'over-loan' to Japanese big businesses. Such bank financing created a foundation for high economic growth before 1973.

Since 1973, the Japanese economy has endured crises and restructuring. There have been, necessarily, parallel changes in the working relationship between banks and large corporations. Low economic growth and the increasing spread of electronic information technologies constrained investment in plant and equipment. Corporations have focused increasingly on repaying loans to reduce debt. By cutting interest payments they hoped seriously to slash their operating costs. This trend, when combined with the rampant asset inflation of the 1980s, meant that as the speculative bubble grew, many firms sat on financial assets whose value exceeded corporate debts. Japanese corporations could be said to have exceeded the 'golden cross'. They could now earn net revenue from their financial operations. Not only retained earnings but also equity finance nurtured these growing piles of net financial assets. An increasing number of large firms accessed funds directly from financial markets rather than through banking intermediaries. Equity shares, straight bonds, convertible bonds and warrant bonds fulfilled financial needs while incurring lower costs. Japanese corporations could tap easily into the international markets for whatever funds they required. In the late 1980s, given the steadily appreciating yen, foreign funds were available (in yen terms) for essentially a negative cost. Rising share prices encouraged firms to rely more heavily on new share issues or hybrid instruments such as convertible or warrant bonds. Not surprisingly, equity finance, as listed by companies on the Tokyo Stock Exchange, increased from 4 trillion yen in 1983 to 28 trillion yen in 1989.[5]

In the late 1980s investment in plant and equipment recovered and increased for the first time in more than a decade. Still, it was only around 5 trillion yen in 1987 and 9.7 trillion yen in 1989 (its highest point). Generally, retained earnings and a portion of the proceeds from equity finance were sufficient to fund such investment. What remained, a not inconsiderable amount, fueled *zaitech* (financial engineering). This translated into speculative trading in domestic financial instruments and real estate, as well as foreign investment and currency speculation. Inevitably, a bubble of speculation formed and grew relentlessly, as shown by the following evidence.

Between 1985 and 1989, market share valuation of listed companies swelled from 196 trillion yen to 630 trillion yen (1.6 times GDP). In almost the same period (1985–90), the number of listed shares grew by an additional 66.6 million (a 21 per cent increase). Business firms held 34 per cent of these new shares, financial institutions 36 per cent, investment trusts 17 per cent, but individual accounts held only 17 per cent. This is in line with the ownership of total listed shares in 1989: financial institutions 42.3 per cent, business firms 24.8 per cent and individuals 22.6 per cent. Corporate capitalism is still very much alive and well in Japan. In contrast, individual shareholders in the US lay claim to 66 per cent of all listed shares. Given that corporations mutually own a large portion of existing shares, the number of shares actively traded remains highly limited, making them more vulnerable to speculative rises in price. Business firms and life insurance companies injected a large quantity of money into shares, either directly or indirectly, quite often in the form of designated trust funds via trust banks and security companies. A reasonable estimate shows these designated trust funds growing from a modest 5 trillion yen (1985) to a not so modest 37.6 trillion yen (1987). As I have pointed out previously, the share price bubble was to a large extent precipitated by *zaitech* speculative trading among big business firms and financial institutions, though individuals were also involved.

Meanwhile, big businesses were no longer borrowing primarily from Japanese banks. Increased competition eroded the banks' retail base as the post office and insurance companies lured away individual consumers by using new techniques to sell new financial instruments.

In response, Japanese banks expanded their business activities overseas.

This tendency became more pronounced in the latter half of the 1980s, made increasingly attractive by the appreciating yen. Between the end of 1985 and the end of 1989, for example, the amount of Japanese international banking assets outstanding increased by 30 per cent annually, eventually reaching 1,967 billion dollars. Japan's share of total international banking assets sharply increased from 26 to 38 per cent during this same period. Such rapid expansion of Japanese international banking operations caused concern among international financiers, worried as they were by the increasing fragility of the international system. To help defuse a potential flashpoint, the Bank of International Settlement (BIS) set new capital adequacy requirements (the Basel Agreement) in 1988. By the end of the fiscal year 1992, banks with international business would be required to maintain a capital base of more than 8 per cent of total assets (adjusted according to the relevant different kinds of asset groups) held. Japanese banks requested and subsequently received permission to include as part of this base 45 per cent of any unrealized capital gains generated by their shareholdings. Given this key concession, rising share prices rendered the Basel requirement unproblematic. Japanese banks responded by assuming that they could continue to increase their loan portfolio unconstrained by the Basel accord.

Unfortunately for the banks, this was not the Japan of the high growth period. Medium and small-sized businesses had replaced large corporate borrowers. Banks lent largely to real estate agencies, construction companies, specialized housing finance companies (non-banks which did not receive deposits, called *jusen*) and even individuals. Despite substantial changes in composition, the annual average increase in total assets (mainly loans outstanding) held by 151 Japanese major banks (including city banks, regional banks and trust banks) rose from 9.6 per cent in the period 1980–84 to 16.6 per cent between 1985 and 1989. It reached 28.9 per cent in 1989. The annual average rate of increase in total loans was 12.2 per cent in the period 1985–89 and 16.1 per cent in 1989. Real estate business loans increased annually by 14.1 per cent between 1985 and 1989 and by 24.3 per cent in 1989. Loans to non-bank and other financial businesses averaged an annual increase of 30.4 per cent during the 1985–89 period, though achieving only a 21 per cent increase for 1989. A Ministry of Finance survey traced the total flow of loans into the real estate market. It amounted to 120 trillion yen by the end of 1991. Major banks owned 59 trillion yen of those loans, and non-banks most of the rest. Given that non-bank loans were largely financed by bank borrowing, it is safe to conclude that the huge real estate bubble was substantially facilitated by money flows coming directly or indirectly from the banks.

In 1988, capital gains from rising land prices alone amounted to some 416 trillion yen, or 1.21 times the GNP of that year.[6] Although a similar bubble in land prices also occurred in the US, capital gains remained at only 3 per cent of GNP. By comparison, the Japanese bubble in land prices was enormous. In 1989, the total value of Japanese land was estimated to be four times that of US land. Since the total area of Japan is one twenty-fifth of that of the US, the average price of Japanese land stood at a hundred times that of the US. Of course, land prices in the Tokyo area and other large cities were much more expensive than the national average.

The average price of residential units also rose. For instance, the price of a typical condominium in the Tokyo metropolitan area increased from 35.8 million yen in 1987 to 61.2 million yen in 1990.[7] By comparison, the annual income of a representative worker's household, in Tokyo, only rose from 5.5 to 8 times the national average income. An unfair and uneven redistribution of wealth, unrelated to personal industry or diligence, took place on a grand scale between existing owners and new purchasers of land and housing units. As real estate prices rose rapidly, the average loan made to those purchasing houses without first buying the land on which these were built, or to those who built houses on plots they already owned, increased. Starting at 16.7 million yen in 1987, the amount increased to 23.4 million yen in 1990 and reached 27.4 million yen in 1992. Since it had become too difficult for a single person to secure a large enough loan to cover the purchase of a residential unit, banks and other financial institutions began offering housing loans that could be repaid over two generations.

Speculation dominated not only the real estate market. Banks and other financial institutions positively promoted the reckless expansion of loans that supported the speculative trade in office buildings, houses, condominium units, empty land and even memberships in golf clubs. Banks and other financial institutions increasingly offered, expanded or renewed loans to business firms, real estate agencies and individuals based on inflated stock prices and land values.

2 THE BURSTING OF THE BUBBLE AND THE PRESSURES WHICH DEPRESSION BRINGS

2.1 The Bubble Bursts

Asset inflation, fueled by speculative transactions, had far outstripped real economic growth. The subsequent collapse was inevitable. The trick was predicting the course of the bubble, what would trip the collapse and, more importantly, the effects such a collapse would precipitate in Japan's economy.

The turning point came in 1989. The appreciation of the yen peaked in 1988. The yen began sliding downward just as the dollar price of oil turned upward. The Japanese wholesale price index began to rise, starting with import prices. Domestically, the sustained and broadly based economic recovery pushed unemployment rates down to 2.2 per cent with the active vacancies ratio (the ratio of vacancies to applicants) exceeding 1.3 in 1989. Labor was in short supply. As expected, wages in the manufacturing sector rose fairly rapidly (by 6.5 per cent).

Meanwhile, the US Federal Reserve Bank gradually raised its official lending rate from 5.5 per cent in 1986 to 7 per cent in 1989. International capital flowed into the US, reflecting the widening rate differential. The yen consequently fell relative to the dollar. Yen prices of imported raw materials and oil began to rise. To prevent inflation, the Bank of Japan raised the official discount rate three times, from a level of 2.5 per cent in mid 1989 to 4.25 per cent by the end of that year. Further increases were anticipated. The official rate rose to 5.25 per cent in February 1990, subsequently holding at 6 per cent between the summer of 1990 and the autumn of 1991.

As mentioned, the Nikkei average of 225 shares listed on the Tokyo Stock Exchange had risen from 13,137 at the beginning of 1986 to 38,915 by the end of 1989. The lowered interest rate had promoted speculative *zaitech*, though mainly among business firms and financial institutions, which resulted in a huge share price bubble. In a parallel fashion, the rise in interest rates lowered the same prices decisively. Japanese share prices started to decline from the very beginning of 1990. By March 1990, the Nikkei average had fallen by about 10,000 yen (or 25 per cent). Capital losses in financial assets were then reckoned to amount to 160 trillion yen. The fall in share prices did not level off in the following years. By the later half of 1992, the Nikkei average declined further to approximately 15,000 (only 38 per cent of its peak). Estimated capital losses from the share market alone were estimated to exceed 430 trillion yen. The Nikkei average slid below 13,000 in the autumn of 1998.

The Japanese bubble economy had started to fold by 1990, with the collapse of share prices. Land prices did not immediately follow in sync with share prices. Land prices peaked in 1990. Even in 1991, prices in three major urban areas remained only somewhat below that peak. This level was still higher than that achieved in 1989. Therefore, the decline in land prices occurred more slowly than that in share prices. A distinct drop did not become conspicuous until 1992, but then persisted throughout the rest of the decade. Despite the fall in share prices, real economic growth managed to continue at a comparatively healthy rate of 5.1 per cent in 1990. Only in the spring of 1991 did Japan drop into a cyclic sequence of economic depression and stagnation.

What caused the difference and delay in the way that different parts of the huge Japanese bubble deflated? The following are important factors.

Initially, business firms and financial institutions resisted realizing substantial capital gains in the shares that firms of the same *keiretsu* group held in common. Firms also held sufficient cash reserves to weather a standard economic squall. Most firms did not need to overreact by dumping shares, selling land, abandoning projects to acquire additional real estate or scrap further investment in plant and area development. Banks felt comfortable assuming that, despite BIS regulations, they could continue to hold on to loan portfolios that were largely secured by land and other varieties of real estate. They still had a cushion of safety largely composed of unrealized capital gains on the shares they held. Even if they had opted to make something like a quick exit, real estate projects, such as the plan to construct a Tokyo Bay area business center, take a long time to complete and cannot be stopped easily in mid construction. Individuals' and even business firms' belief in the myth of the land remained unshaken. Over the long haul, land prices were expected to rise steadily. Speculative real estate ventures continued, often based on a belief that any losses in the share market could be offset by gains in the real estate market.

Despite the share price collapse, investment in plant and equipment also continued at fairly high levels until the spring of 1991. These projects frequently cannot be rushed. Nor was there any urgency to do so. Many firms already had their construction financing in place, which allowed them to continue with ongoing construction projects. At least initially, investment demand still appeared to be robust.

Unfortunately, land prices (swollen by speculative trading and sustained only by easy credit) could not survive an environment characterized by falling share prices and slow economic growth. Ministers, politicians, Bank of Japan officials and the great majority of people working in the financial sector grew increasingly nervous about the worsening quality of real estate loans. After witnessing a recent wave of bank failures in the US, the Ministry of Finance in April 1990 had advised banks to regulate the total quantity of their real estate loans. Despite this concrete expression of worry, banks, at least initially, continued to roll over, and even to expand, such loans. To avoid possible regulatory hindrances, they often chose to channel such dubious loans through loosely supervised non-banks. If sooner or later prices would recover, then time would resolve the temporary embarrassment of deteriorating real estate loans. Beliefs of this sort postponed any abrupt bursting of the land price bubble. Such convictions were still not sufficient to erase the more widespread effects of asset deflation. The capital base of Japanese banks, relative to the total assets they held, could not help but crumble.

Even at this point, real estate loans continued (increasingly through non-bank institutions) but returns diminished regularly. Property purchased at highly speculative prices became increasingly difficult to sell. As a result, the quality of loan collateral seriously declined. Plunging stock prices eliminated the bulk of unrealized capital gains. The capital base supporting banking activities necessarily shrank still further. Since Japanese banks were steadily expanding their international banking activities, they increasingly had to abide by the BIS Basel Agreement. The reduction of banks' latent capital gains in the prices of shares also added to the decline in the ratio of their capital to their assets. Since Japanese banks were expanding their international banking activities, they increasingly had to abide by the BIS Basel Agreement. After April 1993, their capital base had to represent at least 8 per cent of their total assets. Banks could meet this binding constraint by restraining or even calling in loans. But doing so would only exacerbate the worsening credit crunch.[8]

Heavily reliant on borrowed funds, increasing numbers of medium and small-sized firms, especially in the field of real estate, were forced to restrict and reduce their business plans and activities. These were the firms that had depended greatly on borrowing from banks and non-banks to expand their activities. But even big firms, such as Toyota, with a huge recently constructed plant in Kyushu Island, had to reduce investment in plant and equipment. All this newly built capacity came on stream just in time substantially to increase supply in an already depressed market. The resulting increased competition affected profitability. When a drop in investment demand inevitably followed, asset deflation spread further.

When the Japanese economy clearly entered an actual depression in the spring of 1991, effective demand for offices, vacant land, residential units and golf club membership began to plummet, forcing a decline in prices. The striking drop in Tokyo land prices and in three other major urban areas in 1992 clearly illustrates this more general movement. Land prices continued falling following this initial plunge, though at a much slower rate than corresponding share prices. Still, by 1996 land prices had fallen to one half of their peak in the Osaka area and to about 60 per cent of their peak in Tokyo and three other major urban areas. After 1996, prices maintained their drift downward, though at a much slower rate. Throughout the 1990s, this large-scale fall in asset prices was a major factor sustaining economic stagnation in Japan.

2.2   The Complex Linkages Defining the Spiral of Stagnation and Depression

The subsequent asset deflation in Japan (mainly visible in collapsing land and share values) reduced wealth by an estimated 1,000 trillion yen (about one half of that from financial assets and the other half from real estate).

This underlying reality driving the complex depression of the 1990s affected economic stocks and flows in Japan.[9]

As unrealized capital gains (shares and land values) melted away, many business firms found expanding their activities difficult, either by self-financing or by using mortgage-type borrowing. They largely lost the flexibility required to withstand the deflationary pressure exerted by the credit crunch. As business firms subsequently restricted and reduced their activities, employment conditions became more severe and real wages stagnated. By 1993, real wages had actually declined and cuts in overtime income were common. As a result, in 1993 real disposable household income (real household income minus taxes and social security payments) began to fall. Domestic consumer demand cooled down, corresponding to the depressed state of household income.

Consequently, in the first half of the 1990s capacity utilization in Japanese manufacturing declined by more than 20 per cent. With huge and growing excess productive capacity, competitive pressures in Japanese markets became sharper. A widening circle of falling prices fueled a deflationary spiral. Stock prices and land prices fell, labor income dropped, and the prices for goods and services wobbled and fell as well.

Japanese firms reacted by resorting to their traditional export strategy. They hoped that increased exports could essentially counter depressed domestic markets. However, as the trade surplus increased the yen appreciated sharply, undercutting the efforts made by Japanese exporting industries. The yen in dollar terms appreciated from an average rate of 145 to the dollar in 1990 to 127 to the dollar by 1992, reaching as high as 100 to the dollar late in 1994. As 1995 began, a monetary and financial crisis in NAFTA (North American Free Trade Agreement) precipitated by the collapse of the Mexican peso shook confidence in the US dollar. The yen climbed to unprecedented heights against the depreciating dollar, reaching 79.75 in April 1995. The difficulties created for exporters by the strong yen encouraged a shift to overseas factories. Japan's legendary manufacturing industries were now in danger of becoming hollowed out.

For both domestic and international reasons, Japan faced a deepening depression. While the US and other advanced economies enjoyed a worldwide economic recovery and boom after 1993, Japan remained the odd man out. The great Kobe earthquake of January 1995 hardly helped, delivering an especially sharp blow to the Kansai region. After Tokyo, this is Japan's major business center. Added to these woes, adverse demographic trends, caused by a declining birth rate, required more resources to be shifted to sustaining a rapidly aging population. Every turn of events seemed to conspire against economic growth in Japan. The Japanese economy in the 1990s in fact subsided into a sluggish state even when using the less ambitious benchmarks of the 1970s and 80s. The Japanese miracle had come to a shuddering stop.

With asset deflation generating bad loans for banks and other financial institutions, the impediments to long-run accumulation not only continued, but also intensified. Japan was reluctant to acknowledge this. In May 1992 the London *Financial Times* reported that bad loans held by Japanese banks totaled somewhere between 42 and 56 trillion yen (approximately 10 per cent of total outstanding loans of 450 trillion yen). The Bank of Japan immediately labeled this report 'an objectionable exaggeration'. In March 1994, an official estimate proposed that total bad loans (those impossible to collect and those whose payments had been deferred for more than six months) held by city banks, long-term credit banks and trust banks to be no more than 13.57 trillion yen. This figure in retrospect can be seen only as a deliberate underestimation aimed at avoiding financial unrest. It clearly ignored problem loans serviced only after receiving fresh infusions of cash from non-banks. As long as the value of assets backing these loans were expected to recover, such fresh loans could be somewhat rationalized. There was a natural limit as to how long this pretense could be maintained. In any case, the expectation of recovery failed to materialize. Even after several years of attempting to reduce bad loans, in January 1998 a Ministry of Finance survey revealed total bad loans as still composing approximately 12 per cent of total bank loans. This represented some 76 trillion yen (bad loans are defined here as loans which are impossible, or very difficult, to collect, namely loans requiring appropriate risk control). This figure will continue to grow if asset deflation is not seriously ameliorated.

Step by step, the Bank of Japan reduced the official discount rate from a high of 6 per cent in 1990 to 1.75 per cent in 1993 and then down to 0.5 per cent in September 1995. It maintained that unprecedented low interest rate for more than four and a half years, before making a minor adjustment in the summer of 2000. Promoting an earning-out and a growing-out policy seems clearly to be the objective of this monetary policy. The hope is that a policy of low, nearly zero, interest rates will eradicate the difficulties faced by those banks (and other financial institutions) sapped by a huge number of bad loans.

Supportive monetary policy did not keep the banks' security cushion, provided by unrealized capital gains, from becoming distressingly thin. The cherished loophole in BIS regulations, allowing 45 per cent of unrealized gains to count as part of the banks' own capital, now provided torment rather than relief in all ensuing attempts to resolve the bad loan dilemma. In a falling share market, to achieve the required 8 per cent ratio, Japanese banks were forced to shrink their total assets by contracting their loan portfolio. The resulting credit crunch not only weakened an already wobbly real estate sector but also undercut the viability of medium and small-sized firms. A floundering real estate market meant that the quality of mortgages deteriorated and loans turned sour as prices plummeted. This in turn chipped away at the financial health of banks and non-financial institutions, completing this particularly vicious circle.

Economic deterioration increased the woes of the financial sector. The unabated dilemmas faced by these institutions brought into the open several illegal financial operations executed in the belief that a recovery in the value of assets would keep such activities hidden. The general belief that Japanese banks and other financial institutions were impervious to failure lost all credibility. Failures have occurred, though still only sporadically, among banks and other financial institutions. In 1996, seven specialized housing loan companies (*jusen*) failed. In November 1997, Hokkaido Takushoku (the former Taiyo-Kobe-Mitsui) Bank (Hokkaido's leading bank), Yamaichi Security Company (one of the top four security companies), Sanyo Security Company and Tokyo City Bank all failed. These failures, when combined with the Asian monetary and financial crisis (then in full swing), overwhelmed the Japanese economy, pushing unemployment still higher.

To avoid jeopardizing the economy by allowing a continued financial crisis, in February 1998 emergency legislation sought to steady this sector by injecting 30 trillion yen of public money into the banking system. After considerable debate, the Law for Emergency Measures to Revitalize Financial Functions passed in October 1998, setting the upper limit of monetary support at 60 trillion yen. This figure was set in response to the failure and subsequent nationalization of the Long Term Credit Bank. Since then, the upper limit has been further expanded to 70 trillion yen.

Public support still fell short of full stabilization. Japanese banks lacked the confidence needed to compete successfully in international markets. Since 1999, the banks have responded by discussing large-scale merger possibilities and rationalization. The Ministry of Finance supported these key economic reforms, estimating that they might be capable of restoring financial health and defusing further instability. Daiichi-Kangyo Bank, Fuji Bank and Nihon Kogyo (Industrial) Bank are in the process of transforming themselves into the Mizuho Financial Group. Sumitomo Bank and Sakura (former Taiyo-Kobe-Mitsui) Bank have decided to merge into the Mitsui-Sumitomo Group. Tokyo-Mitsubishi Bank and Mitsubishi Trust and Banking Corporation have agreed to form Mitsubishi-Tokyo Financial Group. Sanwa Bank, Tokai Bank and Asahi Bank have also decided to merge. By 2001, four integrated mega-banks should emerge, capable of covering not only commercial banking but securities and insurance activities as well.

Despite these powerful legislative measures and ambitious restructuring projects, a strong recovery eludes Japan. Almost a decade after the end of the bubble, Japan's financial sector is still fragile. Bad loans and persistent asset deflation have not vanished. Japan's problems are complicated by a looming fear of a global crisis. A further collapse might occur if prices on the New York Stock Exchange were to tumble precipitously. Japan is still waiting to enter a safe haven, one in which the economic environment is stable and reliable.

3 CONFUSIONS IN ECONOMIC POLICY

3.1 The Failure of Neo-liberalism

For clear evidence that 'neo-liberalism' fails, one need go no further than the previous analysis of the Japanese economy. Neo-liberalism translates into a belief that competitive markets can establish a rational and efficient economic order. Faithfully following in the wake of the UK and US experience (starting some time in the early 1980s), neo-liberalism has defined Japanese economic policy making as well. It is in direct contrast to the sort of Keynesian approach which dominated most policy thinking until the 1970s. By providing policy with a theoretical foundation, neoclassical economics, as defined by Friedman and Hayek, gained a greater degree of credence. A policy program of neo-liberalism required deregulation of a wide range of business activities, especially in the banking and financial sector. Privatization of public enterprises and an overall reduction in the economic role of the state were also essential. This was, to express my own opinion, not a simple reaction to the practical failure of Keynesianism's attempt to cope with the economic crisis of the 1970s. Instead, neo-liberalism appropriately responded to a distinct corporate need for more suitable economic policies. New information technologies had intensified international market competition. Proliferating product models, internationally rationalized locations for production and operations, and the increased use of part-time and temporary works continued to characterize this new global market. Corporate strategy demanded greater individual flexibility and an economic policy that was more conducive to business activities.

While neo-liberal policies were attempting to promote free competitive market principles, big Japanese firms adjusted to this new environment by introducing and making greater use of information technologies, 'rationalizing' labor management and suppressing real wages in order to maintain international competitive power. Workers cooperated in these company-centered endeavors to improve profitability. As expected, such initiatives increased trade surpluses and strengthened the yen. The Japanese management model attracted global attention in the 1980s. It seemed to represent a particularly successful strategy when faced with the type of crisis characteristic of those times. Major Japanese corporations improved their financial positions and accumulated large cash reserves. These improved positions were generated by an expanded level of retained profits and also by successfully placing equity issues in both domestic and international markets. Japanese firms expanded their foreign investment, which rapidly increased Japan's total external assets. This overseas strategy swelled foreign exchange reserves. In terms of the noticeably appreciated yen, national income per capita surpassed that of the US during the 1980s. The newly restructured Japanese firms, reflecting the essential tenets of neo-liberalism, presented what seemed to be a story of miraculous success.

However, a simple neo-liberal belief in competitive market principles failed to produce either a rational, efficient or fair economic order. The wide and sometimes even anarchic fluctuations in foreign exchange rates associated with enormous speculative flows of international funds economically damaged a wide range of firms and their employees. Simultaneously, the search for ever greater profits by more profit-oriented firms helped to fuel the economic bubble as it formed in the mid 1980s. When it burst, the sizeable collateral damage reflected the intensity of the asset inflation plaguing the Japanese economy and the preceding rapidity of its formation. This history demonstrates the fundamental instability of the sort of speculative development that is intrinsic to a free, competitive, capitalist market economy. Neo-liberal economic policies could do nothing to prevent this irrational and inequitable economic disaster. Rather, they promoted a political and social environment in which company-centered speculative profit making became acceptable, if cloaked in the name of market principles. These principles inevitably spilled into and corrupted the policy arena, fermenting and encouraging private money-making interests to dominate political and administrative duties. Exposures revealing corruption and graft became a commonplace. In the postwar era, Japanese bureaucrats had been regarded as architects of, and key movers behind, the Japanese economic miracle. By the 1990s, whatever credibility and prestige remained to them, as well as their ability to function confidently, was in tatters.

Standard procedures adopted by the Ministry of Finance came under attack for being insufficiently transparent, overly protective of financial institutions and burdened by overly restrictive administrative regulations. Consequently, in 1998 the Financial Supervisory Agency was formed within the Ministry to investigate and regulate the financial sector. The hope is that an agency of this type will force Japan's financial institutions to become more transparent, especially to operate according to clear-cut rules. To further this objective, the Agency will gain its independence from the Ministry of Finance in July 2000. Complementing this policy thrust, additional legislative reform initiated in 1998 amended The Bank of Japan Act. The reform provided more independence for the central bank, but in such a way that it remains subject to at least some governmental influence.

Neo-liberalism not only failed to achieve its promises, but it also failed to provide a consistent foundation for economic policy. Market intervention using fiscal and monetary policy was not eliminated. Of course, even in the classical peak of liberalism, capitalist economies could not dispense entirely with political regulation. The implementation of Peel's Act (19th century England) and the way in which periods of discretionary relaxation synchronized with phases of financial crisis exemplify this. When compared with other industrialized economies, intervention by the Japanese government and the Bank of Japan was more influential, less consistent and also operated in a manner frequently at odds with free market principles.

For instance, the Japanese government and monetary authorities actively sought to lower the interest rate from the end of 1986 onward. Starting from the spring of 1987, Japan simultaneously expanded public expenditure by a substantial amount. These policies were partly a response to strong US pressure, especially after the Plaza Accord. Expansion of Japanese domestic demand would (it was hoped) mitigate trade friction. As discussed previously, these policies initiated and continued to generate an ever swelling economic bubble. Even if the Bank of Japan had simply responded to the monetary demands of the private sector (as Okina underlined in his response to Iwata's monetarist critique[10]), monetary demand by itself still represented a level of corporate political influence potent enough to promote speculative asset inflation. The Bank of Japan, as well as the government, deliberately ignored the danger posed by the rapidly swelling asset bubble. These ministry bureaucrats regarded the relative economic stability and the steady rate of price inflation as evidence of sound monetary policy.

Inevitably, a severe economic setback followed the tightening of monetary policy in 1989–90. Contrary to the neo-liberal creed, Japanese economic policy actively influenced the way in which markets responded during this period. However, policy measures could not, and did not, effectively control the destructive volatility of Japan's market economy. Instead they initiated and widely amplified any inherent instability.

In the subsequent depression of the 1990s the Japanese government continued strongly to intervene in financial markets. This policy dominated Japan's actions despite a continued neo-liberal policy stance, meaning promises to deregulate working conditions and to reduce public support for welfare and education. We next need to pose two additional questions.

What specific political and economic characteristics, domestic as well as international, define Japan's financial instability? How can we best describe Japan's current efforts at economic reform?

3.2   How Can Financial Stability Be Restored?

3.2.1   The floating exchange rate system

By now it should be clear that, after 1973, wild exchange rate fluctuations caused monetary and financial instability in Japan and other countries. The floating exchange rate system had been expected to harmonize and rationalize international economic stability by means of a competitive market balance between the demand and supply of national currencies. Instead of fulfilling such hopeful (perhaps naive) expectations, floating exchange rates served only to increase speculative instability in the world economy.

Especially in Japan, repeated cycles of yen appreciation constrained manufacturing industries even while rationalizing and intensifying the global competitiveness of Japanese manufacturing. Combined with the capital saving available from utilizing information technologies more intensively, the size of investment in plant and equipment shrank, becoming insufficient to absorb total saving. Instead, a large portion of the subsequent idle balances provided the wherewithal for staking out speculative international positions in foreign currencies and securities. Saving merely added to idle money capital. In turn, idle money capital was injected into speculative international investment in foreign currencies and foreign securities. Such speculation made use of wild exchange rate fluctuations (the yen against the dollar and other currencies) while also exacerbating these trends. The rapid and economically unjustified appreciation of the yen in 1994–95 added to the depression in the aftermath of the bubble bursting. This action clearly deepened the difficulty faced by the Japanese financial sector. The subsequent depreciation of the yen heightened the level of international competition provided by Japanese industries in the aftermath of the 1997 Asian crisis. The weak yen served only to deepen that crisis, as did the speculative movement of Japanese money capital out of overseas (particularly Asian) investments. These reversed flows could only rebound back on Japan by producing even more serious financial and real economic difficulties.[11]

Despite the wild currency swings, the Japanese economy still managed to earn large trade surpluses. These surpluses created the world's largest foreign exchange reserve (217 billion dollars in 1998), as well as the single largest net external portfolio of assets (1,130 billion dollars in 1998). A high saving rate in combination with a diligent and very productive Japanese workforce generated this sustained outflow of capital. Although serving to stabilize and sustain debtor countries such as the US, these capital outflows ultimately did little to mitigate Japanese economic distress. Instead, the surplus exacerbated financial instability and accelerated a trend leading to the hollowing out of domestic industries. When 'casino capitalism', operating in a global market, feeds on increasing amounts of speculative funds, the result must be counter-productive and even destabilizing for large capital exporting countries such as Japan.

A failure to recognize these issues fully has caused the current Japanese politico-economic focus to be far too inward looking. The officially sanctioned debate centers on (and is narrowly limited to) the proper way in which to restructure the Japanese financial order (easing and eventually eliminating its current difficulties). The practice of Japanese political and business leaders has been to take their lead from the US when formulating international initiatives. However, Japan would be better off establishing its own alternatives, which might stabilize international monetary flows domestically, as well as in the surrounding Asia-Pacific region. For instance, it might be worthwhile considering the use of a Tobin tax on foreign currency transactions, which would increase the cost of frequent financial speculations but leave real trade and travel basically untouched.[12] An Asian Monetary Fund might serve not only as a lender of last resort but also could stabilize exchange rates in cooperation with the EU and NAFTA. This is a viable policy alternative that would serve to establish Japan's independent stance. Political cooperation, aimed at achieving stability among the euro, dollar and yen, would be a desirable move away from pure 'casino capitalism'.

3.2.2   The effect of BIS regulations

The new restrictions regulating capital/asset ratios (applied to international banks) reflected a decision made by the 12 leading central bankers at a 1988 meeting of the BIS. Japanese banks traditionally worked with lower capital/asset ratios, as they could gather deposits easily from domestic households with high saving rates. As a compromise, Japan requested and received the right to allocate 45 per cent of unrealized capital gains in its securities portfolios as Tier II capital.

When the bubble expanded in the late 1980s, this BIS regulation did not act as an effective restraint but instead promoted the exact asset inflation it was meant to constrain. As long as unrealized capital gains continued to increase in line with each rise in share prices, Japanese banks could easily achieve BIS regulations. Resorting to equity finance would also increase their required Tier II capital, either by issuing their own new shares or by selling convertible bonds. Japanese city banks issued about 1.2 trillion yen of such shares and convertible bonds in 1987, and 2.2 trillion yen of these securities in 1988.

When the bubble burst, Japanese banks found it increasingly difficult to fulfill these same BIS regulations. They could no longer easily resort to equity finance, and lost a large part of their unrealized capital gains. For instance, between March and September 1990, the amount of unrealized capital gains held by Japanese city banks dropped from 12.8 trillion yen to 7.1 trillion yen. Their average capital/asset ratio declined from 9.98 per cent at the end of 1989 to 7.68 per cent by September 1990. To meet BIS regulations, Japanese banks had to reduce assets essentially by liquidating a portion of their outstanding loans. For medium and small-sized firms (especially for real estate operations and construction businesses), which relied heavily on bank credit, the resulting financial crunch was devastating. Belt tightening crippled economic activity and aggravated the subsequent degree of asset deflation. As bad loans increased, the resulting loss had to be met initially by banks dipping into their own reserve funds composed of Tier I capital and the unrealized capital gains characterizing Tier II capital. Thus BIS regulations promoted a vicious circle, which succeeded only in exacerbating incipient depression, asset deflation and bank crisis.

Although BIS regulations were by no means the only contributing factor causing Japanese financial problems, clearly such rules became counterproductive when they amplified rather than ameliorated fundamental instabilities following the burst of the asset bubble. It simply may not be appropriate to apply the same capital standard to all banks, in all countries. Realistically, banks operate in different economies characterized by households and firms with heterogeneous habits and distinct historical backgrounds. Given this, the Japanese government, in consultation with its own Ministry of Finance and its banking sector, needs to be more flexible when concretely applying BIS regulations. To overcome its current and critical difficulties, Japan needs to request a special exemption valid for some years, which would provide sufficient time to resolve its pressing financial crisis. Just as in the 19th century, England suspended Peel's Act when faced with a particularly acute phase of a crisis, banking regulations need to allow for exceptions which would prevent them from otherwise becoming unintentionally destructive. Distracted by the progressive globalization of the Japanese economy, neither the Japanese government nor the banking sector attempted to remove or mitigate the destructive effect of BIS regulations. They chose to adhere strictly to BIS requirements. Perversely, they even tried to generalize these prescribed capital/asset ratios by insisting on a minimum above 5 per cent even for strictly domestic banks.

If the BIS truly intended to promote international stability, then the actual regulations accomplished exactly the opposite result when applied to the Japanese financial crises. BIS strategy would seem to need a serious revaluation before it can be seen as supporting global economic stability and growth.

3.2.3   Rescue operations for financial institutions

When the Japanese financial crisis deepened, the government conveniently forgot its neo-liberal stance and resorted to a wide range of political measures in the hope of rescuing Japan's ailing financial institutions. These measures have been three-fold.[13]

First, despite mounting budget deficits, the State resorted once again to stopgap emergency policies in the form of increased public expenditure. The size of public investment, in terms of government fixed capital formation as a percentage of GDP (total investment in public utilities, including attached facilities and the equipment of central and local governments minus the costs of purchasing necessary land), totaled approximately 4 per cent prior to 1970. This ratio increased to 6 per cent after 1972. The commencement and subsequent deepening of the 1978–79 economic crisis triggered a standard Keynesian-type response, pushing up capital spending to 6.6 per cent. With the decided turn to neo-liberalism in the 1980s, such expenditure subsided to 4.9 per cent in 1985. However, in the late 1980s capital spending surged once again as policies aimed at expanding domestic demand became dominant. Subsequent increases in the 1990s reflected emergency (and apparently ad hoc) economic policies seen as the best or at least the only politically viable way of grappling with persistent and seemingly ineradicable stagnation. By 1996, the public investment ratio had sneaked back up to 6.9 per cent. In yen terms, such spending equaled more than 30 trillion. In terms of GDP, this is comparatively almost four times the level of outlay found in the US and more than three times that of Germany.[14] If we add to this sum the public costs of purchasing necessary land and the further expenditure involved in highway construction, total investment reaches 50 trillion yen. This amounts to 10 per cent of GDP, or close to the 55 trillion received as total tax revenue in 1996. It is not much of an exaggeration to characterize Japan as a civil engineering kingdom or as a state of construction.

Since a significant percentage of bad bank loans were made to real estate operators and construction businesses, public expenditure was clearly meant to rescue financial institutions weighed down by non-performing loans of this type. The government hoped, and perhaps even expected, a *growing out policy* to solve these pressing financial difficulties. The Japanese government firmly believed it could mitigate deteriorating mortgage quality by engineering a general economic recovery.

However, the ability of public investment to prime this particular Japanese pump largely failed in the 1990s. Asset deflation stemming from the demise of the speculative bubble was pronounced and persistent. Consumption demand, occupying about 60 per cent of total demand, continued to slump as Japan's economic future dimmed. Moreover, construction and repair of roads and highways became less effective in boosting the volume of domestic car sales. The employment effect produced by public investment became increasingly small as civil engineering and construction industries introduced additional heavy machinery to economize on direct labor costs. The multiplier effect of public investment in civil engineering and construction was substantially reduced.[15] A growing out policy as an effective way to rescue banks and other financial institutions proved to be less than a total success.

The second strategy (also attempted with scant success) was an *earning out policy* employing an extremely low official interest rate. The Bank of Japan reduced the official rate from 6 per cent in 1990 to an extremely low level of 0.5 per cent in 1995. The Bank maintained that level until midway through August 2000. This monetary policy formed not only another aspect of a reflationary growing out policy, but was also intended to function as an earning out policy for banks and other financial institutions. By borrowing money easily available from the Bank of Japan at such low rates and then purchasing State bonds offering something like a 2.0 per cent rate of interest, banks could earn a significant return without bearing any risk. Such profits could then offset losses from bad loans. Unfortunately, Japan's monetary policy also encouraged large sums of money to flow overseas (especially to the US, where it could earn a higher return). Such flows fueled the bubbly booms in the surrounding Asian region and added additional froth to the New York Stock Exchange. Domestically, however, it failed to achieve the objectives of either a reflationary growing out policy or as an earning out policy.

In fact, the difficulty of accumulating capital when faced with excess capacity depressed consumer demand. Asset deflation created a persistent and particularly vicious circle. Even dramatically lowered interest rates could not encourage significant borrowing. Idle money balances continued to find an insufficient number of profitable domestic outlets. A large proportion of these balances simply leaked overseas. Even during the short 1996 recovery, which artificially brought forward purchases by announcing a pending increase in consumption taxes (April 1997), bad loans by Japanese banks still increased as real estate prices drifted ever downward.

The third and last measure involved the direct *injection of public money*. This type of rescue operation for banks and other financial institutions became increasingly necessary. The failure of seven specialized housing finance corporations (*jusen*) in 1996 marked the initial public recourse to this option. The bail out required 680 billion yen. Initially the government's rationale focused on the need to protect innocent depositors of related financial institutions. However, rescuing a group of financially weak but politically well connected Agricultural Credit Cooperatives formed the reality behind the rhetoric. Public opposition labeled this maneuver as an unfair attempt to protect Agricultural Cooperatives and particularly their managers. Depositors were perceived as a pretext rather than a concern. Politicians reacted to this widespread distrust by not using public money when the Hokkaido Takushoku Bank (Hokutaku) failed in November 1997. Hokutaku was the tenth largest city bank and by far the leading bank in the Hokkaido region. Its collapse caused problems including regional business failures. Financial distress then spilled over to the rest of the economy. The Japanese government responded by making available a fund of 30 trillion yen to protect depositors and to provide capital injections to 'sound' banks facing a liquidity crunch. The amount was subsequently increased to 60 and then to a further 70 trillion yen.

A policy which provides banks with capital injections can be labeled as being either a 'too big to fail' or 'too big to liquidate' strategy. Neither Keynesian nor neo-liberal analysis provides a theoretical justification for such an approach. Its theoretical foundation is hard to find in either traditional Keynesian or neo-liberal economic theories. It is difficult to achieve consistency or fairness when putting such a policy into practice, except to the extent of providing depositors with some given level of protection. In the recent past, there has been no noticeable consistency in the employment of this policy whatsoever. Logically it could be used as a 'financial life-line' to maintain business activity and to assure employment for workers. In this case, the Japanese government should not have cut loose Hokutaku without first transferring the sound portion of its business to another bank. In 1998, under strong government prodding, all major banks applied for additional capital injections, aiming to establish credibility by restoring capital/asset ratios. They were much less eager to accept the type of responsibility entailing strict rationalization of operations, setting up clear disclosure policies and agreeing to abide by effective administrative supervision. The Japanese government failed to demonstrate clearly the dire necessity that required all major banks to accept public funds simultaneously. The rationality of applying this strategy even to the failing Long Term Credit Bank and Nippon Credit Bank must itself be questioned. The newly nationalized Long Term Credit Bank received some 7 trillion yen from the public coffers. Almost immediately after, an American investment group, Ripplewood, snatched up this bank, including assets valued at over 10 trillion yen, for a mere billion yen. The failed and nationalized Nippon Credit Bank received some 3.5 trillion yen in public funds. Softbank (a software holding company) is now negotiating its purchase for 1 billion yen. From the perspective of the average Japanese citizen, he or she has suffered increased taxes and reduced pensions while politicians eagerly employ government resources to protect the ailing financial sector, big business and wealthy investors. To avoid future failures, the financial industry and the Ministry of Finance are actively promoting mergers among city banks, aiming ultimately to form four mega-banks. At best it is still ambiguous if mere mergers among city banks can solve in any substantial sense the dead-weight loss created by the pile of remaining bad loans or improve the banks' competitive profitability. An estimated 13.6 trillion yen in bad loans held by all banks (9.7 trillion yen held exclusively by all major banks) still existed as a major economic impediment at the end of March 1998. The total loss due to bad loans (including 45.7 trillion yen worth which has been treated already as a cumulative loss) would amount to 62 trillion yen for all banks (49 trillion yen for major banks alone). Currently it is difficult to conclude whether these amounts could easily increase if asset deflation continues and worsens. At this time it is difficult to conclude whether the emerging mega-banks will benefit a majority of the Japanese public. On the one hand, a 'too big to fail' policy requiring massive injections of public funds could be more easily and urgently applied to such mega-banks. On the other hand, such banks may more easily segregate markets by applying differentiated interest rates on deposits according to their size or by charging fees for small deposit accounts. This would nourish non-egalitarian, class-like aspects in the Japanese economy.

4   CONCLUDING REMARKS

Summarizing a continuing process, like the state of economic reform in Japan, is difficult. Financial reform sought to follow the US model. This implied such mutually related transformations as:

- a neo-liberal emphasis on competitive market principles;
- a reduction in the main banks role of financing *keiretsu* (affiliated) groups of enterprises;
- an expansion of financing directly from capital markets;
- an abandonment of the convoy policy of protecting all banks equally.

A financial big bang seeks to lift restrictions on specialized financial institutions to promote business deregulation. Such reforms are also strongly backed by the US, which seeks to facilitate the entry of its own banks and other such financial institutions into the Japanese market. But to a great extent these financial reforms also reflect a set of internal necessities in

Japan. For instance, as many manufacturing and other big businesses increasingly relied upon retained earnings and equity issues, the characteristic functions of a main bank system had become to a great extent meaningless by the 1980s.

These correlated transformations in the Japanese financial system have been broadly in accord with my understanding of contemporary capitalism. The impact of new information technologies is generating a spiral reversal of the historical trends, which characterized the 20th century, by moving towards a more competitive market order. Neo-liberalism expressed and promoted this underlying trend of contemporary capitalism. Just as classic liberalism failed in the mid 19th century, neo-liberalism is also unable to achieve a rational, harmonious and efficient economic order. Nor has it successfully managed to refrain from market intervention when faced with problems in the monetary and financial system. Instead it provides fertile ground that nourishes the fundamental speculative instability inherent in market economies. The swell and burst of the economic bubble was consistent with contemporary features in Japan's political economy.

After the 'lost decade' that followed the end of the bubble economy, we now realize the destructive and persistent pressure that bad loans can exert in the financial sector. As we have seen, the financial difficulty facing Japan has been exacerbated by international financial instability. The floating exchange rate system and BIS regulations have both contributed to this instability. Despite these serious problems, Japanese politicians and business leaders have not seriously attempted to imitate US practices. But neither have they seriously challenged the international aspects of these financial issues. The persistent asset deflation, which has torpedoed the Japanese financial system, is closely related to the persistent depression in the real economy. Japanese domestic consumer demand has continued to flounder largely due to increasingly severe working conditions, which have reduced disposable income and increased worries concerning future life in an aging society. With the birth rate dropping from more than two children per woman at the beginning of the 1970s to 1.38 in 1998, economic growth may not be much above the 1990s' level in this new century.

The debate over policy and reform options facing the Japanese financial system should not be confined to a narrow view embracing only technical issues. A popular argument claims that financial reform should more rapidly follow the US model. (Failure to do so has been instrumental in making a bad situation worse.) Some commentators assert that an unwillingness whole-heartedly to embrace reform has seriously impeded Japan on its road to recovery. This is the reason given for Japan's failure to have enjoyed any real share in the US economic boom. Although I have critically examined the inconsistent and confused economic policies employed to cope with Japanese financial distress, I cannot help but see a considerable amount of difficulty in setting up more effective or more timely policies. The reasons are as follows. First, the size of the Japanese bubble and its resultant destructive effect were huge when compared with similar events in the US, or other advanced countries, during this period. Secondly, the amount of bad loans held by banks and other financial institutions fluctuated with trends in the real economy. It was hard to predict or to estimate reasonably the dangers posed by such loans. In this case, an initial growing out policy and earning out policy can be labeled only retrospectively as an error on the part of the monetary authority. Thirdly, the factors generating persistent depression and asset deflation were not limited to those defining the domestic financial system. They also extended to broader conditions underpinning real capital investment and to concomitant international circumstances. In this regard, the recent 'too big to fail' policy, implying an automatic injection of public funds, or even the possible formation of four mega-banks, may not entirely resolve the Japanese financial crisis. An overhang of uncertainty emanating from the precarious condition of the New York Stock Exchange remains.

Despite the inconsistency, even confusion, which defined Japanese economic policies during this post-bubble period, Japan still managed to avoid any catastrophic or acute financial and economic crisis. Instead, the Japanese depression of the 1990s was prolonged, but relatively stable, partly due to the economic policies in place. However, the relative stability of the Japanese economic and financial order has not been sustained solely by economic policies. The costs of those emergency economic policies, including funds funneled into the banks, has been borne directly or indirectly by the mass of people in the form of increased consumer taxes and cuts to welfare schemes. The continuous high rate of household saving, as well as a sustained and diligent repayment of most consumer (and housing) loans, have also contributed to the relative stability of the financial system. Since households are major creditors in terms of a macro-economic financial balance, it is clear that the zero interest rate policy promoting earning out and growing out policies has caused a substantial redistribution of income to borrowers.

Economic reforms and the restructuring of political processes prescribed by neo-liberalism allegedly encourage a fairer and more competitive market order. Japanese society has strengthened its company-centered capitalistic system to suppress workers. During the high growth period, the Japanese economy tended towards a somewhat egalitarian social order. This tendency has now been reversed, supporting instead an increasingly unequal economic order favoring the rich, big business and large financial institutions. A 'too big to fail' policy dependent on emergency public funding should be limited to protecting depositors (up to a reasonable limit). It should not deepen the State's fiscal crisis or shift the burden of repayment to the working population. Younger generations understandably have lost faith in economic explanations since mainstream economists seem more willing to justify than criticize recent confused policies. The crisis lies not only with the Japanese economy, but also with economic analysis itself.

Even when considering the types of highly technical and complex reform measures appropriate to a financial system, we cannot lose sight of more fundamental issues. Neo-liberalism implies the acceptance of certain assumptions and limitations that will constrain the direction that economic reform can take in Japan. Globalization may itself be inevitable, but not the policy options meant to cope with this increasingly international form of competition. Reforms (even including those of a financial nature) can be diverse in practice. Desirable options for the general population based on sound political economy principles should be more widely debated. Japan's future, including the possible difficulty of permanently lifting its long-run economic growth rate, needs more open discussion. A lack of social concern for the well being of the Japanese people unfortunately defines current attempts to reform the financial system. This attitude remains the most worrying aspect in all the confusion surrounding recent economic policies in Japan.

NOTES

*A large part of this chapter depends on Chapter 4 of my forthcoming book, *The Japanese Economy Reconsidered* (Houndmills: Macmillan). Craig Freedman's suggestions, together with several comments by Masato Masuda and other participants in the Centre for Japanese Economic Studies' Fifth Biennial Conference, were helpful in extending and finishing the chapter.

1. See Minsky, 'The Financial Instability Hypothesis; A Restatement' (1978) among other essays in Minsky (1982).
2. For more detail see Chapter 5 of Itoh and Lapavitsas (1999).
3. Housing loans increased from approximately 17 trillion yen in 1986 to around 28 trillion yen in 1990 (Imura, 1997, p. 161). Though that figure includes both public and private loans, private loans provided mainly by banks were the overwhelming proportion of both the total amount and the increment. When Japanese banks began to expand housing loans in the late 1970s, they initially set up specialized housing loan companies as financial institutions, which could channel their loans. However, they soon began to extend housing loans directly so that these specialized housing loan companies were forced to extend riskier loans for real estate to business firms.
4. There are two series of statistics on the rate of saving in the Japanese economy: one based on the GNP statistics (S-GNP) and the other based on a survey of working households (S-SWH). While these two indices for decades showed roughly similar movements, they became noticeably different in the 1980s. We refer here to the movement of S-GNP,

which is lower than S-SWH. Adachi (1993) analyzes the factors that generated this gap. For instance, interest charges on, and principal repayment of, household debts are counted as saving in S-SWH. The relatively high rate of saving among Japanese households may roughly be understood using the following model. Assume that all workers spend a sum five times their average annual income in order to procure a house in a span of 35 working years. Assume also that their saving is to be used only to procure houses either by purchase or construction. Then, on average, they have to save one seventh or 14.3 per cent of their annual income to procure a house by retirement. This saving rate closely matches that actually observed in the Japanese economy.

5. Haga (1993, 1994, 1995) has presented a detailed analysis of the Japanese bubble economy in this period, with useful statistical data, to which I owe much.

6. Tsuru (1990), p. 5. In so far as the great proportion of land was not brought to market, the major part of these capital gains was in fact unrealized. As for the realized part of these capital gains, its source should not be confined to the annual flow of income, or surplus value, produced by society's surplus labor. A significant part of it must have originated in the redistribution of monetary assets. This also seems applicable as being the source of capital gains obtained by rises in share prices. Conversely, capital losses occurring after destruction of fictitious asset values may not directly mean a reduction in income flows or reductions in surplus value. The Marxist theory of surplus value should not be applied too directly to such gains and losses. This point relates to our critique of Hilferding's (1981) explanation of founder's profit in Itoh and Lapavitsas (1999, pp. 114–16).

7. Fudosan Kenkyusho (Research Institute of Real Estate 1997).

8. Lapavitsas (1999) analyzes financial instability in the current Japanese economy by underlining the central position of banks in its economy.

9. Miyazaki (1992) presented a pioneering analysis characterizing the 1990s' depression as a complex depression of stocks and flows where financial stock adjustments induced negative growth in the flows of GNP. His analysis was, however, insufficient since it identified the flow elements as only short-term inventory adjustments. The actual depression in the flows of the economy was more serious, reaching deeper levels of excess capacity and unemployment along with depressed consumer demand and investment. Takumi (1998) defined the 1990s' Japanese depression as belonging to a 'Great Crisis (1929) type', where the deflationary spiral does not have a cyclical nature. This definition is, however, dubious, since monopolistic behavior by big businesses has not been crucial to the difficulties of the contemporary Japanese economy (unlike the 1930s). The functioning of the monetary and financial system under floating exchange rates and managed currencies also differs from that in place at the time of the Great Crisis. Historically, a comparison with the great depression of 1873–96 is also persuasive. That depression was non-explosive but also more persistent than the Great Crisis of the 1930s.

10. A series of arguments on this issue was published mainly in *Toyo-Keizai Weekly*, starting with the debate between Iwata (1992) and Okina (1992).

11. Taking advantage of the extremely low interest rates offered in the mid 1990s, Japanese banks and other financial companies rushed into the surrounding Asian region hoping to recoup their domestic losses. By June 1997, just before the Asian crisis, Japanese bank loans to five Asian countries hit by the crisis (Korea, Indonesia, Malaysia, Thailand and the Philippines) amounted to 97.2 billion dollars, more than four times those from the US. This is estimated from data appearing in Yoshitomi (1998, p. 247).

12. Tobin (1978) presented this idea and Dornbush (1995) theoretically extended its feasibility. See also Haq, Kaul and Grunberg (1996).

13. For a more detailed description of the policy response to Japan's banking crisis, see Corbett (1999) and other papers in Freedman (1999). A chronological table in the Appendix to Corbett's paper also presents a convenient reference.

14. See Okonogi (1998), pp. 139–40.

15. On this issue, Jichitai-mondai Kenkyusho (Research Institute of Local Communities' Problems 1998) presents an input–output analysis showing that public investment generates a much reduced multiplier effect.

BIBLIOGRAPHY

Adachi, Makiko (1993), 'On the Trends of the Rate of Households Savings' [in Japanese], in Daiichi Kangyo Research Institute, *Research Report 7*, October, pp. 17–35.

Corbett, Jenny (1999), 'Crisis? What Crisis? The Policy Response to Japan's Banking Crisis', in Freedman, Craig (ed.), *Why Did Japan Stumble?*, Cheltenham, UK, Lyme, USA: Edward Elgar, pp. 191–229.

Dornbush, Rudiger (1995), 'Cross-Border Payments Taxes and Alternative Capital Account Regimes', Report to the Group of Twenty-Four, UNCTAD, September.

Fudosan Kenkyusho (Research Institute of Real Estate) (1997), *Trend of Condominium National Market* [in Japanese], Tokyo: Fudosan Kenkyusho.

Haga, Kenichi (1993), 'Political Economy of the Bubble Economy' [in Japanese], *Quarterly Mado*, 16, June, pp. 51–94.

Haga, Kenichi (1994), 'Contemporary Japanese Capitalism and Financial Instability' [in Japanese], *Monthly Forum*, April, pp. 22–37.

Haga, Kenichi (1995), 'Financial Instability and the Financial System' [in Japanese], *Keizai to Shakai*,Winter, pp. 65–94.

Haq, Mahbub, Kaul, Inge and Grunberg, Isabelle (eds) (1996), *The Tobin Tax*, Oxford and New York: Oxford University Press.

Hilferding, Rudolf (1981), *Finance Capital*, London: Routledge & Kegan Paul.

Imura, Shinya (1997), 'Housing Loan in Japan and the USA with Changing Roles of the Governments', in Shibuya, Hiroshi, Imura, Shinya and Nakahama, Takashi (eds), *The Welfare State System in Japan and the USA* [in Japanese], Tokyo: Nihonkeizai-hyoron-sha, pp. 137–70.

Itoh, Makoto (1990), *The World Economic Crisis and Japanese Capitalism*, London: Macmillan, New York: St. Martin's Press.

Itoh, Makoto (1992), 'Japan in a New World Order', in Miliband, R. and Panitch, L. (eds), *Socialist Register 1992*, London: Merlin Press, pp. 197–211.

Itoh, Makoto (1995), *Political Economy for Socialism*, London: Macmillan, New York: St. Martin's Press.

Itoh, Makoto and Lapavitsas, Costas (1999), *Political Economy of Money and Finance,* London: Macmillan, New York: St. Martin's Press.

Itoh, Makoto (forthcoming), *The Japanese Economy Reconsidered*, Houndmills and New York: Palgrave.

Iwata, Kikuo (1992), 'Abandon "the Bank of Japan Theory"' [in Japanese], *Toyo-Keizai Weekly*, 12 September, pp. 124–28.

Jichitai-mondai Kenkyusho (Research Institute of Local Communities' Problems) (1998), *The Economic Effect of Social Security is Bigger than that of Public Works* [in Japanese], Tokyo: Jichitai-mondai Kenkyusho.

Johnson, Chalmers (1982), *MITI and the Japanese Miracle*, Stanford: Stanford University Press.

Lapavitsas, Costas (1999), 'Financial Instability and Japanese Capitalism' [in Japanese], in Itoh, Makoto (ed.), *Dynamism in Contemporary Capitalism*, Tokyo: Ochanomizu-shobo, pp. 171–94.

Minsky, Hyman P. (1982), *Can 'It' Happen Again?*, Armonk, New York: M.E. Sharp.

Miyazaki, Giichi (1992), *Complex Depression*, Tokyo: Chuokoron-sha.

OECD (1989), *Government Policies and the Diffusion of Microelectronics*, Paris: OECD.

Okina, Kunio (1992), '"The Bank of Japan Theory" Is Not Wrong' [in Japanese], *Toyo-Keizai Weekly*, 10 October, pp. 106–11.

Okonogi, Kiyoshi (1998), *Reforming the Structure of Public Finance*, Tokyo: Iwanami-shoten.

Tachibanaki, Toshiaki (1998), *Japanese Economic Inequality*, Tokyo: Iwanami-shoten.

Takumi, Mitsuhiko (1998), *The Depression of a 'Great Crisis' Type*, Tokyo: Kodan-sha.

Tobin, James (1978), 'A Proposal for International Monetary Reform', *Eastern Economic Journal*, 4, July–October, pp. 153–9.

Tsuru, Shigeto (1990), *Rethinking Land Prices*, Tokyo: Iwanami-shoten.

Wade, Robert and Veneroso, Frank (1998), 'The Asian Crisis: The High Debt Model versus the Wall Street–Treasury–IMF Comlex', *New Left Review*, 228, March/April, pp. 3–22.

Yoshitomi, Masaru (1998), *Truth about the Japanese Economy* [in Japanese], Tokyo: Toyokeizai-shinpo-sha.

COMMENT ON 'JAPAN'S CONTINUING FINANCIAL DIFFICULTIES AND CONFUSED ECONOMIC POLICIES'

Masato Masuda

Professor Itoh's chapter fully provides an empirical analysis explaining how and why the huge economic bubble swelled and burst. It does so by developing the insight that a vicious circle inexorably led to a spiral of depression in Japan. Next it critically reviews recent economic policies under the guiding light of neo-liberalism. Itoh labels this approach as a failure. It was unable to achieve anything resembling a consistent policy framework but instead introduced an unprecedented level of economic intervention in the vain hope of stabilizing the financial system. Despite all of these heroic efforts, government policy has not effectively succeeded in moving the economy out of its depression. Finally Itoh suggests that Japan should change its current economic policies to better reflect the needs and hopes of the mass of working people. His chapter is based on Japan's empirical experience, but some theoretical conclusions are drawn throughout his analysis.

As Itoh argues, Japan's financial difficulties that resulted from a burst of the huge asset bubble continue to be serious and are regarded as a major cause of the continuing depression in Japan. I'll begin by giving you an overview of the current situation of bad loans. Then I'll go on to comment on Professor Itoh's main arguments.

The situation facing Japanese banks in regard to bad loans is still severe.

Total credit exposure and Category 1 loans, which means normal loans, have rapidly decreased from 545 trillion yen at the end of March 1998 to 470 trillion yen at the end of September 1999. There was a decrease of 75 trillion yen (a drop of 14 per cent) in the space of only one and a half years. We can compare this to bank loans in Australia, where the total loans held by Australian banks as of April 2000 are about $A506 billion (nearly 33 trillion yen). The decrease in loans held by Japanese banks is more than twice the total of loans held by Australian banks. This shows that Japanese banks, at the present time, are cutting loans rapidly.[1]

On the other hand, total losses on the disposal of bad loans are about 15.9 trillion yen, and about 9.5 trillion yen of public money has been directly injected into banks during this period. Moreover, the sum derived from adding Categories 2, 3 and 4 (risk management loans) has decreased by only 3.4 trillion yen. This means that some normal loans have turned to bad loans.[2] The proportion of bad loans to normal loans is increasing even at the present time. As Professor Itoh emphasizes, the problem originates with the huge asset bubble and its subsequent bursting, as well as the suitability of Japan's economic policies to deal with the aftermath.

As he argues, Japanese economic policy triggered the process that swelled the huge asset bubble. The introduction of neo-liberal policy was expected to change the Japanese economy into a freely competitive, capitalist market. The reality of the asset bubble bursting resulted in a subsequent bout of financial instability and severe depression in Japan. The cause of this collapse lay in an unsound accumulation of bad loans held by financial institutions. As Professor Itoh emphasizes, the bubble was so huge and so many financial institutions were deeply involved in the growing speculative fever that the problem of bad loans is still far from solved. This remains true despite a decade of implementing measures intended to cope with financial instability.

Although the main target of current economic policies has been focused on redressing this financial instability and kickstarting an economic recovery, Japan has yet to succeed. Contrary to expectation, the fiscal crisis in Japan, stemming from the enormous (and often wasteful) amount of public investment, has become even more serious. This translates into increased burdens for working people in the form of a higher consumer tax and additional cuts to welfare programs. Furthermore, the general public has begun to lose faith in economic policies, which are regarded as serving only rich people and big banks. People are worried that Japanese society is becoming not only an aging society but also an inequitable society. As their concern mounts, they are forced to save more and more money to provide for their own future needs. The result is that consumer expenditures, which compose the main part of domestic demand in Japan (approximately 60 per cent), have been decreasing for the last seven consecutive years (1992–1999) in spite of record fiscal spending. Professor Itoh describes this situation as a vicious circle of depression. This is the reason that Japan has not succeeded in pulling out of its tenacious depression. He suggests that it is first necessary to change the basic direction of economic reform policies if the economy is ever to achieve a sustained recovery. This conclusive viewpoint is very important and concurs with my own assessment. I think that Itoh's paper should become a standard reference for all people who are researching the Japanese economy.

Next, I would like to comment on four issues: the basic causes of policy failure, how to restore financial stability, the necessity of reforming the floating exchange system, and some measures for expanding domestic demand.

The existing economic situation in Japan clearly demonstrates that current policy measures, for all practical purposes, have resulted only in failure. Indeed Professor Itoh points out that the economic policies adopted in Japan were both inconsistent and confusing. However, a neo-liberal critic could respond by claiming that the policies have been in the right direction, but that implementation and subsequent progress have always been too little and too late. The main cause of failure flowed not from the underlying economic theory but from the political process employed to adopt the requisite theory. As I read the chapter, keeping such arguments in mind, Professor Itoh seems to respond by utilizing three succinct points: the historical characteristics of markets, the underlying premises for markets to operate efficiently, and the inherent financial panics that define a capitalistic system.

He emphasizes that Japanese financial policy and reform have tried to follow the US model in an almost mindless fashion, even though the Japanese financial system has developed in its own historical way, leaving it with significant differences from the US system. If you adopt this point of view, then you can more easily comprehend how the immediate introduction of BIS regulations could be harmful by helping to precipitate a credit crunch in Japan. Most small and medium-sized businesses, which have long been the backbone of the Japanese economy, still rely heavily on bank credit to float their business operations. Alternative financial markets, which might provide needed funds, have yet to develop in Japan. As a consequence, when evaluating the reform process, historic characteristics should be taken into account and carefully considered.

On the second point, Japanese banks are struggling with such a distressing amount of bad loans that they are forced to cut back on lending in order to fulfill BIS regulations. These are the same regulations which caused the credit crunch and worsened the depression in the first place. Banks could only opt to take the obvious course. Non-performing loans are difficult to collect; it is always far easier to collect debts from relatively solvent borrowers even though in this case they were also forced to struggle under depression conditions. Although BIS regulations can work effectively when operating in normal financial situations, they fail to function effectively when most banks already have a substantial number of bad loans. It is clear that the purpose of injecting public money into the banking system in 1998 was to alleviate the distress created by the blind implementation of counterproductive BIS regulations. Even this one piece of history clearly shows that the reform process has been promoted impetuously without due consideration given to economic conditions.

On the third point, Professor Itoh warns against the inevitable cycle of speculative bubbles and subsequent busts characteristic of financial markets. This cycle has repeatedly appeared in the history of capitalism and has reappeared with redoubled force as of the late 1980s. He carefully discusses the Japanese case as an example of this problem. Professor Itoh fails to express clearly the causes of such reappearances, but he seems to recognize one of the main causes as the attempt to implement neo-liberal economic policies. The former two arguments seem to be compatible with neo-liberal capitalism on a long-term basis, but the last remains stubbornly incompatible. I would like to know then what in fact Professor Itoh views as a desirable financial system. In my opinion, a real financial market is essentially unstable. If we assume that a financial market is always rational, then a financial crisis can only be explained as rational despite the actual market participants seeming to act irrationally in a crisis.

If we accept that in exceptional circumstances markets can act irrationally, then we need to depend on some form of public rationality, such as a central bank, operating outside of the market in order to stabilize the system. If this is the case, why and how can we suppose that such levels of required rationality reside in the public sector? In a fractional banking system, if we try to explain the type of mob action demonstrated in a crisis as rational, for instance by employing Nash equilibrium analysis (usually characterizing a strategic game approach), we need to suppose that the mob action is determined somehow outside of the market system. If it is inevitable to admit that the determinant of a crisis must exist outside the system, the system itself is essentially fragile and unstable. Empirically we know that some appropriate combination featuring a guaranteed safety net together with prudential regulation would be an effective solution resulting in more stable financial markets. The problem lies with the inherent difficulty of locating the appropriate combination in each country. Is our only option to learn to coexist with financial instability (assuming that such instability remains even after completing a serious program of reform)? Or should we delay following the direction that leads irresistibly to a US-style system?

Let us move on to the second issue. In his chapter, Professor Itoh examines ways in which financial stability could be restored. He focuses on three points: the floating exchange rate system; the effect of BIS regulation; and the rescue operations for financial institutions. I have already looked at BIS regulations. I will discuss the floating exchange rate system later. Therefore, at this time I wish to focus on Professor Itoh's third point. He categorizes three different types of measure:

- emergency economic policies mainly in the form of public expenditures;
- the earning out policy by means of an extremely low official interest rate;
- public money injections into financial institutions.

It is not clear whether Professor Itoh recognizes that these policies were not enough.

Currently, the policy of restoring financial stability at any cost is given the highest priority. By reforming the financial system and bringing about financial stability, Japanese officials believe they are laying the necessary groundwork for economic recovery. This priority has been accepted almost as an unquestionable tenet of faith. However, we do need to reconsider such priorities and even the propriety of these measures.

Professor Itoh distinguishes reform from stabilizing the financial system. He argues that stabilization must precede any attempts at reform. He contends that trying to implement reform measures after the effect of financial distress only worsened the crisis. But will simply stopping the reform process stabilize the financial system? I agree with his idea of requesting a special exemption from BIS regulations for a substantial period, as well as some measures that might stabilize exchange rates. Are these measures enough? If not, what types of measure should we adopt? Or do we need to change our priorities (stabilizing the financial system even at the cost of weakening our national finances and alienating the general public)? If so, then financial stability cannot be attained only by financial policies but requires economic policies which would increase consumer spending and pull Japan directly out of its extended stagnation. I look forward to hearing Professor Itoh further elaborate these ideas.

Thirdly, the experience of operating a floating exchange rate system demonstrates two serious and rather embedded problems: volatility and misalignment. The repeated appreciation of the yen coupled with the extreme fluctuations between the yen and the dollar contributed to the huge asset bubble and its burst. In addition, the same fluctuations exacerbated financial instability and contributed to the growing industrial hollowing out of Japanese firms. Speculative and short-term capital movements prove to be destructive rather than economically helpful in the modern world. Given this point of view, Professor Itoh strongly suggests that Japan take the initiative in stabilizing the international monetary order. In his view both a Tobin Tax and the institution of an Asia Monetary Fund would successfully assist this process.

I agree with his view, at least at a theoretical level. However, two types of empirical problem still remain. One is the difficulty of realizing either an enforceable Tobin Tax or an effective Asian Monetary Fund. The other issue is whether these two instruments could actually stabilize the exchange rates between two major currencies to any degree. For example, a Tobin Tax would increase costs for frequent speculative transactions and decrease the influence of speculators under normal conditions. Most sudden fluctuations in the exchange rate seem to result from irrational mob actions triggered by unexpected news, policy changes and financial panics. A Tobin Tax is not very useful under such circumstances. Unfortunately, given the present economic conditions, I think there is no viable alternative to the floating exchange rate system. We cannot stabilize exchange rates and can only mitigate sharp fluctuations at best.

Table 5.1 Japan's direct investment in Asian countries

Year	Amount ($US billion)	Year	Amount ($US billion)
1951–1979 (total)	9.316	1989	8.261
1980	1.178	1990	7.045
1981	3.331	1991	5.894
1982	1.38	1992	6.339
1983	1.778	1993	6.602
1984	1.618	1994	9.681
1985	1.429	1995	12.246
1986	2.319	1996	11.64
1987	4.862	1997	11.901
1988	5.552		

We do however have an urgent need to establish an Asian Monetary Fund. Under the current system there still remains a more than reasonable possibility of further and future currency and financial crises. In a crisis, it is necessary to supply foreign exchange to countries suffering a currency crisis. Otherwise, they might be forced to adopt an extremely tight monetary and/or fiscal policy despite the economy being in recession. An Asian Monetary Fund might mitigate exchange rate fluctuations by producing an internationally cooperative atmosphere. But it is risky to give it that stabilization role because countries in the Asia-Pacific region could so easily clash on this issue. We also need to be able to distinguish between those exchange rate fluctuations due to the floating rate system and those generated by a currency crisis. The latter is far more destructive to any given economy.

Lastly, in his chapter Professor Itoh does not fully depict a policy that could successfully expand Japanese domestic demand. This missing story has to be one of the most important tales whenever we provide policy prescriptions.

In my view, one of the main reasons why the economy has resisted repeated emergency policies is the persistence of Japan's excess production capacities. Japan's economy has been export oriented. This has traditionally led to a considerable percentage of production facilities being heavily dependent on export levels. Since the late 1980s, many Japanese firms have rapidly shifted their production bases overseas and closed mass production factories in the country itself. Japanese direct investment in Asian countries remained high even during the stagnation of the 1990s (see Table A5.1). The figures in Table A5.1 show only capital movements for direct investment from Japan. In many cases, funds to finance these investments have come from international and local financial markets as much as from Japanese sources. Therefore, the actual total investments could easily be three times as much as the figures shown in Table A5.1.

As a result of increasing overseas production, many firms are not only switching from export to overseas production, but also increasing the amount that they re-import from their overseas factories. This helps them to survive serious price competition in Japan. Many factories in Asia used to produce manufactured goods not only for Asian regional markets but also for export to the US. This served to mitigate Japan/US trade conflicts. Now the role of Asian factories is changing. In a sense, we can say that the meaning of 'excess' in excess production capacity has changed drastically. The hollowing out of the industrial structure has begun in earnest in Japan despite its huge trade surplus. Japan's version of hollowing out is thought to be more extensive than that of any other country. The process itself is likely to move more slowly in Japan because of its huge trade surplus. If so, Japan will take a longer time to move out of its extended economic stagnation and to restore financial stability than expected. Although I have not as yet read his forthcoming book, I am sure Professor Itoh refers to this problem. I look forward to reading his views.

Notes

1. These figures (as Mr Wakatsuki pointed out at the conference) include the securitization of bank loans; cutting loans to big companies that have previously been advanced only to strengthen *keiretsu* relations; and cutting 'ryodate' transactions (involving a compulsory redepositing of part of the loan into the lending institution) that have been advanced to small and medium-sized businesses. The percentage of each item has not been published.
2. According to the Teikoku Data Bank (a private research institute in Japan), bad loans held by city banks decreased by 12.2 per cent in 1999, whereas those in regional banks increased by 10.9 per cent in 1999 and those in tier 2 regional banks increased by 17.9 per cent (*Mainich Shinbun*, 14 July 2000).

PART III

Japanese Firms: Happy Families or Anonymous Corporate Structures?

Happy families are all alike, but unhappy families are unhappy each in their own way.
Anna Karenina, Leo Tolstoy

6. Can the Japanese change? Organizational, psychological and evolutionary perspectives

Koichi Hamada

INTRODUCTION

Until the end of the 1980s, the Japanese economy was considered to be a miracle of economic development. It was compared to the sun implacably rising up over the horizon. Observers from the rest of the world could not help but praise the quality of its human capital, the cooperative spirit of its workers, the intricate organizational systems and the implicit guidance provided by the Japanese government. Total quality control, the placard (*kanban*) system, *keiretsu* organizations, main bank financing, seniority wage compensation and all-powerful J-firms (Aoki, 1988) became key words linking Japanese strategy to economic success.

Now the pendulum is swinging the other way. After barely surviving ten long years of economic stagnation only the faults of the Japanese system seem to stand out. Mentioning such concepts as a convoy system for protecting financial sectors, the lifetime employment system and the parachuting of bureaucrats into retirement sinecures (*amakudari*) draws only withering criticism.

Different prevailing economic shocks can begin to explain why the same system might prove functional in one period and nonfunctional in another. Thus it was very timely that the previous (Fourth) Biannual Conference of this Center was entitled, *Why did Japan Stumble?*

Starting from the supposition that the Japanese system has to change in some new direction, this present Conference questions whether Japanese economic and social systems can adjust to what is now the current environment. Our powers of crystal ball gazing are limited. It is not easy to answer this question 'Can the Japanese Change?' by peering into the future. What we can take note of are facts from the past and the direction that events are currently taking.

Instead of engaging in guessing games, wishful statements or religious credos (cf. some discussions in Freedman (ed.) 1999), I will start by describing some basic facts about the instantaneous gradients of change in Japanese society that we can observe today. By viewing snapshots in time, like freezing selected frames of a movie, we can reconstruct images of the course that future Japanese development may take.

I will use an interdisciplinary approach to tackle this most difficult of tasks. As always, the impetus for change cannot be one dimensional. Economic motives remain one of the most important factors, but political, organizational, sociological and psychological dimensions should not be disregarded. I will concentrate on these latter three aspects.[1]

In Section II, I trace past and recent trends in the components of Japanese society. In particular, I pay close attention to current changes in institutional features that have been considered to be typical ingredients of the Japanese economy and society. In other words, I explore how labor market customs, such as lifetime employment, the bonus system and seniority wages, have changed recently. I also evaluate changes that have occurred to the custom of cross-shareholding and to the role that main banks play.

Many new changes are taking place in almost all sectors. However, these changes are not necessarily one dimensional. This requires a careful examination that considers the microeconomic composition of their nature. The pace of change does not proceed by abrupt or dramatic jumps. It is often gradual and frustratingly slow for those who welcome such changes.

In Section III, I concentrate on organizational approaches. I begin with Lincoln's (1999) remarks that social consistency in Japanese society hinders changes directed towards a more functional and market-oriented society. I explain the factors that change Japanese institutions by employing theoretical foundations found in standard economics and in evolutionary economics. The already classic ideal-type classification of firms, the A-firm and the J-firm (Aoki, 1988), forms the basis for an evolutionary analysis of Japanese firms. These categories originate in the extensive research (e.g. Koike (1981)) which compares skill formation and information flows in Japanese firms with those in their American counterparts. The A-firm abstracts and generalizes American firms by positing a hierarchical and vertical structure that controls decision making as well as channels information flows. Division of labor is based on functional roles. In contrast, the J-firm uses Japanese firms as its starting point to analyze a decision-making structure and an information architecture that involves more horizontal elements – what might be labeled a rhizome structure. Contextual decisions characterize and define the division of labor (Aoki and Okuno (eds), 1996).

In Section IV, I will discuss the decaying process of organizations by referring to the well-known work of Olson (1982) and to an insightful book by Taichi Sakaiya,[2] *ASoshiki no seibou* (1996) (*The Rise and Fall of an Organization*). In this book, mainly aimed at a general audience, the author claims that the propensity to favor *Gemeinschaft* generates an excessive adaptation to the existing environment. Indulging current success is then an initial symptom signaling future organizational decline. He illustrates his points by using the examples of Hideyoshi Toyotomi in the 16th century, the Japanese Army and Navy before World War II, and the coal industry during the 1950s and 1960s.

In Section V, I examine the nature of game equilibrium and its dynamic adjustment process. According to Aoki and Takizawa (eds) (1996) (see also Okazaki and Okuno, 1993), both J-firm behavior (or strategy) and A-firm behavior (or strategy) can be an evolutionarily stable strategy (ESS) as defined by Maynard-Smith (1982). The equilibrium generated by the firms that adopt the J-firm strategy can be named the J-equilibrium. The J-equilibrium will not be dissipated by a small number of firms that defect from the J-firm strategy (e.g. by adopting the A-firm strategy). The same is true for the A-equilibrium, generated by A-firm behavior. The J-equilibrium is stable even when a marginal number of firms defect to A-firm behavior or to any other alternative. If a large number of firms defect in an economy composed of J-firms to the A-firm form, then that economy will become an A-firm type.

However, Aoki and Okuno (eds) (1996) further contend that there can be a better state than either the J-equilibrium or A-equilibrium. A superior alternative would use a hybrid marriage that employs the J-firm structure when a horizontal feedback of information is desirable (such as feedback received in the production process of automobiles). It would then utilize the A-firm structure when a functional division of labor is preferable (such as the division of labor operative in the purchase of financial derivatives). Aoki and Okuno (eds) (1996) named this kind of correlated equilibrium a P (for Pareto?) equilibrium. They claim that this P-equilibrium is proposed as being superior to either the J- or A-equilibrium. They suggested that proper policy guidance could shift an established J-equilibrium to a P-equilibrium instead of to an A-equilibrium.

I will also question the prevalence of firm-specific skills as the basic driving force behind the J-firm structure. I will argue that the importance of firm-specific skills is declining in the age of modern information technology (IT). Utilizing the analytical technique developed by Kandori, Mailath and Rob (1993), I will analyze the relevant transition mechanism behind this change.

Finally, in Section VI, I will deal with the communicational and psychological aspects defining the question of whether, and, how if so, the

Japanese organization can change. Toshio Yamagishi (Yamagishi and Yamagishi (1994) is just one of many other references) conducts some interesting inquiries into the nature of trust within and across the borders of a community. Contrary to a more commonsense understanding, he presents the experimental result that the Japanese, nurtured in a cozy, homogeneous community (a *Gemeinschaft*), are less likely actively to trust each other than Americans, trained to build trustful relationships through the careful monitoring of their partners. In this section, I will explore the linkages among behavioral, organizational, psychological and perhaps even biological bases for institutional changes.

II OBSERVATIONS ON THE DIRECTION OF RECENT CHANGES

Objective data on these changes and their direction are available in labor statistics and statistics describing firms' financial behavior. Let us start with labor practices, where lifetime employment, seniority wages and enterprise-based unions have been the three pillars that support the Japanese labor system.

A rapidly aging population faced with rapid technological change characterizes the current Japanese labor market (see Genda and Rebick, 2000). Software companies and information systems providers account for about 10 per cent of the increase in service sector jobs. Health care and particularly care for the elderly are responsible for about another 20 per cent.

Despite clear incentives to reduce their number of middle aged and older employees, large firms have made only modest progress. Between 1991 and 1998 the proportion of full-time male employees in large firms actually rose from 31 to 36 per cent. Probably because of that, the hiring of new college graduates declined. The so-called 'parasite single' phenomenon, young college graduates who still live with their parents, attracted social attention (cf. Yamada, 1999). According to Genda and Rebick (2000), this is not the result of any behavioral change in the younger generation, but instead demonstrates a lack of demand for young workers. However, this drop in large firm employment was at least partly buffered by a corresponding rise in small firm hiring.

Yashiro (1997) offers a longer-term view of these structural changes that is more or less consistent with this characterization of the labor market. Average tenure is increasing (see also Chuma, 1995) for members of the older generation. The younger generation faces a decreasing average tenure of employment. The wage profile flattened consistently between 1980 and 1993. Genda and Rebick (2000) argue that this flattening is not a function of the current recession but more accurately represents a general trend.

Enterprise-based labor unions form another characteristic feature of Japan's labor relations. One can hardly recognize any conspicuous changes on this front. However, as one possible indicator, participatory employment practices, as Takao Kato (2000) points out, have been steadily playing a more minor role since about 1988. This tendency, though somewhat subtle, is consistent.

In spite of these changes, the basic characteristics defining the Japanese labor market appear generally intact. Mobility is still low according to Japan's labor statistics. Both the seniority wage and the lifetime employment systems continue to survive and be maintained. But young employees are less likely to believe that these systems will continue. In the economy as a whole, Japan's rapidly aging population and increased foreign competition will make maintaining this system difficult. Foreigners can, and often will, offer more attractive spot wages to younger employees. In my opinion, although the framework of these systems still remains, the near future will likely see their substance largely eroded.

Next, let us turn to practices prevalent in financial sectors, the cross-holding of company shares and the main bank system.

In principle, by mutually holding shares in one another, firms could maintain effective management control against take-over threats while also diversifying risks. This explains at least part of its charm for Japanese corporations. Hirota (1999) shows that the ratio of cross-shareholding characterizing financial institutions slightly increased rather than decreased during the last half of the 1980s. In their forthcoming book, however, Hoshi and Kashyap report a quite different and more recent finding by the NLI Research Institute. The average proportion of shares in a company held by companies whose shares are also held by that company declined from 20.31 in March 1996 to 16.02 in March 1999. Interestingly, foreigners, pension funds and individual domestic investors bought the shares released. Does this indicate that foreign influences are gradually eroding the Japanese system?

The main bank system is another hallmark of Japanese financial practice. In my opinion, this system serves as an implicit co-insurance policy for the banking sector. Banks can avoid duplicating monitoring costs by relying on the main bank's capacity to rescue troubled borrowers. In this type of repeated game setting, incentives work well given normal conditions. The threat of triggering effective sanctions motivates a main bank to fulfill its role. Other main banks of those companies to which the bank extends credit as a non-main bank lender will penalize that bank if it does not meet its own obligations (a classic tit-for-tat strategy). I propose the following theoretical prediction: if a financial crisis deepens, then the repeated game will turn into an end game situation. The main bank will find it more profitable or unavoidable to defect and the main bank system will be discontinued.

Available data fail to show, however, evidence of such institutional changes. Hirota (1999) reports that any change remains marginal. In the late 1980s, the ratio of main bank holding to total outstanding equity issues declined slightly, but during the 1990s the ratio stayed about the same. The frequency of main bank reshuffles is very small, only around 2 per cent of the sample. This actually declined between 1996 and 1998. The system is still quite robust.[3]

Changes are taking place but only very slowly. Some continue to maintain that the traditional system is worth defending.[4] Kentaro Aikawa, Chairman of Mitsubishi Heavy Industries, said in the *Nikkei Sangyo* newspaper (January 1999), 'I have always said that Mitsubishi always values jobs before profit. We don't give a hoot about things like return on equity' (quoted in *Fortune*, 30 March 1998, p. 82). On the other hand, Taichi Sakaiya, whose theory of organization I will introduce in the next section, explicitly contends, 'Instead of trying to hold on to the "Japanese" employment system that supports lifetime employment, we should aim for a labor market that supports frequent turnover. This would in turn result in higher efficiency' (*Nikkei Bijinessu,* 7 June 1999, p. 33).

III AN ORGANIZATIONAL APPROACH TO THE TRANSFORMATION

The complementarity of institutional features is an important theme that has been broached already and will crop up again. In this section I introduce two major arguments. The first is by Ed Lincoln (1999) and emphasizes the need for the institutional components of Japanese society to be mutually consistent:

> Institutional systems for organizing economic activity vary among market economies in ways that are closely related to broad social norms and behavior. Indeed, since economic institutions and rules are created by political systems, it would be surprising if the outcomes were not influenced by social or cultural factors. Rarely are economic choices made solely on the basis of economic efficiency. When a society experiences economic problems that are attributable to some aspect of the existing institutional or regulatory system, a desire to improve economic efficiency may well be an important driving force for change and notions of efficiency may inform or partially shape the outcome. Nevertheless, non-economic social factors will also play a role in shaping change. (p. 3)

In other words, social factors affect the shape of the overall framework within which economic activity occurs. Lincoln mentions typical features of Japanese society as being group orientation, hierarchy, reliance on personal relations, avoidance of uncertainty,[5] the importance of facades (e.g. *honne to tetemae* – inside truth and facade), and a preference for indirectness and informality. He argues quite convincingly that all of these features prevent an effective transformation of Japan's economic system. For example, the labor market is under outward pressure to change, but these inherently Japanese features at least slow down the pace. The *keiretsu* should also transform themselves, but only do so very gradually because Japanese people pay obeisance to the basic protocols already described. Finance, corporate governance and administrative reform are other examples where those social norms are slowing down, if not obstructing, the speed and direction of necessary change. Although Lincoln (1999) refers only briefly to education in this particular chapter (apparently intended to be a chapter in a forthcoming book), the role of education in helping to reproduce these norms and behavior needs to be emphasized.

In sum, Lincoln (1999) suggests that the requirement for social consistency is a potential hindrance to changing Japan's society and economy smoothly to one more clearly dominated by open markets. The facts described in Section II echo his observation that minor changes in economic indicators do not affect basic Japanese social structures.

The second argument for complementarity comes from correlated game theory. Markets can achieve many wonders, but in certain situations more deliberate coordination of behavior is essential for a society and an organization. Aoki, Sekiguchi and Hori (1996) illustrate this by using a simple example of traffic rules. A society should choose either a right-hand-side drive or a left-hand-side drive but not a combination of the two. Two coordinated equilibria exist, and market competition is incapable of choosing between them. Direct coordination or even coercion can ensure that only one will prevail.

Using the well-known concepts of the J-firm and the A-firm, Aoki and Takizawa (1996) develop the following argument. When functional collaboration within an institution is important, then the A-firm is relatively more effective. In that kind of world, coordination between A-firms will create a desirable social equilibrium. On the other hand, when a contextual collaboration is important, then coordination between J-firms creates a desirable social equilibrium.

For the past half-century in Japan, contextual or collaborative situations dominated. J-firms (and the associated J-firm equilibria) promoted economic development and growth. However, the current economic environment demands more functional collaboration. One Japanese option is to align both economic and social structure to an A-firm equilibrium. Aoki and Takizawa (1996) (see also Okazaki and Okuno (1993)) seem to contend that a hybrid approach could be a third and probably better option. Firms that are structured in an A-firm way coordinate to achieve an A-firm equilibrium. Firms that more closely reflect J-firm structure and strategy might still retain their coordination with a J-firm equilibrium. Both A-firms and J-firms could coexist within a larger system. Moreover, Aoki and Takizawa suggest that this ideal and smooth transition to a preferred (Pareto superior) P-equilibrium mix could be assisted by public policy.

In contrast to Lincoln's point of view, the consistency or coordination requirement is not necessarily an obstacle to a smooth transformation. On the contrary, the government may be able to guide the transition towards an effective equilibrium.

IV   THE WAX AND WANE OF AN ORGANIZATION

Let us review organizational approaches to institutional change. In his analysis of the rise and decline of nations, Mancur Olson (1982) considers the possible causes of declining economic power. At a certain stage of economic development, vested labor interests and those of other sectors prevent the economy from adjusting to new institutional developments and from benefiting fully from free trade. This undermines macroeconomic as well as microeconomic policies, setting the stage for industrial sclerosis.

From his policy experiences and his own historical observations, rather than as a result of scholastic inquiry, Sakaiya (1996) presents a refreshing view on the rise and fall of institutions. Three enormous Japanese institutions that waxed and waned in dramatic fashion illustrate his ideas. His first example is Hideyoshi Toyotomi, a dominant figure of the 16th century. Despite starting as the son of a low-ranking samurai, he rose to become ruler of Japan. Though Toyotomi's ascent was amazing, soon after his death Iyeyasu Tokugawa destroyed his empire. Sakaiya's second example is the Japanese Army and Navy before World War II. These military forces achieved many military successes only to be dismantled after World War II. The coal industry during the 1950s and 1960s is his last example. Despite enjoying government protection (and partly because it enjoyed such protection), this industry was unable to arrest its decline.

Although addressed more to a general than a scholarly audience, Sakaiya's insights manage to shed light on the hidden mechanisms that define organizations. In his book, he claims that three features characterize large decaying institutions:

- a propensity to lean towards *Gemeinschaft* (community atmosphere);
- an excessive adaptation to a foregone or disappearing environment;
- indulging in past successes.

Gemeinschaft is motivated by natural will, in contrast to *Gesellschaft* (functional entity) where rational will prevails (Toennies, 1887). *Gemeinschaft* requires the following conditions:

- membership is lifelong;
- members feel comfortable in the group;
- the objectives of members are held in common;
- evaluation is made by insiders.

If environmental shocks are perverse, such an institution may misallocate personnel and foster a secretive community.

Dinosaurs responded to their environment by evolving into behemoths. This over-adjustment subsequently led to their own extinction. Any excessive adaptation to a specific stimulus can make an institution too fragile to respond effectively to different kinds of shock. In that sense, success can prove to be fatal. A successful experience, if over-emphasized, can cause an organization to lose the flexibility required to cope with adverse shocks.

Hideyoshi hacked his way to the top, starting as a poor, low-ranking samurai and eventually becoming the ruler of Japan. Both his ascent and his territorial expansion were fast and surprising. His method of taxation based on land surveys, and his strategy of confiscating firearms, formed the foundation of subsequent governments. Confidence, nurtured by his continued success, led him to invade Korea, a decision that ended disastrously. Ten years after his death, his empire collapsed, falling into the hands of Iyeyasu Tokugawa.

The Japanese Army and Navy also developed very rapidly. They rarely experienced a defeat prior to the end of World War II. As a result, they became tight communities with their own strict hierarchies. The Army imposed its will on the government by withdrawing the Army Minister whenever it was displeased. The Navy believed that a naval battle would be the decisive confrontation of World War II, just as it had been in both the Sino-Japanese and Russo-Japanese Wars. Accordingly, the Navy built extremely heavy battleships. Due to this approach, Japan was not prepared when the decisive weapon changed from battleships to airplanes.

After World War II, Japan regarded the coal industry as the key to economic success. The Ministry of International Trade (MITI) heavily protected the industry when cheaper oil threatened coal's dominance. The coal miners' union had grown strong and prospered under the same prevailing success syndrome. The famous *Miike* strike symbolized the end of the 1950s, that is, the demise of the pre-rapid-growth era.

These are only excerpts from Sakaiya's (1996) attempts to analyze the rise and particularly the fall of a large institution. The analysis can also be applied to:

- the Japan National Railway (Kokutetsu) before its privatization;
- the Ministry of Finance empire that dominated the economic landscape before the outbreak of financial crises in the banking sector during the 1990s;
- Japan's universities that now desperately need to change.

This story does not seem to be completely congruent with the complementarity or the consistency school. Some Japanese organizations now in trouble may not exactly be following J-firm-styled adjustment, or any other rational adaptation, to the economic environment prevailing *at this moment*. Japanese practices were, to be sure, a rational adaptation to previous environments. Now, they may reflect a process of excessive adaptation. From this point of view, using subsidies to maintain an overall J-equilibrium only subsidizes the over-adjustment of existing firms. Instead, the government could lift the barriers that impede the movement of agents from a J- to an A-equilibrium. If in fact the environment happens to favor the J-equilibrium, genuine practices by J-firms will survive solidly.

This does not deny the relative merits of Japanese-type employment practices (Fukao and Morita, 1997):

- The fact that a majority of corporate executives are picked from an existing pool of employees provides a sense of cooperation between employees and management.
- A firm has more incentives to invest in human capital because it can expect to reap a return from such investment. Japanese firms could send their employees to study abroad without worrying (too much) that an employee might not return when studies were complete.
- Employees are less likely to resist relocation to another working unit.

On the other hand, Fukao and Morita (1997) also note:

- The Japanese system cannot deal adequately with those who have special talents such as software designers, financial dealers and copywriters.
- The emphasis on teamwork prevents employees from taking paid vacations and women from being employed with men in competitive job categories.

In particular, the first point may well be the factor that retards the development of new IT industries.

This perspective leads me to doubt fundamentally the type of statement found at the end of Chuma (1994, p. 269): 'the Japanese style employment system, involves sufficient rationality. It is necessary for us not to destroy an employment system that should be defended. We should try to rescue the system through a joint effort by management and labor.' Could it not be true that this system was possibly rational only in the context of the specific external disturbances that defined labor relations during Japan's high growth period? Is a blind defense of the present system tantamount to subsidizing past over-adjustments to past external disturbances? Take, for example, labor relations and employment practices, as well as aspects of the banking industry. These reflect deliberate adjustments to the administrative guidance provided by the Ministry of Finance (MOF). Many agree that they were over-adjustments. By promising a seniority wage, which offers higher wages later on, can a bank hope to retain a young employee of the Internet technology generation?

Incidentally, Chuma (1995) himself documents the 1920s transformation of American corporations into an A-firm pattern in response to the severity of the Great Depression. According to him, American firms in the 1920s practised something closely analogous to the J-firm employment model. Only the harsh reality of the depression prevented firms from continuing these employment practices. As a result, trust vanished from American labor relations. Instead, the current American system replaced those more traditional elements that relied on trust. Japan should study these kinds of transition process rather than proclaiming that the Japanese employment system is rational and needs to be continued. Finally, we have to examine the idea of firm-specific knowledge and firm-specific skills. The effectiveness of the J-firm configuration depends on the existence of firm-specific skills. I do not doubt the existence of firm-specific skills or the use of such an important concept. May I ask, however, what exactly are these skills that cannot be transferred from one firm to another? Most recently developed computer technology cannot be firm specific if it is machine or program specific. Examples of firm-specific technology often come from manufacturing firms where job rotation, quality improvement and information sharing can be carried out effectively in a community-like environment. There Japanese firms, as well as their *ideal typus* J-firms, have demonstrated clear advantages. Some 30 or 40 years out of the second half of the 20th century alone make up Japan's days in the sun. Japan's technological strength could legitimately be described as flowing from firm-specific industries.

We've heard such phrases as, 'This can be done only at Toyota', 'This is a system unique to Honda'. Is it also possible to say, 'This is the Sumitomo

Bank method', 'Only the Industrial Bank of Japan can achieve such an accurate screening of projects'? If there really is such a meaningful differentiation, then the distinction between the J-firm and the A-firm types remains a powerful analytic tool for understanding our present situation. If not, the Japanese banking industry would be unable to transfer its incentive scheme internationally because this incentive scheme is in reality configured to the Ministry of Finance's administrative guidance, rather than the result of a transition process.

V   AN EVOLUTIONARY APPROACH TO THE ADJUSTMENT PROCESS

Evolutionary game theory attributes economic and social development to fitness strategies adopted by agents operating in a given system. They are usually unaware of the implications of their strategies. They simply inherit their behavior from their forebears or adapt it as the result of mutation. Those who instinctively choose a desirable fitness strategy survive (Maynard-Smith, 1982; for a more rigorous treatment see Osborne and Rubinstein, 1994).

Table 6.1 Strategies and firm types (Pay-offs are for illustration)

	Strategy I J-firm (or MC)	Strategy II A-firm (or GE)	Strategy III P-strategy?
Strategy I (J-firm) (or MC)	(3, 3)	(0, 0)	(0, 0)
Strategy II (A-firm) (or GE)	(0, 0)	(4, 4)	(0, 0)
P-strategy?	(0, 0)	(0, 0)	(5, 5)?

An Evolutionary Stable Strategy (ESS) equilibrium is defined as a situation where any activity which mutates from equilibrium behavior will be weeded out. Consider the situation in which everyone chooses an identical equilibrium strategy and a mutant chooses a different strategy. Mutant behavior should earn fewer benefits than those provided by the equilibrium strategy. In Table 6.1, Strategy I is the J-firm strategy and Strategy II is the A-firm strategy. Both the J-firm equilibrium and the A-firm equilibrium are ESS equilibria. These exclude the survival of mutants because J-firm behavior within an A-firm environment is not as effective as J-firm behavior within a J-firm environment. These represent coordination equilibria like the choice mentioned earlier of choosing which side of the road to drive along. Needless to say, if J-firm land is invaded by A-firm land and the A-firm strategy is dominant in the system (no longer mutant), then the A-firm equilibrium will prevail.

One can substitute male chauvinistic (MC) strategy for Strategy I and gender equality (GE) strategy for Strategy II. Since the system is complementary, it is hard to break the male chauvinistic equilibrium. Career women employees encounter substantial pressures: lack of day-care or nursery facilities, opposition from the family to long-distance job transfers, and the expectation that they will be subordinates serving tea to men. Statistical discrimination takes place during a woman's job interview, because even she does not know whether a future spouse will insist that she quit her job. Advocates of male chauvinistic practice use this logic when declining to hire women.

Okuno (1993) argues that there is a Pareto superior solution that combines and *coordinates* features of the A-firm equilibrium with those of the J-firm equilibrium. This is an innovative idea, but the concrete way to achieve this P-equilibrium still needs clarification. One possibility would recommend that manufacturing firms employ the J-firm strategy but that IT firms adopt the A-firm strategy. Most importantly, firms should choose the right strategy in a manner that does not disturb the prevailing coordination. However, the concrete image of this reality still needs to be presented.

Okuno (1993) maintains that this required coordination could be accomplished by government policy. In the presence of multiple equilibria, government policy can be more effective, at least in principle. Given Japan's probable future (slow economic growth), I cannot help but think that any positive room for government intervention is quite limited. In the mid 1960s, MITI surrendered a substantial part of its leverage over industry. No longer could it control the licensing of material and technological imports or influence tariff rates. Instead, the Ministry resorted to drawing up blueprints for the future. This was obviously only one way of influencing the choice among multiple equilibria (as explained later). MITI achieved only mild success.

On the other hand, until recent times the MOF created and sustained an incentive system for the financial industry that proved incapable of coping with either increased worldwide competition or IT advances. As the words 'MOF-*tan*' (watcher) and the 'BOJ-*tan*' indicate, banks, security companies and insurance companies focused more on anticipating the intentions of their supervisory agencies than on market opportunities or developing new products. Companies such as Nissan and Toyota are free to design and develop their own new products. The introduction of new financial products was highly constrained by the MOF. Ministry approval often reflected average industry needs and advantages represented by financial institutions such as Bankers' Associations and Insurance Associations.

Kano (1991) documents many cases where government regulations prevented or tried to prevent innovations in the private sector. Following MITI's example, the very brightest MOF officials[6] should develop something like a blueprint detailing the future of the financial industry, especially those parts that the Ministry has distinctly handicapped in the past. Practices in the financial sector have been nothing like a rational J-firm strategy. Any attempt to maintain, support or resurrect this *ancién regime* of financial oversight will deprive Japan's financial institutions of the opportunity to re-establish themselves in world markets.

If there are more than two equilibria, what determines the ultimate choice? People see sunspots and coordinate their choice accordingly. How do people know that this particular sunspot appearance corresponds to a J-equilibrium instead of an A-equilibrium? Matsuyama (1991) shows that either history (the society happens to be at a J-equilibrium) or expectations (the society will converge to a gender equality equilibrium) can determine the choice made from among multiple equilibria. Blueprints could help to influence expectations by providing a standard of guidance.

As you no doubt can comprehend, we desperately need an analysis detailing the transition process from one equilibrium to another. In this context, Kandori, Mailath and Rob (1993) provide an interesting analysis of the transition process. I will summarize this analysis without going into its detailed mathematics. Kandori *et al.* construct a mechanism for creating mutations in a world where information is imperfect. Since information cannot be accurate, agents behave myopically. Moreover, changing strategies is not costless. In this case, the probability of mutation is small. A chain of mutations leads to a new, stable state when the transition probability from the old state to the new state approaches unity.

I do not know exactly how to translate this insight into real situations. However, let me try. Certain IT shocks become too strong for agents to stick with the same (e.g., the J-firm) strategy. Despite the cost, agents want to defect from the old system. Only when these defectors gather sufficient momentum will the system shift towards a new structure.

VI A PSYCHOLOGICAL APPROACH TO GROUP BEHAVIOR

Psychology provides interesting answers to the question, *Can the Japanese Change*? In his many experiments, Toshio Yamagishi finds that Japanese participants in psychological experiments behave in a less trustful manner than do their American counterparts. When a Japanese individual is in a closed and safe relationship, he functions well regulated by the group norm to which he subscribes (Yamagishi, Jin and Miller, 1998). The system relies on the concept of control over others in the group (Hayashi *et al.*, 1999). On the other hand, when he is 'emancipated' from a closed relationship, he cannot find a better interaction since all other relationships are closed to outsiders. For an employee in a closed system, developing a high level of general trust and becoming emancipated from the confines of established relations brings little benefit (Yamagishi and Cook, 1993). Americans would start with a higher level of general trust because better opportunities abound outside already established relations.[7]

Yamagishi (1998) claims that he is acting as the representative of 'modernists' such as Masao Maruyama, whose influence was not fully appreciated or accepted some 20 years ago. Now the worldwide communication and technology environment makes those 'modernists' sound increasingly accurate. We find in this work a rather unqualified manifesto supporting a complete modernization of Japanese society (Yamagishi, Cook and Watabe, 1998).

People may choose to stick with the status quo and continue to limit their contacts to group members. They may opt to lower psychological and institutional barriers to encourage more frequent exchanges with outsiders and to exploit opportunities lying outside narrow group boundaries. The choice ultimately depends on the relative balance between *transaction* and *opportunity cost*. How much do they stand to gain by excluding outsiders in order to focus on promoting mutual cooperation within their closed group? How much do they potentially lose by giving up outside opportunities? The strategy of closing doors to outsiders in order to seek harmony and efficient cooperation within is a good strategy if opportunity costs are small or, more accurately, insofar as the savings of transaction costs within closed relationships exceed the opportunity costs incurred by closing relationships to outsiders. In this sense, so-called Japanese management practices, such as *keiretsu* networks and permanent employment systems, might have helped the Japanese economy to prosper in the way some economists claim.

However, once opportunity costs increase beyond a certain level, that kind of social system becomes a liability. It especially becomes an obstacle to economic efficiency. As outside opportunities increase (and this is what seems to be happening in and around Japan), the maintenance of commitment relations such as *keiretsu* networks and the permanent employment system becomes increasingly costly. In this instance, societies which are lumbered with a 'collectivist strategy' for tackling the problems of social uncertainty will be losers, not only in economic spheres but also in other social and personal domains. Once this change occurs (and I believe the change will occur fairly quickly), Japanese society will be left with less stable social and personal relations. It will lack the type of moral principles which are congenial with that kind of new and open social environment, principles that are related to fairness and trust (Yamagishi, Cook and Watabe, 1998).

I cannot believe in any straightforward fashion that a complete transformation to an A-equilibrium would result in full 'emancipation'. Some part of the feedback information structure of the J-firm should still be preserved. The community orientation characteristic of Japanese society may save us from making Japan into a 'legalistic' society like the United States. However, my previous discussion provides a sufficient warning against using traditional Japanese collectivism as a pretext for defending the overadjusted practices dominating its business and financial systems.

VII CONCLUDING REMARKS

The question *Can the Japanese Change?* has two facets. One is the question as to whether the Japanese social and economic systems will change under stress. The other is whether the behavioral and cognitive patterns of the Japanese people will change because of various circumstantial alterations in society. The two questions are of course interrelated because the Japanese system can only change if behavioral patterns at the deepest human level change to support an alteration in the social and economic systems. I emphasized the importance of human issues and communication problems in the previous section of this chapter. To accommodate a new, or at least different, system, human perception and behavior need to change. Keeping this in mind, let us start with the first question I posed.

I began my analysis by reviewing the current status of changes in Japan. Definitely, Japanese systems and individual economic behavior have not remained the same. The speed of change is still slow and the directions that change takes are not uniform. We are unable to point to a clear trend that would indicate a straight-line transformation from a community-oriented society to one that bears a Wall Street-type complexion.

Instead, current signs of change are subtle and complex. Many piecemeal changes seem to indicate a move towards a more market-dominated economy. For example, young people increasingly lack gainful employment, as the term 'parasite singles' symbolically indicates. On the other hand, employment practices for middle and older ages remain largely intact. One may interpret this as a symptom that reflects the universal efficiency of the Japanese system. Equally it could be a sign that Japanese firms are warm-hearted, leading them to honor their previous commitments to workers. A more realistic view would be to characterize Japanese society as being caught by the tension and torn between the pressure to accommodate outside environmental changes and an acute desire to fulfill commitments shaped by old promises. Japanese businesses find they must tread an ever-narrowing road between efficiency and social consistency.

The Japanese economy grew so fast because its elements were congenial to an environment which could foster efficiency and growth. Japanese management practices emphasized:

- feedback loops and sharing of information;
- on the job training as a response to firm-specific technology;
- less hierarchical firm structures.

These practices did succeed in providing tools that promoted effective adaptation to the environment, particularly when applied to the manufacturing sector. The Japanese approach to management also possessed the ingredients that could sustain this coordinated equilibrium.

Now the tide of the worldwide economy is becoming dominated by IT technology in the service sector, especially in the banking, securities and insurance sectors. These sectors are where Japan is lagging behind the most. Is there enough room in these sectors for firm-specific technology to justify the continuation of Japanese practices? Otherwise, the penetration of Western business practices into the service sector, or at least their piecemeal adoption, seems inevitable.

Nobody doubts that the Japanese management style was effective during the high growth era. To exaggerate its past effectiveness and minimize the difficulty of continuing to employ it as a component of the current social system may involve, I am afraid, a danger of encouraging the 'unwarranted success syndrome' that revels in past glories. In spite of the difficulties that stem from the complementary nature or consistency of institutional arrangements, Japanese organizations need to keep exploring changes that might best cope with this new environment. They should try piecemeal changes if a systemic change is too difficult. As an example, the American auto industry resurrected itself in the early 1980s and 'came back' by adopting elements of Japan's high productivity regime, but in a very piecemeal fashion. Both the Placard (*kanban*) System and Total Quality Control were introduced without holding morning meetings or even singing the company song! In order to restore economic flexibility, American industry took advantage of only those components most conducive to its own structure and behavior. Japan's public as well as private sector need to work towards easing those constraints imposed by a once successful but now outdated social system.

NOTES

1. Political factors are crucially important because any real change in an organization needs an appropriate level of political recognition. The reason I emphasize the latter three aspects is that they are relatively more neglected than political factors.
2. Taichi Sakaiya is the State Minister of Economic Planning in the Mori (and formerly Obuchi) Cabinet.
3. Summarizing his interviews, Hirota (1999) observes that the main bank serves as a good monitor of the firms to which it lends, but hardly functions as a good monitor of its own stock holding.
4. I owe the following sources to a senior essay at Yale (Inoue, 1999).
5. In my opinion, the Japanese still face a substantial degree of uncertainty, whether or not they like to think so. More to the point, they are not trained to cope with uncertainly in a deliberate manner.
6. They are extremely adept at passing difficult examinations. Some doubt the effectiveness of this type of intellect, but the intensity of intellectual power and the capacity for concentration are certainly valuable to society.
7. Cason and Saijo (1999) report that Japanese subjects in an experiment showed more grudging or spiteful reactions to the gains of their partners than did American subjects.

BIBLIOGRAPHY

Aoki, Masahiko and Masahiro Okuno (eds) 1996, *Keizai Shisutemu no Hikaku Seido Bunseki (Comparative Analysis of Economic Systems)* Tokyo: Tokyo University Press.

Aoki, Masahiko and Hirokazu Takizawa, 1996, 'Kigyo Shisutemu no Seisei: Shinka Geimu teki Apurochi (Evolution of Firm Systems: Evolutionary Game Approach)', Chapter 3 in Aoki and Okuno (eds), 1996.

Cason, Timothy N., Tatsuyoshi Saijo and Takehiko Yamato, 1999, 'Voluntary Participation and Spite in Public Good Provision Experiments: An International Comparison', OHP Sheet, July 1997; revised August 1999.

Chuma, Hiroyuki, 1995, *Rodo Keizaigaku (Labor Economics)*, Tokyo: Shinseisha.

Chuma, Hiroyuki, 1994, *Kensho: Nihongata 'Koyo Chosei' (Employment Adjustment: The Japanese Style)*, Tokyo: Shueisha.

Dawkins, R., 1989, *The Selfish Gene* (2nd edn), Oxford: Oxford University Press.

Freedman, Craig (ed.) 1999, *Why Did Japan Stumble? Causes and Cures*, Cheltenham: Edward Elgar.

Fukao, Mitsuhiro and Yasuko Morita, 1997, *Kigyo Gabanansu Kozo no Kokusai Hikaku (International Comparison of the Structure of Corporate Governance)*, Tokyo: Nihonkeizai Shinbunsha.

Genda, Yuji, 2000, 'Youth Employment and Parasite Singles', *Japan Labour Bulletin*, The Japan Institute of Labour, March.

Genda, Yuji and Marcus E. Rebick (forthcoming), 'Japanese Labour: Rapidly Changing Markets in a Stable Institutional Setting', *Oxford Review of Economic Policy*.

Hamada, Koichi, 1999, 'The Incentive Structure of a "Managed Market Economy": Can it Survive the Millennium?', *American Economic Review (Proceedings)*, **88**(2): 417–22.

Hayashi, Nahoko *et al.*, 1999, 'Reciprocity, Trust and the Sense of Control: A Cross-Societal Study', *Rationality and Society*, **11**(1): 27–46.

Hirota, Shin-ichi, 1999, 'Ginko Chushin no Kinyu Shisutemu wa Henka Shiteiku noka (Can the Financial System Based on Banking Change?)', *Waseda Shogaku*, February.

Hoshi, Takeo and Anil Kashyap (forthcoming), 'The Banking Crisis and the Future of the Japanese Financial System', mimeo.

Inoue, Yoshiko, 1999, 'Road to Recovery: The Changing Corporate Structure of Japan', Senior Essay, New Haven: Yale University.

Kandori, Michihiro, G. Mailath and R. Rob, 1993, 'Learning, Mutation and Long Run Equilibria in Games', *Econometrica*, **61**: 21–56.

Kano, Yoshihiro, 1991, *Min-ei-ka ga Nihon o Kaeru* (*Privatization Changes Japan*), Tokyo. The PHP Research Institute.

Kato, Takao, 2000, 'The Recent Transformation of Participatory Employment Practices in Japan', paper presented at the NBER Japan Project Meeting in Cambridge, MA, May.

Koike, Kazuo, 1981, *Nihon no Jukuren* (*Skill Formation in Japan*), Tokyo: Yuhikaku.

Lincoln, Edward J., 1999, 'The Social Consistency of the Japanese Economic System and the Implication for Institutional Transformation', paper presented at the Japan Economic Seminar (New Haven), August.

Matsuyama, Kimihiro, 1991, 'Increasing Returns, Industrialization, and Indeterminacy of Equilibrium', *Quarterly Journal of Economics*, **56**: 617–650.

Maynard-Smith, John, 1982, *Evolution and the Theory of Games*, Cambridge: Cambridge University Press.

Okazaki, Tetsuji and Masahiro Okuno, 1993, 'Gendai Nihon no Keizai Shisutemu to sono Rekishiteki Haikei (The Modern Japanese Economic System and its Historic Background)', in Tetsuji Okazaki and Masahiro Okuno (eds), *Gendai Nihon no Keizai Shisutemu no Genryu* (*The Origin of the Modern Japanese Economic System*), Tokyo: Nihonkeizai Shinbunsha.

Osborne, Martin J. and Ariel Rubinstein, 1994, *A Course in Game Theory*, Cambridge, MA: The MIT Press.

Sakaiya, Taichi, 1996, *Isoshiki no Seisui* (*The Rise and Fall of Organizations: What Determines the Destiny of Corporations?*), Bunko: PHP.

Toennies, Friedland, 1887, *Gemeinschaft to Gesellschaft*, Lepzig: Reisland.

Yamada, Masahiro, 1999, *Parasaito Sinuru no Jidai* (*Days of Parasite Single*), Tokyo: Chikuma-shobo.

Yamagishi, Toshio, Nobuhito Jin and Toko Kiyonari, 1999, 'Bounded Generalized Reciprocity: Ingroup Boasting and Ingroup Favoritism', *Advances in Group Processes*, **16**: 161–97.

Yamagishi, Toshio, Nobuhito Jin and Allan S. Miller, 1998, 'In-group Bias and Culture of Collectivism', *Asian Journal of Social Psychology*, **1**: 315–28.

Yamagishi, Toshio, Karen S. Cook and Motoki Watabe, 1998, 'Uncertainty, Trust, and Commitment Formation in the United States and Japan', *American Journal of Sociology*, **104**(1), July: 165–94.

Yashiro, Naohiro, 1997, *Nihonteki Koyokanko no Keizaigaku* (*The Economics of Japanese Employment Practice*), Tokyo: Nihonkeizai Shinbunsha.

COMMENT ON 'CAN THE JAPANESE CHANGE? ORGANIZATIONAL, PSYCHOLOGICAL AND EVOLUTIONARY PERSPECTIVES'

Noel Gaston

Professor Hamada's chapter reminds interested spectators of the Japanese economy that narrow and simplified treatments of the recent and ongoing changes in the nature of Japanese corporations are probably just that – too narrow and too simple-minded. Hamada's treatment certainly does not fall into this category. For me, there are three prominent themes in his chapter. Perhaps the central message is that fundamental change will, of necessity, be multi-faceted. Organisational, psychological and sociological dimensions all interact with the more familiar economic and political economic forces on which economists normally train their sights. A holistic approach is required to analyse effectively the key determinants of change in the structure of corporate governance, human resources management and the nature of contracts between a firm's stakeholders (both explicit and implicit).

Another theme, and a factually relevant point worth repeating, is that there is considerable inertia in the Japanese economy.[1] Change is occurring, but from a Western perspective it is occurring at a snail's pace. From a Japanese perspective, change is likely to come with some, not insignificant, cost. Consequently, the slow pace of change is explicable. It is extremely difficult for me to find fault with Hamada's treatment of these first two themes. In my role as discussant, however, I will permit myself the luxury of introspection and raise some issues that may offer slightly different perspectives. Finally, I do have some reservations about what I perceive to be the last of the main themes of the chapter. Specifically, Hamada's sub-text identifies a subtle role for government and public policy in the pursuit of the ideal corporate form, although not necessarily the much touted US-style 'A-firm'.

Some Institutional Realities – Whither the J-Firm?

The first issue that I would like to address is the accuracy, as well as the usefulness, of the popular Western image of a Japanese firm. Just how pervasive *in* Japan is the prototypal J-firm? Are most Japanese firms simply clones of flagship mega-corporations such as Sony, Toyota and NEC? In fact, while corporations such as these are influential and obviously high profile, they are not ubiquitous. Within the Japanese economy, small- and medium-sized companies employ the bulk of the Japanese workforce. In fact, nearly 90 per cent of all private sector workers are employed in busi-nesses with fewer than 300 workers (Sugimoto, 1997, p. 80). As with the small firm sector in the West, there is considerable labour turnover in this part of the economy. Consequently, there is no lifetime employment for the overwhelming majority of Japanese workers (Hiwatari, 1999).[2] Naturally, some of the small businesses are part of *keiretsu* networks. However, these same businesses, particularly small sub-contractors, are likely to face greater exposure to market forces and are unlikely to enjoy the full range of insurance and financial benefits provided to fully fledged subsidiaries.

The large Japanese firms undoubtedly garner the lion's share of the attention of labour and industrial economists due to the contribution that they have made to the Japanese economy's export performance. These firms wield political and economic influence at home *and* abroad. In addition, the governance structure, lifetime employment system and seniority-based wage structure of the large corporations are distinctive. They differ from their Western, particularly US, counterparts, and this fact may well have contributed to the popularisation of the 'types of capitalism' approach to analysis. Such an approach, however, tends to bias the efforts of research-ers towards the study of what is uniquely Japanese, what is uniquely American or perhaps even what is uniquely Australian. It tends to predis-pose one to look first for 'cultural differences' in the way in which corpora-tions are organised. This approach to social science tends to sit uncomfortably with most economists. Of course, such a research concen-tration has both costs and benefits. Aoki's (1990) caricatures of Japanese and American firms are based on observable and static characteristics of large Japanese and American corporations. It should always be kept in mind that the J-firm and A-firm are models – no more than that. They dis-tinguish types of firm on the basis of how information is acquired and pro-cessed; control is exercised; operations are financed; and incentives are provided to employees (the incentives to cooperate or compete, to monitor or to shirk). More generally, these models categorise firms based on the involvement and specific investment by stakeholders in the corporation.

I'm an economist and, of course, I'm extremely fond of models. Models are useful for understanding and focusing our thinking and, hopefully, for also helping us to frame testable hypotheses.[3] In the present case, however, the 'varieties of capitalism' approach provides little guidance on how actual corporations are likely to evolve and transmogrify if they are subjected to a succession of either positive or negative economic shocks. After all, some of the mooted changes that are being bandied about are not marginal changes; for example, they involve calls for the abandonment of the lifetime employment system. As Hamada points out, it is not clear whether the J-firm should strive to look more like an A-firm, an hybrid of the two or, I might add, something else altogether different (a 'yet to be assigned letter of the alphabet type-firm').

The 'New Economy' and the Breach of Implicit Contracts?

The world is dynamic and, of course, corporations must be sufficiently flexible to meet the challenges that arise in a changing environment.[4] A point stressed by Hamada is the pervasiveness of the IT revolution and how it is being implemented at an accelerating rate. Hamada's implication is that, in relative terms, it seems to some at least that it is a revolution that may have bypassed Japan. This is an interesting point to make. I'm not particularly an adherent of the 'New Economy' or the 'never ending increasing returns' school of thought. Still, looking at the phenomenal rise of the NASDAQ index, it would be naïve to argue that we are not experiencing a sea change in the way business is being done and the way in which fortunes are being made.

Baldwin and Martin (1999) describe the distinct characteristics of the 'two waves of globalisation'. The first wave of globalisation (pre-World War I), which generated rapid economic development for First World countries, was characterised by rapid industrialisation. In contrast, the second wave of globalisation (since 1960) that generated rapid income growth for so many OECD developed countries has been characterised by a process of deindustrialisation and an associated steady decline in manufacturing employment. Modern Japan is somewhat the exception. Japan has not deindustrialised to the same degree as other OECD countries. In all likelihood, this is because Japan's comparative advantage still lies in manufacturing. An interesting question, of course, is whether this comparative advantage is being eroded by changes elsewhere in the global economy.

In addition, it's also possible that Japan's outstanding success in manufacturing has had ramifications commonly associated with 'Dutch Disease'. An argument is sometimes made that countries with a strong comparative advantage in mining or agriculture (e.g. Australia) fail fully to diversify their economies. The underlying strength of such a dominant sector of the economy pulls resources from other sectors. Not only does 'Dutch Disease' potentially expose such economies to substantial terms-of-trade shocks, but also the lack of investment in other sectors of the economy may leave them less able to exploit growth opportunities in industries in which 'first mover' advantages may be crucial. While I do not take such a scenario too seriously for a country such as Japan, it's possible that the lack of mobility of factors of production may inhibit development of incipient industries.[5]

What are the costs of overhauling a human resources management system that has apparently served Japan so well? Has its time really come? The firm is often described as a nexus of contracts. Taking the broadest possible definition of contract (i.e. that which encompasses social, economic and legal elements) provides a particularly useful way in which to frame one's thinking about the relationship between a firm's various stakeholders. During the 1980s there was considerable debate in the United States about suspected breaches of implicit contracts during the height of the 'merger wave'. One aspect of the hostile takeovers that attracted considerable attention was the fact that some of the takeovers were financed by 'stripping' excess assets from employee pension funds and renegotiating the wages of long-term (mainly union) employees. Corporate restructuring through takeovers is in large measure value enhancing. However, it was argued, some of the gains to shareholders were redistributive transfers from employees and other stakeholders of the corporation (e.g. Shleifer and Summers, 1988). Of course, the main problem with reneging on implicit contracts is that such opportunism undermines the value of the firm and may create inefficiencies. 'The breach of trust accompanying such deals might spread enough fear of further breach through the economy as to either vastly complicate or even prevent profitable trade' (Shleifer and Summers, 1988, p. 53). Seen in this light it is not surprising that J-firms have been reluctant to embrace drastic changes to lifetime employment and related human resources management practices.[6]

A somewhat more cynical political economic explanation for the resistance to changing the status quo management and human resources system is that employees are the most important and influential stakeholders in J-firms. Directors and managers of J-firms are normally drawn from the ranks of long-term employees. Simply put, resistance by self-interested groups of 'insiders' explains the slow pace of change in the structure of corporate governance (see Miwa, 1998).

Nature Versus Nurture and the Importance of Political Economy

As promised, Hamada concentrates on organisational, psychological and sociological aspects as the mechanisms for change (or inertia). What is very clear, however, is that political economic considerations are extremely important in maintaining the status quo or in realising change. The promise of improved economic efficiency is not a sufficient condition for change. Some authors contend that celebrated institutions (such as lifetime employment, the seniority wage system and enterprise unionism) arose for primarily political reasons. As mentioned previously, Gilson and Roe (1999) argue that lifetime employment evolved in post-World War II Japan for reasons that had more to do with closing external labour markets and ensuring peaceful industrial relations than for the provision of specific human capital investment incentives. Similarly, Hiwatari (1999) argues that enterprise unionism, in large part, arose by historical accident and only in small measure by conscious design. Enterprise unionism generated better employment conditions for its members through such guarantees of lifetime employment. The *quid pro quo* was wage restraint when 'crises' hit their firms. Enterprise unionism became more significant as the export-oriented industries, in which such unions were prominent, became more influential.

Hoshi (1998) describes the heavy involvement of government in Japanese corporate governance through *amakudari* – the placement of retired bureaucrats on the boards of large corporations. In part, this is entirely consistent with the 'industry policy as driving force' view of Japan's economic development. However, Hoshi's (1998) analysis suggests that, rather than being the agent of change, due to its heavy involvement as a stakeholder, the government is often instrumental in resisting change. Outwardly, the role of the government tends to be contradictory at times. Genda and Rebick (2000) note that much government policy has acted to maintain existing employment practices. Weinstein (1997) concludes that the government's tax and financial policies continue to inhibit foreign takeovers through the promotion of stable shareholding. On the other hand, Blomström *et al.* (2000) note that deregulation has opened up much of the industrial and service sectors to foreign multinationals. Overall, it is not clear whether any stakeholder interest group, including public policy makers, is able to provide much practical guidance on selecting the ideal corporate form.[7]

Corporations in every country, including those in Japan, face the need to change due to the very nature of ever shifting dynamic comparative advantages. There is always resistance to change, of course. The mooted changes in organisational direction involve winners and losers. The abandonment of lifetime employment and renegotiation of implicit contracts will undoubtedly adversely affect incumbent employees. On the other hand, the effect of demographics and greater external labour market opportunities for experienced workers may work to offset a portion of these losses. Some of the changes in organisational design are inevitable as the Japanese labour market and corporate environment globalise. Inward FDI into the Japanese economy is small, but is likely to increase as deregulation opens up industrial and service sectors (Blomström *et al.*, 2000). This will serve to modify existing corporate culture. Likewise, the 'tyranny of demographics' may force Japan, with its low rate of natural increase, to rethink its immigration policy or national 'population policy'. For instance, an increased intake of skilled migrants may assist in alleviating the declining capacity of the economy to support an increasing number of ageing and non-working residents. Developments such as these would potentially increase competition in external labour markets, rendering traditional employment practices less defensible than they currently are.

Notes

1. Genda and Rebick (2000) argue that Japan has been undergoing structural shifts in its labour markets, both external and internal, and that these changes have been amplified by demographic factors. However, they also note that the shifts are not particularly notable when compared with European, and particularly UK, developments. In a similar fashion, Kato (2000) describes how Japanese firms have been 'fine-tuning' rather than dismantling their existing employment practices. However, he argues that some of the recent changes have the potential to result in reduced commitment by union officials to rank-and-file workers. This may eventually lead to the 'breakdown of the system'.

2. Interestingly, employer tenure data published by the OECD (1997, table 5.6, p. 139) indicate that Japanese employees spend an average of 11.3 years with one employer. The OECD average is 9.6 years. The fact that average tenure for US employees is among the lowest for OECD countries at 7.4 years may explain the attention given to the purported long tenure of Japanese workers. (That is, it's not that the tenure of Japanese workers is particularly long, rather that the tenure of US workers is relatively short.)

3. An example of the usefulness and testability of the J-firm/A-firm distinction is Ichniowski *et al.* (1997). These authors found that it was unprofitable for American firms to adopt Japanese-style human resource management practices in a piecemeal fashion. The profitability of such changes in 'culture' rested on the adoption of the entire menu of employment and human resource management practices, due to the complementarity of the component parts. Itoh (1994) reaches a similar conclusion from a theoretical perspective.

4. Some management theorists have even argued that organisations should be 'chaotic' by design, so that they can be flexible enough to respond adequately to dramatically changing environments (e.g. see Nonaka, 1988). This view is in stark contrast to those who see organisational change as occurring incrementally or in a more deterministic fashion.

5. Gilson and Roe (1999) describe the lifetime employment system of J-firms as having a 'bright side' and a 'dark side'. The latter involves the lack of exposure to the external labour market and worker immobility. The 'dark side' encourages productivity and commitment (because employees fear the potentially large costs associated with job loss), but the J-firms' lack of 'macro'-flexibility leaves them unable to respond to rapid technological change.

6. Simple versions of implicit contract models imply that wages are equalised across states of nature. Wages can be viewed as part indemnity during poor states and as part insurance premium during good states. Such insurance arrangements are ex-ante optimal for risk-averse workers and their less risk-averse employers. There are two points worth noting. First, the feasibility of such implicit contracts relies on the independently and identically distributed nature of productivity and demand shocks through time (or across sectors of a conglomerate firm). A firm hit by a permanent shift in the underlying distribution of the states of nature it faces may be forced to renegotiate long-term contracts or to abandon implicit contracts in favour of more market-based employment agreements. Secondly, there is a dual moral hazard problem associated with enforcing implicit contracts *ex post* (see Davidson, 1990). Workers have an incentive to breach contracts when external labour market conditions improve and firms have an incentive to renege on implicit contracts when the labour market is slack. Incentive compatibility constraints adjust to reflect these costs of enforcing implicit contracts. For example, if demographic changes in Japan serve to raise the reservation wage of experienced, skilled workers, then this will force contract wages closer to market-determined wages. This requires that the firm offset these wage

increases by collecting an insurance premium from its less experienced workers. If this proves to be infeasible, the only alternative may be to abandon implicit contracting (as well as some of the institutions that support it, such as lifetime employment).

7. As Hamada notes, even the case of multiple equilibria in oligopolistic rent-seeking games does not necessarily signal the need for active government involvement. In dynamic games, identifying the Pareto-optimal strategy is like trying to hit a moving target. Policy makers may get lucky, of course, but this is likely to be an inferior approach to allowing the information provided by market forces to dictate changes. At some stage, the impetus for change may become irresistible. Repeated games may sometimes involve going through a 'slow game' phase in which stakeholder groups try to improve or maintain their own welfare at the expense of the corporation. However, such games eventually progress to an end game scenario in which fundamental change is unavoidable (see Lawrence and Lawrence, 1985).

References

Aoki, M. (1988), *Information, Incentives and Bargaining in the Japanese Econoomy*, Cambridge: Cambridge University Press.

Aoki, M. (1990), 'Toward an Economic Model of the Japanese Firm', *Journal of Economic Literature* **28**(1), 1–27.

Aoki, M. and M. Okuno (eds) (1996), *Keizai Shisutemu no Hikaku Seido Bunseki (Comparative Analysis of Economic Systems)*, Tokyo: Tokyo University Press.

Aoki, M. and H. Takizawa (1996), 'Kigu Shisutemu no Seisei: Shinka Geimu teki Apurochi (Evolution of Firm Systems: Evolutionary Game Approach)', in Aoki and Okuno (eds) (1996).

Baldwin, R.E. and P. Martin (1999), 'Two Waves of Globalisation: Superficial Similarities, Fundamental Differences', *NBER Working Paper No. 6904*, Cambridge, MA.

Blomström, M., D. Konan and R.E. Lipsey (2000), 'FDI in the Restructuring of the Japanese Economy', *NBER working paper No. 7693*, Cambridge, MA.

Cason, T.N., T. Saijo and T. Yamato (1999), 'Voluntary Participation and Spite in Public Good Provision Experiments: An International Comparison', OHP Sheet, July 1997 (revised August 1999).

Chuma, H. (1995), *Rodo Keizaigaku (Labor Economics)*, Tokyo: Shinseisha.

Chuma, H. (1994), *Kensho: Nihongata Koyo Chosei (Employment Adjustment: The Japanese Style)*, Tokyo: Shueisha.

Davidson, C. (1990), *Recent Developments in the Theory of Involuntary Unemployment*, Kalamazoo, MI: W.E. Upjohn Institute for Employment Research.

Dawkins, R. (1989), *The Selfish Gene* (2nd edn), Oxford: Oxford University Press.

Freedman, C. (ed.) (1999), *Why Did Japan Stumble? Causes and Cures*, Cheltenham: Edward Elgar.

Fukao, M. and Y. Morita (1997), *Kigyo Gabanansu Kozo no Kokusai Kikaku (International Comparison of the Structure of Corporate Governance)*, Nihonkeizai Shinbunsha.

Genda, Y. (2000), 'Youth Employment and Parasite Singles', *Japan Labour Bulletin*, The Japan Institute of Labour, March.

Genda, Y. and M.E. Rebick (2000), 'Japanese Labour in the 1990s: Stability and Stagnation', *Oxford Review of Economic Policy, Summer*, **16**(2), pp. 85–102.

Gilson, R.J. and M.J. Roe (1999), 'The Political Economy of Japanese Lifetime Employment', in M.M. Blair and M.J. Roe (eds), *Employees and Corporate*

Governance, Washington, DC: Brookings Institution Press, 239–74.

Hamada, K. (1999), 'The Incentive Structure of a Managed Market Economy: Can it Survive the Millenium?', *American Economic Review*, (Proceedings) May (1999).

Hayashi, N. (et al.) (1999), 'Reciprocity, Trust and the Sense of Control: A Cross-Societal Study', *Rationality and Society*, London: Sage Productions, **11**(1), pp. 27–46.

Hirota, S. (1999), 'Ginko Chusin no Kinyu Shisutemu wa Henka Shiteiku noka (Can the Financial System Based on Banking Change?)', *Waseda Shogaku*, February.

Hiwatari, N. (1999), 'Employment Practices and Enterprise Unionism in Japan', in M.M. Blair and M.J. Roe (eds), *Employees and Corporate Governance*, Washington, DC: Brookings Institution Press, pp. 275–313.

Hoshi, T. and A. Kashyap (forthcoming), 'The Banking Crisis and the Future of the Japanese Financial System', mimeo.

Hoshi, T. (1998), 'Japanese Corporate Governance as a System', in K.J. Hopt, H. Kanda, M.J. Roe, E. Wymeersch and S. Prigge (eds), *Comparative Corporate Governance – The State of the Art and Emerging Research*, Oxford: Oxford University Press, pp. 847–75.

Ichniowski, C., K. Shaw and G. Prennushi (1997), 'The Effects of Human Resource Management Practices on Productivity: A Study of Steel Finishing Lines', *American Economic Review* **87**(3), pp. 291–313.

Inoue, Y. (1999), 'Road to Recovery: The Changing Corporate Structure of Japan', Senior Essay, Yale University.

Itoh, H. (1994), 'Japanese Human Resource Management from the Viewpoint of Incentive Theory', in M. Aoki and R. Dore (eds), *The Japanese Firm: The Sources of Competitive Strength*, Oxford: Oxford University Press, pp. 233–64.

Kandori, M., G. Mailath and R. Rob (1993), 'Learning, Mutation and Long Run Equilibria in Games', *Econometrica*, **61**, pp. 21–56.

Kano, Y. (1991), *Min-ei-ka ga Nihon o Kaeru (Privatization Changes Japan)*, Tokyo: The PHP Research Institute.

Kato, T. (2000), 'The Recent transformation of Participatory Employment Practices in Japan', presented at the *NBER Japan Project Meeting*, May, Cambridge, MA.

Koike, K. (1981), *Nihon no Jukuren (Skill Formation in Japan)*, Tokyo: Yuhikaku.

Lawrence, C. and R.Z. Lawrence (1985), 'Manufacturing Wage Dispersion: An End Game Interpretation', *Brookings Papers on Economic Activity* **1**, pp. 47–106.

Lincoln, E.J. (1999), 'The Social Consistency of the Japanese Economic System and the Implication for Institutional Transformation', paper presented at the *Japan Economic Seminar* (New Haven), August.

Matsuyama, K. (1991), 'Increasing Returns, Industrialization and Indeterminacy of Equilibrium', *Quarterly Journal of Economics*, **56**, pp. 617–50.

Miwa, Y. (1998), 'The Economics of Corporate Governance in Japan', in K.J. Hopt, H. Kanda, M.J. Roe, E. Wymeersch and S. Prigge (eds), *Comparative Corporate Governance – The State of the Art and Emerging Research*, Oxford: Oxford University Press, pp. 877–9.

Nonaka, I. (1988), 'Creating Organizational Order Out of Chaos: Self-renewal in Japanese Firms', *California Management Review*, **30**(3), pp. 57–73.

Okazaki, Tetsuji and Masahiro Okuno (1993), 'Gendai Nihon no Keizai Shisutemu to sono Rekishiteki Haikei (The Modern Japanese Economic System and its

Historic Background)', in Okazaki, Tetsuji and Okuno (eds) (1993), *Gendai Nihon no Keizai Shisutemu no Genryu (The Origin of the Modern Japanese Economic System)*, Tokyo: Nihonkeizai shimbunsha.

Okuno, M., G. Mailath and A. Postlewaite (1993), 'Belief-based Refinements in Signaling Games', *Journal of Economic Theory*, **60**(2), pp. 43–59.

Olson, M. (1982), *The Rise and Decline of Nations: Economic Growth, Stagflation and Social Rigidities*, New Haven: Yale University Press.

Organisation for Economic Co-operation and Development (OECD) (1997), *Employment Outlook*, Paris: OECD.

Osborne, M.J. and A. Rubinstein (1994), *A Course in Game Theory*, Cambridge, MA: MIT Press.

Shleifer, A. and L.H. Summers (1988), 'Hostile Takeovers as Breaches of Trust', in A.J. Auerbach (ed.), *Corporate Takeovers: Causes and Consequences*, Chicago, IL: University of Chicago Press, pp. 33–56.

Sugimoto, Y. (1997), *An Introduction to Japanese Society*, Cambridge: Cambridge University Press.

Toennies, F. (1887), *Gemainschaft to Gesellschaft*, Lepzig: Reisland.

Weinstein, D.E. (1997), 'Foreign Direct Investment and Keiretsu: Rethinking U.S. and Japanese Policy', in R. Feenstra (ed.), *The Effects of US Trade Protection and Promotion Policies*, Chicago, IL: University of Chicago Press, pp. 81–116.

Yamada, M. (1999), *Parasaito Sinuru no Jidai (Days of Parasite Single)*, Tokyo: Chikuma-shobo.

Yamagishi, T. and K. Cook (1993), 'Generalized Exchange and Social Dilemmas', *Social Psychology Quarterly*, **56**(4), pp. 235–47.

Yamagishi, T., K. Cook and M. Watabe (1998), Uncertainty, Trust and Commitment Formation in the United States and Japan, *American Journal of Sociology*, **104**(1), July, pp. 165–94.

Yamagishi, T., N. Jin and A.S. Miller (1998), 'In-group Bias and Culture of Collectivism', *Asian Journal of Social Psychology*, **1**, pp. 315–28.

Yamagishi, T., N. Jin and T. Kiyonari (1999), 'Bounded Generalized Reciprocity: Ingroup Boasting and Ingroup Favouritism', *Advances in Group Processes*, **16**, pp. 161–97.

Yashiro, N. (1997), *Nihonteki Koyokanko no Keizaigaku (The Economics of Japanese Employment Practice)*, Tokyo: Nihonkeizai Shinbunsha.

7. Japan's industries and companies: economic dynamism and social continuity

James C. Abegglen

With still vivid memories of the government, economy and society of Japan in the autumn of 1945, the question of whether Japan can change seems a distinctly odd one, hardly needing an answer. Yet there does appear often, abroad from Japan, a view of the system as rigid and static. Distance and ignorance no doubt play their part in shaping this view, but an issue as well may be the different rates of change in Japan, with quite exceptionally rapid changes in industrial structure and technologies and relatively slow rates of change in social structures and values. These differences in velocity of change are notable in the tensions around the organization and governance of Japan's industrial firms.

RAPIDLY CHANGING INDUSTRIAL STRUCTURE

In industrial structure, no nation has yet changed as rapidly and thoroughly as Japan. The economic growth rate is clear testimony: nominal GDP increased 60 times in the 40 years from 1955 to 1995, and in real terms by 10 times. The increase in GDP measured in US dollars over the 40-year period was more than 200 times, as Japan's currency value increased to reflect the economic wealth created. This kind of economic growth was possible only through exceptional changes in the value-added structure of Japanese industry.

Over this period, once-dominant agriculture dropped to less than 2 per cent of GDP, with a massive shift from the countryside to the cities. Changes within the industrial sector were no less massive. Coal mining is a prime example. In 1950, coal mining was the largest industry measured by number of employees, some 350,000 working more than 800 coal pits. At a rate without parallel in the industrial world (note Ms Thatcher's problems with Britain's mining union), Japan's labor intensive, high cost mines closed. There are now two in operation, with some 3,000 employees at recent count.

Similarly, labor intensive cotton spinning, in the earlier period for Japan as most developing economies a critical source of employment and output, shrank drastically from a peak in 1960 (more than 120 companies to 40 in the mid-1990s; 110,000 employees to 16,000). Japan became the world's largest cotton goods importer.

Industrial change was by no means limited to labor intensive sectors, although the drive to higher value-added output had its greatest impact on those industries. Capital intensive bauxite smelting is an example of a quite different industry from mining and cotton spinning. In 15 years from the mid-1970s, Japan's alumina output went from 1.2 million tons, about 15 per cent of world output, to 18,000 tons in a single surviving small-scale mill, most of this drastic write-off occurring in only five years from 1977 to 1982.

Much – too much – has been made of the role of government in bringing about these changes. The Japanese government, as all political entities, made efforts to slow and ameliorate change, by protective policies for agriculture for example, and relocation assistance stemming from mine closings and other industrial shifts. At the same time, policies encouraged shifts in industrial structure as well. However, the basic force at work was economic growth and the growth in turn made relocations and reallocations much easier. Still, individuals lost jobs, families had to relocate, villages were abandoned, prefectures were in economic trouble and companies disappeared. No one has managed to make industrial change simple or pleasant.

We might then characterize the high growth period from the mid-1950s to the mid-1990s as one of rather straightforward shifts toward greater capital intensity and higher levels of technology. All of this provided higher value-added, both causing and made possible by historic rates of industrial growth. Japan changed, mightily.

FROM GROWTH TO MATURITY

With Japan's economy reaching its highest levels of output, income and technology, an abrupt transition period began in the early 1990s as the economy and society shifted from high growth to industrial and demographic maturity. In demographic terms, 1998 was the first year that the numbers of persons 65 years and older exceeded the numbers of persons 15 years and younger. With this has come a peaking of labor force size and the subsequent constraints on growth brought about by a diminishing labor force and population that will persist over the next decades. As a wealthy, mature and technologically very advanced economy, the potential for growth moves from the very high earlier levels to the 2 to 3 per cent growth rates that characterize mature economies.

This transition from high growth to maturity requires very significant changes in industrial and corporate strategy, and as the present situation in Japan indicates, the changes are not easy to effect. To cite a few, during high growth it is desirable and indeed necessary to have high savings rates (household savings as well as corporate savings/retained earnings). These savings make possible the high levels of capital investment that growth depends on, and the high use of relatively inexpensive debt to fund that investment.

Market share rather than profitability measures corporate success under conditions of high growth. Failure to keep pace with growth is fatal when growth rates are exceeding 20 per cent or more annually. As growth slows, with needed additions to capacity slowing as well, measures of profitability become the appropriate measures of success.

All of this, and more, changes with maturity. High savings choke off growth in a mature economy, and higher levels of consumption are needed – a hard lesson for households to learn after generations of instruction on the need to save. The balance sheet of companies must be strengthened, debt levels brought down, and higher returns on assets achieved as growth slows and stronger balance sheets are required. Success in slow growth businesses is measured by profitability not by market share, as increases in market share become too costly to justify. Finally, under conditions of high growth business diversification is easy – almost any new business undertaken by the firm will achieve some modest success buoyed up by an overall high growth economy. With maturity, however, firms must focus their businesses and concentrate resources where they have established sustainable positions.

This entire massive shift in strategy and in mindset is difficult enough under any condition. It has been made very much more difficult by very costly errors in macro-economic management that precipitated the recession of 1998 and 1999, and a considerable period of substantial deflation. No surprise then that Japanese companies have had several years of very hard going. Basic strategies must change in an economic environment that is in any case a punishing one.

INDUSTRIAL CHANGE WITH ECONOMIC MATURITY

The industrial sector might be divided, in terms of patterns of change now taking place, into three broad groupings. The first, and most conventional in pattern, is a range of what might be called commodity-based industries, including cement, pulp and paper, and petroleum refining as main examples. These are energy intensive, pollution intensive, land extensive, import-dependent industries with little future in a mature and high technology Japan. The pattern here is one of corporate merger. The numbers of players will decline steadily, making desperate efforts to solve basic economic problems with greater scale.

A second, and economically more significant, grouping is that of industries that are now in mature markets and use mature technologies, following a long period of high growth and rapid change. These notably include autos and consumer electronics. The issue is one of too many competitors. There are still some 11 vehicle producers in Japan. Three would seem quite sufficient. Yet sustained high growth served as an umbrella protecting marginal companies in these industries. The most efficient producers, in pursuit of growth, left the marginal firms relatively untouched. With slowed or no growth, the marginal firms go to the wall, as the leading, low cost producers strengthen their market positions.

Thus in autos Toyota and Honda are doing very well, and continue to increase their share in a very slow-growing domestic market. Toyota has moved to consolidate its control over Daihatsu and Hino, further reducing the number of makers. In contrast, the marginal firms (Nissan, Mitsubishi Motors, Mazda, Suzuki and Fuji Heavy) have all been driven into the arms of foreign investors. No doubt it is better for the Japanese economy to have foreign investors prolong the survival of marginal firms than to have to deal with bankruptcies. It is not clear, however, that these foreign investments will materially slow the advance of winners in the industries or profit the foreign investors all that much. (See below for some parallels in the financial sector.) But change there certainly is in these mature industries.

A third group of companies, in terms of industrial change, is those caught in a trap of over-diversification. Very high growth generates opportunities to diversify with low cost and risk (witness the Internet sector in the US currently). While a great many Japanese companies fell into this trap, and are now in process of divesting and consolidating, the major players have been the electronic conglomerates (notably Toshiba, Hitachi, Melco, NEC and Fujitsu).

Mr Taizo Nishimuro, now Chairman of Toshiba, put the problem and remedy as follows:

> In the past, you had only to be in a growing sector and somehow you made a profit. Now you have to rank high worldwide in each sector or you cannot survive. Therefore, what is required is not a management looking at the overall business, but a management ensuring a position in each competitive situation and structuring the company to increase profits[1]

Mr Nishimuro closely followed his own advice, disposing of more than a dozen marginal businesses in an 18-month period, through sale, merger and joint venture options. He followed this series of cutbacks with a reorganization to focus investment on the information technology sectors where Toshiba had achieved a position but was lagging in needed investment. The correction as proposed required a $2.5 billion refocusing program. Fujitsu, NEC and Hitachi have also been following this pattern closely and with increasing success.

CHANGING CORPORATE LAW

Along with the pressures of economic maturity, changes in the ground rules for doing business are also impacting Japan's industrial firms. Some are changes in long-standing, but now obsolete, regulations. Important here is the abolition of the Anti-holding Company Act, rigidly enforced since its passage not long after the end of World War II. Originally aimed against a revival of the huge concentrations of economic power represented by the pre-war holding companies, the act has been a barrier more recently to the rationalization of large Japanese companies. With its abolition rather more than a year ago (1998), industrial firms (such as Toshiba and Hitachi) and financial groups (such as the merging Mizuho banks) can set up separate operating companies under a holding company umbrella. The result will be a much increased potential to consolidate businesses, and to separate out for divestment non-core businesses to an extent not possible until now.

Other rules are changing as well. A critical change is the requirement for consolidated reporting. Until now, for domestic purposes at least, financial reports have generally been of the parent only, although many major companies, especially those raising funds in foreign markets, have for many years reported consolidated results. For many other companies, however, loss-making businesses could be set up as separate, unconsolidated subsidiaries, as could very promising businesses in order to give them autonomous running room. The lack of consolidated reporting has led to extremes in spawning affiliates. The *sogo shosha* have had hundreds of subsidiaries, variously estimated for Mitsui Bussan, Itochu and the like at between 950 and 1,200. No doubt triage is appropriate – a third are only lightly wounded perhaps, a third might benefit from surgical attention and a third might best be left to die. In any case now, with consolidation required, we will see how these myriads of affiliates fare when exposed to the harsh light of public accounting.

An additional change in rules is the requirement to mark assets to market. The investment item on the balance sheet is made up largely of shares in supplier, customer and group companies, and is often very large. These shares could be carried at cost until now, as could real estate, but henceforth must be 'marked to market' (shown at current market values). A third major rule change is the requirement to recognize (and within a defined period to deal with) full pension and retirement liabilities.

These rule changes are all recent. The full consequences for individual companies and for industry organization are by no means evident as yet. However, it might be expected that overall these rule changes are likely to make the strong relatively even stronger and the weak distinctly weaker. Strong companies have tended to set up new and promising businesses as subsidiaries to give them room to develop. Such companies will tend to consolidate their healthy subsidiaries. For weaker firms the result will be the opposite, with loss-making subsidiaries and affiliates worsening the consolidated statements.

So too with pension liabilities – companies such as Toyota and Shiseido have met the problem squarely, using their attractive investment portfolios to fund liabilities, an option generally not available to weaker firms. Broadly then, the outcome will favour stronger firms resulting in fewer (and larger) survivors of these changes. These new regulations will generally work to the disadvantage of already weak competitors.

THE CHANGED SERVICES SECTOR

The massive changes that have taken place and are continuing in the industrial sector now have their counterpart in the services sector, which has long been highly regulated. It has been in this sector that the (very misleading) clichés about the economy, such as the 'convoy system', have had some accuracy. Banking and insurance especially were bound up in regulations that determined product, pricing and distribution channels. With Japan's 'big bang' now moving toward completion, this sector has been undergoing massive change.

The changes have been abrupt and drastic. For the first time in post-war history, with banks assumed to be entirely safe and government guaranteed, three major banks went bust (Long Term Credit, Nippon Credit in 1998 and Takushoku in 1997), along with several smaller banks and other financial institutions. An insurance company went under, the first such bankruptcy in post-war Japan, followed by several others, with still more teetering on the brink. A major brokerage firm died dramatically (Yamaichi Securities), along with the smaller Sanyo Securities. The causes of the problems these bankruptcies symbolize are many, but the overall issue is that of sudden and far-reaching deregulation in a sector that had been too long protected, or so it now, with hindsight, seems clear.

Two main trends might be noted, along with the failure pattern. First, widespread mergers are sweeping the entire financial system. Of the nine main commercial banks, several themselves the result of earlier mergers, only four will remain in a year or two from today (2000), after announced combinations are effected. Trust banks are combining under the aegis of these main bank mergers, as are also life and casualty insurance companies. Long-continued patterns of cross-shareholdings and 'stable' shareholders will change greatly as these mergers are implemented in operations.

Second, foreign investment penetration of the financial sector is beginning to approximate foreign company penetration of manufacturing. Japanese companies in which foreign direct investment is at least 20 per cent of equity account for some 6 to 8 per cent of total sales in Japan. With the deregulation of services, something like this is happening in banking, insurance and brokerage as well. General Electric has invested approximately $15 billion in life insurance, consumer finance and leasing over the past four years (1995–1999), but is still looking for more investments. Including GE Capital's buy into the bankrupt Toho Insurance, six life insurance companies have been acquired by foreign interests, two by French investors, one by a Canadian investor and three by US investors. In addition, foreign interests have acquired and are relaunching the bankrupted Long Term Credit Bank, while Merrill Lynch has bought up large pieces of the bankrupted Yamaichi Securities.

It remains the case however, in the finance sector as it is in industry, that the acquisitions by foreign investors are of failed Japanese companies. Selling to foreign investors remains an alternative to bankruptcy or a solution to bankruptcy, no less in finance than in the auto industry. It needs to be noted that this pattern is not peculiar to foreign buyers, but applies no less to Japanese buyers. Successful businesses in Japan are not yet for sale, at any price, to local or foreign would-be purchasers.

Deregulation, along with other changes in the economy, is producing service sector changes in areas other than financial services. Economic pressures have halved the number of pharmaceutical wholesalers in the past decade, for example, with wholesalers also disappearing from among consumer electronics businesses. Distribution changes are reflected as well in the rise of new types of retailer. The annual report on Japan's excellent companies by Nihon Keizai Shimbun in 1999 had a newcomer, Ryohin Keikaku, a private brand retailer, in 10th place behind Fuji Film but ahead of Matsushita Communication. Another new retailer, Fast Retailing, selling cut-price apparel, was rated 20th most excellent company, tied with Toyota in rank.

The Nikkei listing of excellent companies provides a further note regarding change in Japanese industry. The top three companies in order of excellence in the 1999 listing are Nintendo, NTT Docomo and SevenEleven, in that order, a far cry indeed from the heavy industry-dominated lists of leaders of the 1970s and 1980s. No steel companies, no chemical companies, no electrical machinery companies head the lists. Instead, services, as the economy changes yet again.

CHANGE AS A CONSTANT

As would be the case with any successful economy, Japan's economy has been a dynamic one, perhaps even exceptionally so by world standards. Over about two generations, Japan has gone through the full cycle from agriculture and labor intensity to heavy industry, then to high technologies and now to services. Change has been both the cause and result of very rapid economic growth. With slowed growth bringing economic and demographic maturity, change has become more difficult. Yet it continues to be quite rapid, spurred now by far-reaching changes in the regulatory environment for the services industry and rules regarding the organization and financial reporting of individual companies.

An aspect of industrial change not so far alluded to concerns capacity to innovate. By the late 1970s–early 1980s, Japanese industry had caught up with the highest levels of technology. Purchasing technology abroad as a device for continued change lost its effectiveness. The issue then became the capacity of Japanese industry itself to develop new products and services. Many of the clichés regarding Japan's educational system and its industrial progress belittle the nation's ability to innovate, and suggest that lack of capacity to innovate technologically is a major barrier to future economic growth.

Two sources of data here seem relevant, in an area that is exceptionally hard to measure. One is the continuing research by Porter and Stern, who have developed and for some years applied an 'innovation index'. In their most recent report, in 1999, Japan is rated first in the world in innovative capacity, up from third in 1995, while the US is rated third in 1999 after being first in 1995. Projecting to 2005, Japan continues first, with the US sixth. (Australia was rated in 11th place in 1999 and holds the same position in 2005.)[2]

A rather different measure of innovative capacity is patents awarded. According to the US Patent and Trademark Office, in 1999 patent approvals, to individual companies, were most frequently awarded to IBM, followed by NEC and Canon. Of the top ten companies awarded patents in the US, six were Japanese companies, three US companies, one Korean and none either European or from anywhere else. Patents are not a rigorous measure, by any means, of innovative capacity, but still this marks a major change from 20 years earlier when only one Japanese company, Hitachi, was among the US top ten corporate patent recipients. No better than indicative, still these measures suggest that the capacity to innovate, as a factor making for continuing industrial change, is substantial in the case of Japan.

SOCIAL CHANGE AND SOCIAL STABILITY

Driven largely by drastic economic change, social change in Japan has also been considerable. Most dramatically, life expectancy increased by 26 years for men and 29 years for women in only a 50-year period from 1947, extraordinary testimony to economic success and in itself evidence of great changes in Japanese society.

Along with this has come rapid urbanization, a shift from extended to nuclear families, a drastic decline in birth rate, delays in marriage age and increases in the proportion of the non-married. The young lady in Tokyo carrying the requisite hair-coloring and i-mode phone, with platform soled boots, presents a rather different prospect from her mother at a similar age. How much of all this is economy driven and how much a basic change in social values is not at all clear.

Certainly there is a good deal of continuity. For all of the alarums expressed by the chronically self-critical Japanese, most indices of social disease and health suggest not only a healthy population, but a socially stable and conservative one as well. By standards of other developed nations, crime rates remain low. The family system is relatively intact. Divorce rates remain low and births to unmarried women are only some 1 per cent of total, compared with the US at 30-odd per cent and Sweden at over 50 per cent. Women have much increased roles in business and politics, yet only 21 per cent think they should have the same rights as men, compared with 60 to 70 per cent of women in Europe and the US.[3]

Even as economically related a factor as the savings rate represents continuity, as analyzed recently by Garon: 'As the Japanese economy recovered and then prospered, housewives and their families experienced the benefits of expanding consumption. They did not, however, stop saving at high rates. As in the war, the resourceful housewife "rationalized" consumption, engaged in "life planning", and saved for the future.'[4] Savings continue at a high level and are held mainly in bank and postal savings deposits, along with insurance, rather than in equities as in the US and UK. That is, the savings focus is on security of savings rather than hoped-for appreciation of savings.

Changes in values and attitudes are rather harder to estimate. Writing in the early 1990s, Hiroyuki Nitto reviewed a series of surveys and concluded:

> Research in the 1970s identified the core values of Japanese people as an emphasis on group harmony, consideration for human relations, and responsible actions by the individual as a member of family and society . . . Research in the 1980s, however, revealed that a new and contrary element – an emphasis on the individual – is developing in Japanese consciousness. Research in the early 1990s suggests these two [sets of] values are now interacting and changing.[5]

Research carried out as the economy hit the worst period in post-war history, 1998, suggests that under this stress there was a shift back toward the earlier pattern described by Nitto. The most recent HILL study, carried out in 1998, concludes:

> In spite of the growing [economic] pessimism, the percentage of Japanese who are satisfied in daily life and who consider their lives to be enjoyable has not decreased . . . A growing number of Japanese believe that there are too many changes in Japan and in the world today. They prefer a life style that is simpler and quieter. They are also resorting to traditional values. The percentage of those who feel it is important to adhere to customs and accepted practices rose 10.5 points in two years . . . Increasingly, they feel that the Japanese should focus more on society and the nation than on their individual lives. They think they should look out for the national interest even at the expense of the wellbeing of individuals. And they believe that they should place the interests of Japan above the interest of the international community.[6]

A conclusion from all this might be that attitudes and values have shown considerable continuity over a very long period, despite all the changes in the broad social and economic environment. This should perhaps be no surprise. Japan's is a healthy society on the whole, and healthy societies with effective family systems change rather slowly.

CORPORATE GOVERNANCE: THE ANGLO-AMERICAN VIEW

The high rate of economic change in Japan and the relatively slow rate of social change and of change in social values continue to be a source of tension in many sectors, notably in the management structure of the Japanese corporation. For reasons that seem not to be well explained in rather a-historical management literature, the Anglo-American world has come fully to accept the doctrine that shareholders have full and pre-emptive claim to corporate property. Implicit in this is the view that the value of a corporation is a function only of capital investment, with the roles of ordinary employees, suppliers, customers and the community playing no significant part.

This rather odd view, much encouraged by the success of the US and UK economies in the mid and late 1990s, has been discussed and propagated under the rubric of 'corporate governance'. An advisory committee to the OECD presumed to define public policy in the matter: 'Corporate governance comprehends that structure of relationships and corresponding responsibilities among a core group consisting of shareholders, board members and managers designed to best foster competitive performance to achieve the corporation's primary objective.'[7] The committee goes on: 'Defining the mission of the corporation in the modern economy: Generating long-term capital gain to enhance shareholder (or investor) value is the corporation's central mission.'[8]

With a political bow to diversity, the OECD endorsed the committee's views: 'There is no single model of good corporate governance. Different legal systems, institutional frameworks and traditions mean that a range of different approaches have developed around the world. Common to all good corporate governance regimes, however, is a high degree of priority placed on the interests of shareholders.'[9]

(It might be noted here that this focus on and concern for shareholders takes no note of the fact that shareholding in the United States at least has become a short-term matter, quite like buying a ticket for the local lottery. Each activity has a similar focus on a short-term pay-off from cashing out. These shareholders are 'owners' in a rather odd sense.)

A number of consequences flow from this view that the corporation is the exclusive property of the shareholder. One is the very high incidence of corporate sale and acquisition both in Britain and the United States. The company is a physical property with a price to be negotiated. If the price is attractive in terms of prices of shares, the deal is to be carried out. Consequences for employees, supplier and customers are not at issue in closing the transaction. The corporation is simply a commodity.

A second consequence is the perceived need to align the interests of management with those of the shareholder – whose interest is presumed to be in the price of shares. Thus there are very high levels of compensation for top management, with the additional incentive of stock options on the assumption that these cause management and shareholders to have a common objective. Stock options are a one-way play, with no downside risk, which makes the executive's concern rather different from that of, say, the day-trader. Moreover, since in the US and UK share price is driven by quarterly earnings reports, the time horizon of management is shifted to a three-month perspective, with corporate funds used for share buy-backs as share price may threaten to weaken and thus diminish the attraction of the options.

Best of all, stock options are treated as no-cost compensation items in US accounting. In 1996, if stock options had been correctly treated as a cost of compensation, Microsoft's earnings would have changed from a positive $2.8 billion to a total loss of $10.2 billion.[10] In summary, one consequence of the view of shareholder value as the purpose of the corporation has been to provide the rationale for stunningly high levels of total pay for chief executives, all much buttressed by the promotion of a 'leadership' mystique.

CORPORATE GOVERNANCE: THE JAPANESE VIEW

The considerable discussion of Anglo-American concepts of corporate governance, especially given the confidence – even arrogance – with which they are recommended to others, has of course led to a good deal of discussion in and about Japan where these concepts seem especially prone to neglect. In his excellent book on comparative corporate governance, Jonathan Charkham, a distinguished British specialist, describes Japan in part as follows:

> To understand how corporate governance works requires us to know what the participants perceive their objective to be. In Japan there appears to be a general consensus that although profit is important, the long-term preservation and prosperity of the family (which is how companies are viewed) are and should be primarily the aim of all concerned, and not profit maximization or shareholders' immediate values.[11]

A senior Japanese executive put the matter more bluntly: 'I believe that my mission as an executive is first to maintain employment, and second to be profitable. It is necessary to secure a standard profitability in order to maintain employment and carry out R&D. Is it not strange to have profit as a corporate objective by sacrificing domestic employment?'[12]

In response to the OECD activity and the fashion for discussing corporate governance, a prestigious group of Japanese businessmen organized the Corporate Governance Forum of Japan. In its final report, the Corporate Governance Committee of the Forum offered this view:

> The Japanese management style has been characterized and criticized as one which preserves inefficient and unprofitable divisions only in order to maintain employment. On the other hand, the Anglo-American model admits that the ability to quickly dispose of workers is only 'for the benefit of shareholders,'

which is why the system has tended to be criticized. But it is possible to avoid the damaging effects of corporate downsizing in practice through the fulfilment of management's duty to re-allocate employees to newly created profitable sectors. The Japanese style of management has not been one easily obsessed by precipitate employee lay-offs or the mergers and acquisition syndrome.[13]

The report goes on with a gentle but firm assertion of Japanese values: 'The frequent adjustment of employment during each negative phase of the business cycle is regarded as an irresponsible transfer of business risks to employees . . . We believe this notion could add certain values to the Anglo-American model of corporate governance.'[14] Or, as Hiroshi Okuda, Chairman of Toyota Motors, put it in a different context: 'The source of competitive strength of Japanese companies is management that honors its personnel. Last year, Moody's announced a lowering of the debt rating of Toyota for the reason that Toyota maintains a system of long-term employment (shushin koyosei). This is much too short-sighted an evaluation.'[15]

There is no suggestion in the conclusions of the Forum that shareholders have no place in a corporation or role to play. On the contrary, 'Managers ought to be responsible for the long term maximization of shareholders' profit and should exercise fiduciary duty toward shareholders.'[16]

One of Japan's newer business leaders, Yoshihiko Miyauchi, Chairman of Orix, put it this way:

> I find I have doubts about shareholder capitalism. There are many types of shareholders, ranging from those from the time of the founding of the company to shareholders seeking an overnight large profit. How on earth does one know which shareholders to work on behalf of? I feel I should send a message regarding the desired type. In truth, it is shareholders that seek medium and long-term growth. As a result is it not likely that that sort of shareholder will come to make up the majority? The company will grow by placing the shareholder at the center of the interested parties. Moreover, since the company is the instrument of common interests and common destiny, it is essential to give closest concern to relations with employees.[17]

The consensus view is rather clear. The shareholder is one of the several stakeholders in the company, and management must take a long view in dealing with all the stakeholders. Relations with employees, and honoring obligations to employees and their careers, remain the central focus. The Anglo-American focus on the shareholders' interest as the purpose of the corporation is quite clearly rejected.

While legislation authorizing stock options has been enacted, press reports suggest that only some 10 per cent of companies have introduced stock options, and that in many cases these are offered to the entire workforce. Of course, employee share ownership has a long history in Japan through employee shareholding associations. There is little indication as yet that the stock option will be used as a method of aggrandizing the very top. Similarly, while share buy-backs are now possible, they still seem to be little used. On the contrary, recent reports have indicated that such leading companies as Sony, Secom and Softbank, far from resorting to share buy-backs, are increasing their share issues as a means of increasing equity capitalization.

We see a similar response with still another slice of the Anglo-American model; the outside director. Often the fashion leader, Sony moved to have several outside directors, including even a foreign director or two. Putting it very mildly, there has been no rush to follow Sony's lead. Some 90 per cent of all corporate directors remain insiders, career executives for whom a directorship is the final and highest stage of their careers in the company. True, they serve at the whim of the chief executive, but then so do the directors in Anglo-American companies. At least the Japanese directors have a close and immediate knowledge of the company's interests and problems, unlike the outside directors who make up the majority of directors of US companies. There has been a rather general reduction in total number of directors, along with a delayering of corporate hierarchies, but the directors remain almost entirely insiders.

This may change. The Corporate Governance Committee notes: 'Currently a sufficient supply of independent external directors does not exist in Japan. But in the medium term the uniquely Japanese system of cross-shareholding might begin to unravel, which will necessitate a system of governance more reliant on independent and external directors, in turn leading to a market for such individuals.'[18]

Indeed, all of these aspects of Japanese management may change over time. A persistent candidate for change is the incidence of corporate acquisitions. The problem in assessing the degree of change here is the great degree to which merger and acquisition activities are exaggerated by the firms seeking M&A business in order to keep their large staffs occupied. In fact, acquisitions in Japan remain largely restricted to the purchase of deeply troubled companies, in or near bankruptcy. In the Anglo-American business world, the purchaser seeks growth, success and effective management. Acquisitions in Japan remain few in number, and very difficult to accomplish. The funds available, especially from abroad, for acquisitions and management buy-outs are very large and still growing; the deal flow is minuscule.

More specifically relevant to the corporate governance issue, there still (despite considerable and well-publicized efforts) have been no hostile takeovers in Japan. Given all the money available and the effort invested, surely some change is likely. But there still has been none, and the potential for deals of this sort can only decline as the economy and its businesses recover from the 1998–99 recession.

The Forum referenced cross-shareholdings as an aspect of corporate governance that may be changing. The topic is complex and not easy to measure accurately. The best analyses are by Nissei Kiso Kenkyujo. Its most recent report analyzes shareholdings in 2,426 companies (end of 1998). Stable holders, defined largely as banks, insurance companies and group member companies, declined from about 48 per cent of total share-holders in 1987 to 41 per cent in 1998. The decline was by slight degrees, but steady over the decade. Cross-shareholdings were down from 21 per cent to 16 per cent, also declining steadily. One major increase was in shares held by trust banks – presumably largely pension accounts – that curiously were not considered 'stable', up from 8.5 per cent to 13.5 per cent over the decade. The largest increase was in foreigner shareholdings, up from 4 per cent in 1987 to 14 per cent in 1998. We may assume that these are not 'stable'.[19]

Certainly financial cross-holdings are down, but clearly they remain sub-stantial. What is less clear is the future trend: if balance sheet pressure eases, do sell-offs stop and cross-holding purchases increase? What is the quality of holdings – are core holdings within established groups being held or are they too diminishing? As in so much of this governance discussion, this issue also seems to be going through some change, but not dramatic change – in contrast to frequent press reports.

In sum, if change in business systems is viewed from the perspective of corporate governance categories, the conclusion must be that the special features (both positive and negative) of corporate governance in Japan remain largely unchanged. This is not due to a lack of interest or attention, nor a lack of advice, especially from abroad. However, the system persists; no doubt because for Japanese society and given Japanese values, it is an appropriate, useful and effective system.

THE JAPANESE EMPLOYMENT SYSTEM

A review of corporate governance provides a context for a closer look at developments in the Japanese employment system. The employment system comprehends what is broadly referred to by the term '*Nihonteki keiei*' (Japanese-style management). Usually this refers to three aspects of the system:

- *shushin koyosei*, or life-time employment;
- *nenko joretsu*, or seniority-based pay and promotion;

- *kigyonai kumiai*, or enterprise union – a single company union with membership undifferentiated by skill categories and including all eligible company employees.

The Japanese company is not simply an economic machine to generate cash. It is instead an integrated social organization and as such its patterns are consistent with, and based on, the values and behaviors of the broader society. This is apparent in Japan's employment system, with its emphases on egalitarianism, age grading, economic security and group identification.

The employment system of Japan came together in its current form in the post-World War II period, and was first detailed in English and in Japanese by the present writer in the mid-1950s.[20] The term in English and Japanese, 'lifetime employment', was first offered in these books – although it has come to have a rather different usage from its original definition. Even in the mid-1950s, industries and companies were restructuring and 'voluntary retirement' was in practice as a result, along with contract workers, women with shorter periods of job tenure, and the like. That is, there has always been a good degree of workforce flexibility, important to keep in mind when considering how much change has taken place in the intervening four or five decades.

It perhaps needs to be noted that this system of employment has no legal standing. No law or laws enforce it. Courts will however reserve the right to review dismissals to examine whether they have been reasonable and justified, thus putting the weight of the courts behind job security. Also, it is sometimes suggested that the career employment pattern applies only to that part of the labor force in large companies and/or unionized labor forces. This simply is not so. As any small businessman can attest, the pattern is a general one. Whatever the size of the company, ignoring this pattern entails a real risk.

It has in the past few years become something of a cliché to state that the lifetime employment system has come to an end. Indeed, the end of the system has been announced, especially in the Western press, each year since the term was introduced. Some of this reflects the arrogance of Western observers. Japan is different but will soon see the light and adopt our better, Western ways, a view also common among many Western-trained Japanese. As the above discussion of corporate governance and the role of the shareholder and employee suggests, change is not so rapid or uni-dimensional.

A thorough-going analysis of the question was undertaken by the Ministry of Labour, the results being published in that Ministry's 1999 White Paper. The conclusions are quoted here at some length as providing an informed and objective assessment of the current situation.

Conceptually speaking, there are two aspects to long-term employment practices. One aspect is the idea of a worker working at a single company or corporate group continuously from entrance after graduation (from high school, university, etc.). Another aspect is a corporate philosophy that sees employment as part of a long-term strategy, and does not undertake employment adjustments in response to short-term fluctuations in the economic climate.[21]

The White Paper reviews trends in job tenure:

Trends in long-term employment practices show that the average number of continuous working years has increased through the stable growth period. An analysis of cohorts by age group shows that the average number of continuous working years has lengthened for the baby boomer generation and the generation immediately following it but has not much changed since.[22]

In conclusion:

Support for long-term employment practices currently remains high among both companies and workers. Long-term employment practices will continue to be highly effective with respect to jobs in which teamwork is important, and in relation to vocational abilities that require a build-up over time. For Japanese companies and the Japanese economy and society as a whole, it will be important to focus in particular on stabilizing and maintaining employment, thereby improving employee morale and securing the flexibility needed for corporate growth . . . It is unnecessary for Japan to have the exact same employment system as the US . . .[23]

In further support of the Ministry's conclusions, it needs to be noted that despite the economic stresses of the past two or three years in particular there have been no mass lay-offs or dismissals in Japan. Bankruptcy is of course another matter (the system has not provided a safety net under bankruptcy), but this becomes a powerful spur to employees to work to maintain the health of the company.

Change is taking place. Younger people are likely to change jobs and to seek part-time employment initially. Japan is a wealthy country, families do have a good measure of financial resources, and the pressures for early career decisions are very much less now than a generation ago. Thus for example, one of the companies studied in 1955 by the writer reported recently that it knows when it hires young college graduates (and it hires only from universities), some 15 or 20 per cent have no intention of staying with the company for their careers. In that sense, the 'lifetime employment system' has changed. But the company still maintains its long-held commitment to keep the employee in its service for his or her full career. That is, the corporate social contract remains in place. The Labour Ministry's 1998

White Paper reported, 'the job changing rate for younger workers and female workers has been particularly noticeable. The rise in the proportion of part-time workers, whose level of job changing is high, is a major factor in the overall job changing rate.'[24]

Judging by the increased part-time employment, it appears that younger people are prepared to forgo job security. The applicability and scope of the notion behind lifetime employment may well diminish. A key question still relates to the economy, and how employees and employers will respond to improved or worsened economic circumstances. To date, the social contract has held, to a large extent.

In contrast, there can be little doubt of the diminishing influence of strict seniority on pay and promotion. A great deal of change in pay systems is in progress, with the role of 'merit' and productivity playing an increasing part. Seniority has of course always had its limits – the escalator cannot carry all to the top floor, since space is limited. Job evaluation has always been a standard part of Japanese personnel management, with even slight differences in pay and bonus making for very real rewards and punishments. But it seems quite clear from all reports that the role of seniority, while always a factor in an age-graded, Confucian-influenced society, has very much lessened. Indeed, one might argue that in view of demographic trends, we might well see the day when younger employees, given their high scarcity value, receive pay premiums. All societies have some age grading in their structure, and generally seniority receives some due in compensation and job security. What is perhaps particularly special to Japan in compensation practice is the continuing pattern of relatively egalitarian pay in the Japanese company. The most widely referenced survey of compensation (1999) finds that a Japanese manufacturing worker is the most highly compensated of workers in the major economies ($45,000), but the compensation of Japanese chief executives is only 10 times greater ($486,000). In contrast, the US worker receives $39,000, while the chief executive receives on average $1,351,000, or a spread of 34 times. Germany is rather more like Japan, the difference being 13 times. In contrast, Britain and Australia are nearer the US model, with multiples of 24 and 23 times respectively.[25] (This is another interesting example of the quite close parallels between management in Japan and management in Germany – the role of banks, low dividend pay-out rates, very few acquisitions and, complex and difficult-to-penetrate distribution systems are some of the others.)

The contrast with the United States is clear, especially as income differentials in US companies are continuing to widen as they have for some years now. Extraordinary compensation levels, retirement benefits and separation payments have become a US executive commonplace. Such levels would be quite impossible in a Japanese firm, another instance of the company as family, or village in the Japanese case. It is sometimes argued, defensively, that Japanese executive perquisites are relatively high (car, driver, company house, entertainment and the like), but these are available and widespread in all economies. In the US, private planes and the like supplement the more standard perquisites, which are augmented still further by the quite extraordinary benefits from lavish stock option systems. Japanese firms still have an egalitarian constraint against a flagrant exploitation of the workforce (and indeed shareholders) by one or even a few at the top rank.

There is, by the way, no indication that Japan's more egalitarian system of management compensation works against effective company performance. 'Japanese executive turnover and compensation are related to earnings, stock returns and to a lesser extent, sales performance measures. The fortunes of Japanese executives therefore are positively correlated with stock performance and current cash flows . . . The relations for the Japanese executives are generally economically and statistically similar to those for their US counterparts.'[26]

The third so-called pillar of the Japanese employment system is the enterprise union. Here there has been real change, not in the structure of the union, which remains firm limited and undifferentiated by skill categories, but in union influence. There has been a steady decline in trade union density. The unionization rate stood at around 34 per cent of the labor force in the 1960s and 1970s, but since then membership has eroded to about 22 per cent of the labor force with the decline continuing. Whereas 15 or 20 years ago no discussion about Japan's companies would have been deemed sensible if it excluded a serious consideration of trade union views and policies, the union is now hardly a factor in current considerations.

One analyst spoke of

> the decline in union density and rising apathy of members toward their union's activities. The fall of union density derives mainly from the inherent shortcomings of enterprise unionism. Enterprise unions have concentrated their efforts on problems specific to the firm and have not devoted resources to organizing non-unionized workers . . . The unionization rate in Japan will probably continue to fall.[27]

Retirement age is an additional aspect of personnel management in Japan that is undergoing noticeable change. In the mid-1950s, the retirement age in most companies was 55 years for all employees except those who achieved director status. Depending on exact rank, these employees could stay on longer. In general, only God retired the chief executive. With life expectancy lengthening dramatically, the retirement age has lengthened too. It is now on average rather over 60 years. Both government and unions are pressuring for a further extension, to age 65. Even now some companies are moving to that as the highest age for continued employment. At the same time, there is a considerable increase in companies setting an early retirement age at 50 or even younger. The entire system is becoming more flexible.

Continued employment at older ages poses problems, given seniority-influenced pay. Older workers are expensive and increasingly so as they age. A variety of approaches are being worked on. These include a choice of career lines at age 50 or thereabouts, including retirement with benefits and then re-employment without accumulating benefits. In addition, companies such as Matsushita are establishing work places for older workers where the tasks are less physically demanding and the work hours more flexible.

It is useful when considering retirement ages to remember that Japan's total population will peak in a few years, and that the workforce size has already reached a maximum. In a country that is most unlikely to experience mass immigration, labor shortage will become the issue in the rather near future. Thus, the extension of working careers is likely to be encouraged, and indeed will become necessary over time.

There remains both contrast and tension. Japan presents an economy that has changed in industrial structure and technological level to a truly exceptional degree. That change shows every sign of continuing at a very rapid rate. Yet the systems of governance and personnel management of the Japanese company change slowly and only at the margin. The resulting tensions are real and difficult – and can be taken, mistakenly, to indicate a reversion to Western, especially Anglo-American, systems.

Referring again to Jonathan Charkham:

> There is a great danger that when we think of the modern corporation we do so primarily in terms of its products or factories or offices or advertising. The very word 'corporation' sounds impersonal and inanimate. The term 'company' is better because it has about it the ring of the essential truth, that all enterprises are collections of people with intelligence, spirit and emotions. Their performance together will depend heavily on the way they are treated and led.[28]

Japanese society is unique, as are all societies. Japan's economic success is due fundamentally to its adaptation of introduced technologies and techniques while maintaining organizational and management systems consistent with Japan's own values and beliefs. Management in Japan will change, as it always has, but at its own pace and in its own directions. These directions will not be those developed in other, quite different societies, but will reflect changes in Japan's own social system. Any deviation from this tested pattern would put Japan's entire economic system at very great risk – and is unlikely in any case.

NOTES

1. 'Hashire! Toshiba', *Nikkei Business*, 25 January 1999, p. 21.
2. Porter, Michael E. and Scott Stern (1999), *The New Challenge to America's Prosperity: Finding is from the Innovation Index*, Council on Competitiveness, Washington, DC, US.
3. 'Women's Views Compared', *The Economist*, 9 October 1999, p. 86.
4. Garon, Sheldon (2000), 'Luxury is the Enemy: Mobilizing Savings and Popularizing Thrift in Wartime Japan', *The Journal of Japanese Studies*, 26 (1), p. 76.
5. Nitto, Hiroyuki (1993), 'The Changing Structure of Japanese Values', *NRI Quarterly*, 2 (3), p. 26.
6. Hakuhodo Institute of Life and Living (1998), *The Annual Data Book on the Japanese People* L29 – and English Supplement, Tokyo.
7. Milstein, Ira et al. (1998), *Corporate Governance*, Organization for Economic Cooperation and Development, Paris, p. 13.
8. Ibid., p. 17.
9. Organization for Economic Cooperation and Development (1999), *OECD Principles of Corporate Governance*, Paris p. 10.
10. Morgenson, Gretchen (1998), 'Stock Options are not a Free Lunch', *Forbes Global Business and Finance*, 18 May.
11. Charkham, Jonathan (1994), *Keeping Good Company*, Oxford: Clarendon Press p. 41.
12. Aikawa, K. (1996), Interview, *Nihon Keizai Shimbun*, 21 October, p. 6.
13. Corporate Governance Committee, Corporate Governance Forum of Japan (1998), *Corporate Governance Principles – a Japanese View*, Tokyo, p. 41.
14. Ibid., p. 41.
15. Okuda, Hiroshi (1999), 'Management Necessity of Highly Valuing Personnel', *Nihon Keizai Shimbun*, 29 October, p. 9.
16. Corporate Governance Committee, *op.cit.*, p. 36.
17. Miyauchi, Yoshihiko (2000), 'Kabunushi nomi jushi no keiei gimon', *Nihon Keizai Shimbun*, 12 April, p. 5.
18. Corporate Governance Committee, *op.cit.*, p. 42.
19. Nissei Kiso Kenkyujo (1999), *Kabunushi Mochiai Jokyo Chosa 98 Nen Dohan*, Tokyo, pp. 19–20.
20. Abegglen, James C. (1958), *The Japanese Factory*, The Free Press, Glencoe, Ill., US and J. Abegglen (1958), *Nihon no Keie* (trans. M. Urabe), Daiyamondosha, Tokyo.
21. Ministry of Labour (1999), *White Paper on Labour*, The Japanese Institute of Labour, Tokyo, p. 77.
22. Ibid., p. 79.
23. Ibid., p. 80.
24. Ibid., p. 37.
25. Taylor, Robert (2000), 'Total Remuneration Packages', *Financial Times*, 7 January, Tokyo.
26. Kaplan, Steven N. (1994), 'Top Executive Rewards and Firm Performance: A Comparison of Japan and the United States', *Journal of Political Economy*, 102 (3), p. 510.
27. Fujimura, Hiroyuki (1998), 'The Future of Trade Unions in Japan', *Japan Labor Bulletin*, 37 (7), p. 8.
28. Charkham, *op. cit.*, p. 1.

PART IV

Producing a More Japan-Friendly World

It was a Captainish sort of day, when everybody said, 'Yes, Rabbit' and 'No, Rabbit,' and waited until he had told them.
   The House at Pooh Corner, A.A. Milne

8. Japan and the international economic institutions*

Marcus Noland

INTRODUCTION

Japan has arguably been the prime beneficiary of the post-war liberal international economic order. In the area of trade, the General Agreement on Tariffs and Trade (GATT), and later its successor, the World Trade Organization (WTO), have facilitated the reduction in barriers to international trade worldwide. These institutional arrangements enabled Japan's exploitation of its comparative advantage, contributing to income growth and rising living standards in post-war Japan. The World Bank, along with its Bretton Woods twin, the International Monetary Fund (IMF), contributed even more directly to post-war Japanese economic development, by financing infrastructure projects such as the construction of the *shinkansen*. As the post-war economic reconstruction proceeded, these institutions continued to serve Japan well throughout its evolving stages. Its economic interests broadened from trade and finance, narrowly defined, to encompass a wide range of issues relevant to the expansion of Japanese firms around the world.

Nevertheless, the consensus among both Japanese and non-Japanese observers is that Japan 'punches below its weight'. Despite the efforts of the government of Japan to increase its influence on multilateral institutions, its influence on the architecture of global economic policy remains smaller than one would expect for the world's second largest economy. This chapter examines recent Japanese policy initiatives with respect to international institutions in the area of world trade, finance and development. To the extent that these initiatives have any rationale beyond pure self-interest, they reflect longstanding intellectual tendencies, which, compared with the values embodied in the existing order, place a greater emphasis on the state relative to the market in economic life.

Japan's attempts to exert greater influence on international institutions are limited by three factors:

- the dominance of the US and Japan's unwillingness to risk a rupture with the world's sole superpower;
- the historical legacy of suspicion and distrust of Japan in Asia;
- Japan's own parochial politics.

Growing disenchantment with the status quo, especially in Asia, may create more propitious conditions for future Japanese initiatives, however.

TRADE POLICY

Japan's history of problematical trade relations with the rest of the world extends at least as far back as its forcible opening to trade by the United States in 1854. The 50 years following the Meiji Restoration in 1868 were a remarkable period of modernization in which Japan adapted a myriad of foreign (social and technological) innovations to its own ends.[1] The Japanese leadership of the late 19th century was driven by the exigency of preserving national sovereignty and, indeed, Japan was one of the few non-Western nations to escape colonization. Economic liberalism, which would become the dominant ideology of the world system, never really took hold in Japan. Rather, Japan conformed to the practices and procedures embodied in the international system when it was compelled to do so and deviated when it had the opportunity.[2] This densely populated country with a relatively high level of education and social capacity quickly developed a comparative advantage in labor-intensive manufactures.

In the first instance of a recurrent pattern, Japanese exports were met by discriminatory trade restrictions imposed by trade partners fearing 'import surges'. Japan began raising its own tariffs significantly during the worldwide slump which followed the conclusion of World War I. In the wake of the 1923 Great Kanto Earthquake, Japan raised tariffs to 100 per cent on a number of 'luxury' items. Instead of reducing tariffs to their earlier levels after overcoming the immediate crisis, Japan continued to raise its tariffs throughout the 1920s and, like others, played the 'beggar-thy-neighbor' game once the Great Depression began in the late 1920s.

Japan moved decisively away from economic liberalism with the installation of the Inukai Tsuyoshi cabinet in 1931. Under Finance Minister Takahashi Korekiyo it began a policy of 'regulated reflation', similar to that undertaken contemporaneously in Germany by Hitler's Economics Minister, Hjalmar H.G. Schacht.[3] As the international economic system disintegrated, Japan launched the Pacific War with the aim of creating a Greater East Asian Co-Prosperity Sphere.

The war ended in ruin, defeat and occupation by US military forces. US occupation authorities installed a set of institutions modeled on the New Deal experience in the US, but sided with Japanese conservatives in Japanese economic affairs as the Cold War with the Soviet Union deepened. Again, Japan focused on catch-up and, again, economic liberalism failed to establish itself as the dominant intellectual tendency.[4]

After the occupation ended in 1952, Japan applied to join the GATT. This trade organization initially developed out of US Secretary of State Cordell Hull's attempt to reconstruct the liberal international order during the Roosevelt Administration. It became the fallback option when the Republican-controlled US Congress rejected the International Trade Organization, which had been envisioned as the third leg of the Bretton Woods triad. The Japanese GATT application was initially opposed by a number of countries, but the US strongly supported the application. Japan was granted provisional membership in 1953 and full membership in the GATT in 1955.[5]

Once in the GATT, Japan participated in successive rounds of multilateral negotiations (including the 'Tokyo Round' of the 1970s). Japan was relatively passive, however, in its use of the GATT's admittedly weak dispute settlement mechanism. In cases in which GATT panels found against Japan (in the case of some agricultural quotas, for example), Japan had a good track record of complying with GATT panel decisions (though in some cases removal of trade restrictions was accompanied by the introduction of more direct forms of support). Adverse panel rulings were arguably a constructive form of *gaiatsu* (foreign pressure) from a multilateral organization that Japan had voluntarily joined and supported.

However, due to the GATT's dysfunctional dispute settlement procedure, many trade conflicts continued to be resolved bilaterally, often in a discriminatory fashion. In addition to GATT-consistent forms of protection, such as anti-dumping measures, Japanese exports were subject to gray area measures such as the Orderly Marketing Arrangements (OMAs). Japan and the US invented this type of agreement in the 1950s and applied it to the textile trade. OMAs became the forerunner of the so-called Voluntary Restraint Agreements (VRAs) or Voluntary Export Restraints (VERs), which both the US and EU applied with gusto to Japanese steel and automobile exports in the 1980s. In the 1990s, Japan and the US would pioneer the use of voluntary import expansions (VIEs).[6]

The WTO

The 1 January 1995 establishment of the WTO and its new and improved dispute settlement mechanism marked an important turning point in Japan's trade relations with the rest of the world. This new international institution greatly strengthened Japan's ability to oppose discriminatory trade protection by its trade partners. Japan demonstrated this dramatically that year by calling the US bluff in the automobile dispute. The Japanese refused to acquiesce to US market-opening demands, and threatened to duke it out in the WTO. The US decided to settle out of court (Table 8.1). Since then, Japan has brought cases to the WTO at a rate that slightly exceeds one per year. Around half the cases involve the US and around half involve the automobile industry in some way. WTO panels have yet to rule against Japan in any of its complaints.

At the same time, Japan's trading partners have taken cases to the WTO at a rate of about two per year (Table 8.2). As is often the case in the WTO, many of these disputes are settled bilaterally without going through the complete adjudication process. Of the remaining few cases that have gone through the dispute settlement process, Japan has lost two:

- discriminatory taxation on alcoholic beverages brought by the EU, the US and Canada;
- an agricultural quarantine case brought by the US.

Japan did however win the famous 'Kodak–Fuji' case on photographic film.

Japan has also made use of its third-party rights in 24 cases, mostly in cases involving the US and/or the EU (Table 8.3). Within the Asian region, Japan has brought one case against another Asian country (Indonesian autos) and entered two more (South Korean government procurement and Thai anti-dumping) as a third party. No Asian country has made use of the WTO dispute settlement procedure to challenge Japanese trade practices.

Although the new dispute settlement system represents a noteworthy advance over the old GATT system, the WTO faces a number of challenges. The two most immediate issues are:

- what to do in the aftermath of the debacle in Seattle;
- how to integrate China into the organization.

In the longer run, issues of personnel as well as substantive agenda items will re-emerge.

The 1999 attempt to launch a new round of multilateral trade negotiations in Seattle was driven by a political compromise left over from the Uruguay Round rather than any global groundswell for trade liberalization.[7] To secure a conclusion to the last round of negotiations, the US accepted less than a complete reform of agricultural trade practices on the part of the EU in return for a commitment to revisit the issue in 1999. This

Table 8.1 Cases brought by Japan under the WTO

Case	Case Number/Date	Resolution
United States – Imposition of Import Duties on Automobiles from Japan Under Section 301 and 304 of the Trade Act of 1974	WT/DS6 July 19, 1995	Settled bilaterally
Brazil – Certain Automotive Investment Measures	WT/DS51 July 30, 1996	Pending consultation
Indonesia – Certain Measures Affecting the Automobile Industry	WT/DS55 and 64 October 4, 1996	Panel ruled in favor of Japan
United States – Measures Affecting Government Procurement	WT/DS95/1 July 18, 1997	Panel suspended at the request of the complainants
Canada – Certain Measures Affecting the Automotive Industry	WT/DS139/1 July 3, 1998	Panel ruled in favor of Japan; under appeal
United States – Anti-Dumping Act of 1916	WT/DS162/1 February 10, 1999	Under panel consideration
United States – Anti-Dumping Measures on Certain Hot-Rolled Steel Products from Japan	DS184/1 November 18, 1999	Under panel consideration

Sources: Ministry of International Trade and Industry, Japan; World Trade Organization.

195

Table 8.2 Cases brought against Japan under the WTO

Case	Complainant/Date	Resolution
Tax on Alcoholic Beverages	EU (WT/DS8), US (WT/DS11), Canada (WT/DS10) September 27, 1995	Appellate panel ruled against Japan. The complainants accepted Japanese modalities for implementation of the panel report. Arbitrator determined reasonable time of implementation
Measures Affecting the Purchase of Telecommunications Equipment	EU (WT/DS15) August 18, 1995	Settled bilaterally
Measures Concerning Sound Recordings	US (WT/DS28) February 9, 1996	Settled bilaterally
Measures Concerning Sound Recordings	EU (WT/DS42) May 24, 1996	Settled bilaterally
Measures Affecting Consumer Photographic Film and Paper	US (WT/DS44) June 13, 1996	Panel ruled in favor of Japan
Measures Affecting Distribution Services	US (WT/DS45) June 13, 1996	Pending consultation
Measures Affecting Imports of Pork	EU (WT/DS66) January 15, 1997	Pending consultation
Procurement of a Navigation Satellite	EU (WT/DS73/1) March 26, 1997	Settled bilaterally
Measures Affecting Agricultural Products	US (WT/DS76/1) April 7, 1997	Appellate panel ruled against Japan. Japanese modalities for implementation are under consultation
Tariff Quotas and Subsidies Affecting Leather	EU (WT/DS147/1) October 8, 1998	Pending consultation

Sources: Ministry of International Trade and Industry, Japan; World Trade Organization.

Table 8.3 Cases in which Japan participates as a third party

Case	Complainant/Date	Resolution
Canada – Measures Affecting the Importation of Milk and the Exportation of Dairy Products	US (WT/DS103/1) October 8, 1997	Panel ruled in favor of complainant; modalities for implementation accepted by the complainant
EU – Measures Affecting the Exportation of Processed Cheese	US (WT/DS104/1) October 8, 1997	Pending consultation
EU, United Kingdom and Ireland – Customs Classification of Certain Computer Equipment	US (WT/DS62, 67, 68) February 11, 1997	Appellate panel ruled against the complainants
Brazil – Measures Affecting Payment Terms for Imports	EU (WT/DS116/1) January 9, 1998	Pending consultation
United States – Harbor Maintenance Tax	EU (WT/DS118/1) February 6, 1998	Pending consultation
Turkey – Restrictions on Imports of Textile and Clothing Products	India (WT/DS34) March 21, 1996	Appellate panel ruled in favor of the complainants; modalities of implementation under consultation
United States – Tax Treatment for 'Foreign Sales Corporations'	EU (WT/DS108/1) November 18, 1997	Panel ruled in favor of complainant; modalities of implementation under consultation
India – Measures Affecting the Automotive Sector	EU (WT/DS146/1) October 6, 1998	Pending consultation

Table 8.3 (continued)

Case	Complainant/Date	Resolution
India – Import Restrictions	EU (WT/DS149) October 29, 1998	Pending consultation
India – Measures Affecting Customs Measures	EU (WT/DS150/1) October 30, 1998	Pending consultation
United States – Measures Affecting Textiles and Apparel Products	EU (WT/DS151/1) November 19, 1998	Pending consultation
Canada – Patent Protection of Pharmaceutical Products	EU (WT/DS114/1) December 19, 1997	Panel ruled in favor of complainant; modalities of implementation under consultation
United States – Anti-Dumping Act of 1916	EU (WT/DS136) June 9, 1998	Panel ruled in favor of the complainant
United States – Sections 301–310 of the Trade Act of 1974	EU (WT/DS152/1) November 25, 1998	Panel ruled against the complainant
United States – Section 110(5) of the US Copyright Act	EU (WT/DS160/1) January 26, 1999	Under panel consideration
United States – Import Measures on Certain Products from the European Communities	EU (WT/DS165/1) March 4, 1999	Under panel consideration
Korea – Measures Affecting Government Procurement	US (WT/DS163/1) February 16, 1999	Under panel consideration

EU – Anti-Dumping Duties on Imports of Cotton-Type Bed-Linen from India	India (WT/DS141/1) August 3, 1998	Under panel consideration
United States – Safeguard Measure on Imports of Lamb Meat from Australia	Australia (WT/DS178/1) July 23, 1999	Under panel consideration
Thailand – Anti-Dumping Duties on Angles, Shapes and Sections of Iron or Non-Alloy Steel; H-Beams from Poland	Poland (WT/DS122/1) April 6, 1998	Under panel consideration
United States – Anti-Dumping Measures on Stainless Steel Plate in Coils and Stainless Steel Sheet and Strip from Korea	Korea (WT/DS179) July 30, 1999	Under panel consideration
United States – Import Prohibition of Certain Shrimp and Shrimp Products	India, Malaysia, Pakistan and Thailand (WT/DS58) October 8, 1996	Appellate panel ruled in favor of the complainants. Modalities of implementation are under consultation
United States – Measure Affecting Government Procurement	EU (WT/DS88/1) June 20, 1997	Panel suspended at the request of the complainant
Hungary – Export Subsidies in Respect of Agricultural Products	Argentina, Australia, Canada, New Zealand, Thailand and the United States (WT/DS35) March 27, 1996	Settled, pending grant of waiver

Sources: Ministry of International Trade and Industry, Japan; World Trade Organization.

is the origin of the so-called 'built-in agenda' of talks on agriculture and services motivating the new round. A certain sense of urgency was attached to the negotiations over agriculture inasmuch as the 'peace clause', which prohibits WTO cases against certain practices (principally undertaken by the EU and US), is due to expire at the end of 2003.

This built-in agenda shaped participants' negotiating strategies heading into the Seattle ministerial. Japan argued that a successful round would have to have three characteristics:

- it would have to be 'comprehensive';
- it would have to be a single undertaking;
- it would have to strengthen rules and disciplines as well as market access.

The recognition that Japan needed to broaden the overall agenda to hide its inevitable concessions in agriculture, and to use gains in other areas to make an agreement emerging from the new negotiations politically palatable at home, motivated the notion of a 'comprehensive round'. Specifically, Japan made tightening the anti-dumping provisions a high priority (strengthening 'rules and disciplines'), and in the weeks leading up to the meeting had stitched together a broad international coalition which clearly had the US on the defensive. On agriculture, Japan found an eager ally in the EU, which jumped on to the Japanese 'multifunctionality' bandwagon to distract attention from its increasingly indefensible export subsidies.

In the run-up to the meeting, the US showed little flexibility, largely trying to limit the agenda to agriculture and services where the US would not be expected to make major concessions. Meanwhile, the US simultaneously tried to force on to the agenda relatively new and controversial issues such as the relationship between trade and labor standards, and environmental concerns.[8] As Japan's Ministry of International Trade and Industry (MITI) correctly observed, such an approach jeopardized progress on even the built-in agenda, as it left most participants with no incentive to move forward (MITI, 1999). Once in Seattle, the degree of public mobilization against the talks caught officialdom off-guard. The protest was led by a wild melange of groups whose motivations and aspirations appeared at times only tenuously connected to the issue at hand. Despite police intelligence, the authorities in Seattle appeared unwilling or unable to comprehend the violent tendencies of some of these groups.[9]

Yet in the end, the traditional US–EU dispute over agriculture (the same dispute that nearly scuttled the launch of the prior round of negotiations and nearly torpedoed those negotiations a half dozen times), not the shenanigans of the Raging Grannies or the Ruckus Society, sank the Seattle negotiations. Japan appeared content to hold the EU's coat on agriculture. Its sin was one of omission (passively allowing an opportunity to slip away) rather than one of commission.

In the aftermath of Seattle it has principally been the EU, and to a lesser extent, Japan, which has moved to right the organization. Various attempts have included:

- restarting the agricultural and services negotiations (though the EU did block the consensus on selecting the chair of the agriculture talks);
- undertaking a series of 'confidence building' measures, which included possible extensions of the 31 December 1999 deadline for developing countries to implement WTO agreements on intellectual property, investment measures and customs valuation.

This effort has garnered a greater sense of urgency with the prospective membership of China, following the successful conclusion of the EU–China bilateral talks. Pascal Lamy, the EU Commissioner for Trade, has admitted publicly that it would be easier to conclude the next round of WTO negotiations if China were not a full participant. Meanwhile, the US pursued the quixotic agenda of re-launching the round before the Okinawa Summit. Some within the US government regard a Japanese proposal to set up a distinguished persons group to assess the most propitious path for future progress as no more than a delaying tactic.

In the longer run, the organization will have to deal with both personnel and more substantive issues. With regard to the former, Japan actively backed Thailand's Supachai Panitchpakdi over New Zealand's Mike Moore in a protracted dispute over who would succeed Italy's Renato Ruggeiro as the WTO Director General. The eventual compromise reached allowed Moore and Supachai to split the term. This haggling did nothing to promote the institutional development of the organization. Another such brawl can be expected in 2005 when the Moore/Supachai term ends. The search for Supachai's successor could become entangled with person-nel decisions made in other international organizations, as will be discussed further below.

Beyond personnel issues, the WTO has a series of intellectually and politically challenging issues that it must confront. Most immediate will be the built-in agenda of agriculture and services. In agriculture, Japan typi-cally sides with the EU against the US and the Cairns Group.[10] It pros-aically has observed that current tariff levels 'reflect particular domestic situations' and has expressed an interest in strengthening disciplines on the use of export restrictions, reflecting its concerns about food security.

On services, developed countries typically demand liberalization of financial and professional services on the part of developing countries. Developing countries have countered by demanding the possibility for an increased movement of people, so that, for example, a service firm in a developing country could bring its workers into a developed country (on a temporary basis) to work on a project (in construction or maintenance, for example). In reality, though, they are more interested in reforming anti-dumping restrictions and in stretching out their Uruguay Round obligations than in negotiating service agreements. Similarly, Japan is relatively uncompetitive in much of the service sector, and has not pushed as hard as the US or EU for liberalization in this area.

Beyond this built-in agenda, traditional tariff cutting and the need better to integrate rules governing anti-dumping and competition policy dominate the industrial products trade agenda. The tariff-cutting exercise is a well-understood process, amenable to traditional WTO tariff offer negotiations. It is simply a matter of reaching an international consensus on an acceptable formula, not a trivial task but not one fraught with the conceptual problems of the other agenda items.

Reform of anti-dumping rules and the creation of a more coherent international competition policy regime present greater challenges. Japan has led the international coalition demanding reform of anti-dumping procedures, which it regards, with significant justification, simply as process protectionism. Its major opponent has been the US. Within the US there is little intellectual consensus as to what the goals of a desirable international competition policy might be beyond prohibiting horizontal collusive practices such as cartels. Politically, the issue has been captured by import-competing firms, which regard competition policy as prospectively a much less protection-friendly alternative to the existing, and WTO-consistent, anti-dumping laws. Within the US government, the bureaucracy is split. The Antitrust Division of the Justice Department fears that any multilateral accord would amount to a dumbing down of US law, which would weaken US antitrust practices. The United States Trade Representative, stung by its defeat in the WTO (losing the Kodak–Fuji case), opposes narrowing anti-dumping laws in the interests of its import-competing clients. Unless there is a significant shift in domestic politics, it is hard to envision much constructive activity on this issue emanating from the US in the foreseeable future.

The anti-dumping competition policy issue is an inside-the-Beltway matter compared with the hot-button issues inextricably linked with the social clause. The US agenda on labor and environmental issues of recent years has found little support in Japan, which has not experienced the degree of public and NGO mobilization on these issues as has the US and

EU. The Japanese have been on the defensive in a number of international disputes involving endangered species. However, these issues tend to be relatively partisan in nature in the US, and one could imagine significant ratcheting up or down in emphasis, depending on the outcome of the November 2000 elections.

Taken together these observations suggest that the WTO may face some difficult times ahead. Although the system has served Japan well, it typically displays a lack of leadership. On a number of issues looming on the horizon, Japan's positions conflict with those of the US, the organization's dominant member.

Regional Initiatives

Japan stands alone as the only major WTO member that does not participate in preferential regional trade arrangements. However, dissatisfaction with the WTO could encourage Japan and other countries in Asia to go their own way, creating regional preference arrangements similar to those that exist in Europe, North America and Oceania.

The sole major existing regional initiative, the Asia-Pacific Economic Cooperation (APEC) forum, includes countries from outside Asia, most notably the US. Indeed, APEC was originally an Australian initiative. At least some Asians wanted a US involvement to act as a counterbalance to Japan, which had made a similar proposal. APEC's first meeting was held in Canberra in 1989. The next big step was in 1993 when, at the first APEC 'leaders meeting', the US hosted history's first pan-Asian summit, which was held, ironically enough, outside Asia. APEC's membership accounts for more than 2 billion people (40 per cent of world population) and more than half of world output. An officially appointed Eminent Persons Group issued a report calling for free trade and investment in the region by 2020 (2010 for rich members, 2020 for poorer ones). Governmental leaders adopted this goal in their Bogor Declaration of 1994.

Due to the great political-economic diversity among the membership, no one anticipates 'deep integration' along the lines of the EU. Rather, much activity has been in terms of 'business facilitation' (streamlining procedures, etc.). Progress on trade and investment implementation has been uneven. Agriculture is still a highly sensitive issue. Japan had, almost habitually, attempted to carve out agriculture from any accelerated liberalization commitments, both at the Bogor (1994) and Osaka (1995) leaders' meetings. Later, in November 1998, Japan torpedoed the Early Voluntary Sectoral Liberalization (EVSL) initiative, which would have required it to eliminate over a ten year period its relatively low tariffs on forest and fishery products. Japan is not unique in this regard: South Korea and others have

been willing to let Japan take the lead in opposing agricultural trade liberalization within APEC, in much the same way that Japan stands behind the
EU in the WTO. For its part, the Clinton Administration lacks the statu-
tory authority to implement early tariff cuts in several of the EVSL sectors
(though it has residual authority from the Uruguay Round negotiations for
others).

The growth of regionalism outside Asia, and the failure of the WTO
meeting in Seattle, have encouraged Asian countries to take a second look
at regional schemes for economic integration. The old East Asian
Economic Caucus idea has been revived as the ASEAN+3 (Japan, China
and South Korea) initiative.[11] In Japan, MITI is actively studying the possibility of free trade areas (FTAs) involving Japan, Singapore, South
Korea, Mexico, China and possibly others.[12] Article 24 of the GATT
agreement and Article 5 of the General Agreement on Trade in Services
(GATS) specifies the conditions under which preferential trade arrangements are consistent with the WTO obligations of its members. The
WTO:

- must be notified of the intent to form an FTA;
- must not raise barriers to other parties;
- must reduce tariffs within the FTA to zero after 'a reasonable time
  period' (codified in the Uruguay Round agreement as ten years);
- must abolish trade restrictions in 'substantially all sectors';
- must liberalize the service sector per the GATS.

For Japan and its potential partners, the problem is the 'substantially all
sectors' requirement. Because of its inefficiency in agriculture, Japan is constrained to look to partners that either do not have an agricultural sector
(Singapore) or have similarly inefficient agricultural sectors (South Korea).
Otherwise, Japan must be willing to run the risk of a WTO challenge if it
attempts to exclude agriculture from an agreement (Mexico).[13] Japan's
search for regional alternatives to the multilateral system is hamstrung by
its own agricultural policy.

Of the FTAs that Japan is considering, one with Singapore, a city-state
which pursues virtually free trade today, would be the easiest to complete
and, perhaps unsurprisingly, convey the smallest benefits to Japan. More
interesting is the possibility of an FTA with South Korea, and the two
governments have commissioned studies of this possibility (Cheong, 1999;
Yamazawa, 2000).[14]

Both studies use static computable general equilibrium (CGE) models to
evaluate a prospective Japan–South Korea FTA. These models have
significant limitations, notably their inability to capture dynamic economic

effects and the absence of any reaction functions on the part of other trading nations.[15] Nevertheless, they are the obvious starting points for any serious analysis of a prospective FTA.

Yamazawa's conventional model generates the result that when Japan and South Korea enter into an FTA, Japan's bilateral surplus with South Korea increases. The US is adversely affected by trade diversion (unfortunately, no separate results are reported for Australia). As would be expected, the impact on the smaller economy is bigger than the impact on Japan. South Korean real GDP increases 0.3–0.4 per cent, while the effect on Japan is 'marginal'. The implicit message is that an FTA would have little impact on either economy and could well create problems with the US.

In a search for bigger numbers, Yamazawa then presents another variant in which he assumes large, sectorally non-uniform, productivity increases accompanying the formation of the FTA. In this variant, he obtains qualitatively similar results (e.g. Japan's bilateral surplus increases and the US is adversely affected by trade diversion). However, both Japan and South Korea experience large real national income increases (in the order of 10 per cent). Unfortunately, this latter result appears to be driven by assumed productivity gains rather than anything intrinsic to the FTA.

Cheong's results are, if anything, even less supportive of the desirability of a Japan–South Korea FTA. In his model, not only does Japan's bilateral surplus with South Korea increase, but South Korean welfare actually declines. As in the case of Yamazawa's original model, these effects are quite small. Cheong then sets out to reverse the latter result, and comes up with two possibilities: unspecified 'preferential rules of origin' and the inclusion of China in the FTA.

Ultimately, these models may badly misspecify the workings of a Japan–South Korea FTA. They do, however, point to something that could be problematic politically. Levels of protection are generally higher in South Korea than in Japan. Moreover, South Korea has pursued a policy of actively discouraging imports from Japan through its 'import diversification program'. Only the IMF conditions attached to the December 1997 standby package caused the termination of this policy in June 1999. When the policy ended, imports from Japan surged in a number of sectors, causing public protest in South Korea. Any FTA with Japan will be a hard sell politically in South Korea. Japan is similarly disunited on this issue. MITI supports an FTA with South Korea, but the Ministry of Foreign Affairs reputedly opposes it (championing instead the WTO). The Keidanren (the big business association) is also antipathetic to such an arrangement. Its members fear a possible South Korean penetration of the steel sector.

INTERNATIONAL FINANCIAL POLICY

The other important area in which Japan interacts with international economic institutions is in the area of finance and development. (These two
have to be discussed together if for no other reason than the IMF, the most
prominent of the international financial institutions, has evolved into an
institution that is relevant mainly to developing countries. The debate over
bilateral foreign assistance programs is beyond the scope of this chapter,
however.) In the finance and development sphere a similar set of themes –
disagreement over substantive and key leadership issues, and a possible
Japanese and Asian desire to go their own way – reoccurs. The focal points
have been:

- Japanese and Asian dissatisfaction over the performance of the US
  government and the Washington-based IMF during the Asian
  financial crisis;
- subsequent debates concerning possible reform to what has come to
  be known as the international financial architecture;
- proposals for regional initiatives that could run counter to policy
  emanating from 'Washington'.[16]

Asian Regionalism

On the first point, Tokyo and Washington clearly reacted differently to the
Asian crisis. Reactions reflected differences in ideology, national interests
and perhaps idiosyncratic understandings of the crisis. The US government
initially underestimated the severity of the crisis, with President Clinton
describing it as 'a glitch in the road' at the APEC summit in November
1997.[17] Furthermore, relative to Japan the US was unsympathetic to the
capital channeling and cronyism that had contributed to the crisis. As well,
relative to Japan, US financial institutions and banks had less at stake in
the region. Crudely put, the US government initially regarded the crisis as
a modest regional affair, largely of the Asians' own making. The initial US
refusal to come to its financial assistance stunned Thailand at the onset of
the crisis. This included a refusal to participate in the 'second line of
defense' associated with the initial IMF program.[18] Only the spread of the
crisis to South Korea (and the threatened spread to Brazil and Russia)
shook the US out of its complacency.

What are widely regarded as fundamental mistakes in the IMF programs
(actually exacerbating the crisis instead[19]) compounded Asian disappointment in US reticence. Asian countries came to believe that the US was an
unreliable ally, and that the economic prescriptions being written by

Washington were at best incompetent and at worst malevolent. This disillusionment created an opportunity for Japanese leadership on regional financial issues, despite the fact that the yen depreciation of 1995–97 and the weakness of the Japanese banking sector contributed to the crisis in the first place.[20] Japan proposed an Asian Monetary Fund (AMF), but US, IMF and Chinese opposition blocked this initiative; 'Washington' feared that an AMF would degrade the global financial system by undercutting the IMF, while China opposed it out of geopolitical rivalry.[21] (It did have the effect of spurring the US Treasury to redouble its efforts to secure an IMF quota increase, as discussed below.) The Japanese Ministry of Finance (MOF) countered with the 'New Miyazawa Initiative', named for its Minister, Kiichi Miyazawa. This proposal incorporated a $30 billion financial assistance plan for the region, consisting largely of sovereign debt guarantees, trade credits and low-interest loans.[22] Cynics claimed that this was simply a backdoor means of providing public funds to Japanese banks and corporations through their Asian subsidiaries. There is probably some truth to this, but whatever the motivation Japan extended more official assistance to strapped economies in Asia than did the US. At the same time, it should be noted that during 1998–99, exports from the most heavily affected Asian economies to the US rose, while those to Japan fell. In essence, the US enabled trade while Japan provided aid.[23]

After two years of dormancy, MOF resuscitated the AMF proposal in the spring of 2000 (Kuroda, 2000). The Japan-dominated Asian Development Bank (ADB) floated a report stressing the need to 'seriously consider' an AMF (a position from which it subsequently backed away[24]). The problem was in some ways similar to the one that confronts Japan with respect to FTAs. The Japanese did not want to be perceived as originating the policy proposal, but rather as responding to the entreaties of others. In the case of the AMF, Japanese officials invariably described the AMF as an ASEAN and Japan proposal.[25] ASEAN finance ministers did indeed consider the proposal in their March 2000 meeting in Brunei, but shelved it in favor of a less ambitious regional currency swap arrangement involving Japan, China and South Korea. At the same time they did agree to conduct 'a study on the modalities and mechanisms for a regional financing arrangement to supplement the existing international facilities'.[26]

The countries of East Asia possess enormous foreign exchange reserves (of the order of $600 billion) and financing such an organization would not be a problem, especially if Japan were willing to commit a significant amount of funding. Rather than resources, the real constraint in Japan may be political. Japan is a major source of saving for the region. Some Japanese would like their country to play a greater role as an international center of financial intermediation. Yet despite the highly touted 'Big Bang' plan which introduced financial market deregulation, the government has been ambivalent about undertaking actions necessary to promote the inter-nationalization of the yen. Even regionally, it is unclear whether Tokyo could ever play the roles that Hong Kong and Singapore play today and Shanghai may play some day in the distant future. Politically Japan remains oriented fundamentally inwardly. Its own domestic parochial political interests, financial markets and institutions dominate, not global markets. As a consequence, Japan appears unwilling or unable to act in ways that would reassure non-Japanese institutions that it would play a responsible role as an efficient and unbiased regulator.

The Global System

Parallel to this discussion of greater regional cooperation in Asia, there has been a more general discussion about what should be done to reform the financial architecture (in general) and the IMF (in particular). Again, the US has dominated the international debate (though the US, Japan and the EU did cooperate in the formation of the Group of 20 (a framework for systematically evaluating international financial architectural reform). As mentioned earlier, in the spring of 1998 the specter of an AMF spooked the US Treasury into pushing the US Congress to increase the US quota commitment to the IMF. The argument favored at that time suggested that while the existing set of institutions might be sub-optimal, it was unwise to reorganize the fire department in the midst of a fire.[27] The political *quid pro quo* for congressional approval of the quota increase was the establishment of a panel of outside experts. The government created the International Financial Institutions Advisory Commission, whose sole task was assessing those international financial institutions in the public sector. This Commission, chaired by longtime IMF foe Professor Allan Meltzer, was time bound to issue its report in March 2000.

Anticipating that the Meltzer Commission, as it came to be known, would issue a strongly 'market oriented' critique of the international financial institutions, the US Treasury attempted to pre-empt the Commission by issuing its own reform recommendations. The US govern-ment proposal, contained in Summers (1999) and US Treasury (2000), calls for the IMF to phase out long-term lending and take on a more narrowly defined crisis-prevention mission than its current activities encompass. In particular, it calls for the Fund to play a quasi-lender of last resort func-tion, lending significant amounts at 'prices to encourage rapid repayment' (Summers, 1999, p. 6). At the same time, this report seems to support the same kind of intrusive conditionality that proved so controversial in the Asian crisis:

- it argues that issues of social cohesion and inclusion 'should be addressed as a condition for IMF support' (ibid.);
- it cites approvingly the inclusion of labor standards conditionality in recent IMF programs (US Treasury, 2000).

These two thrusts would appear to be contradictory. If the IMF is offering short-term finance at penalty rates, then there is a reduced need for policy conditions (much less the kind of deep conditionality embodied in the Asia crisis packages).[28]

When the Meltzer Commission report was released in March (IFIAC, 2000), as expected, the majority report reflected a near obsession with the notion of moral hazard. Its conclusions called for greatly restricting IMF lending activities, a wholesale downsizing and reorganization of the present system of multilateral development banks. The report went on to recommend the abolition of such institutions as the Multilateral Investment Guarantee Agency (traditionally headed by a Japanese national) and the multilateral development banks' private sector arms, such as the World Bank group's International Finance Corporation.

Japanese government reaction, as might be expected, has been sympathetic to neither the 'less money with more conditions' thrust of the Treasury proposal nor the 'moral hazard über alles' stance of the Meltzer Commission. In his address to the March 2000 meeting of the Manila Framework group, MOF Vice Minister Hirohiko Kuroda called for the IMF to limit the inclusion of structural reform conditionality in its assistance packages. The Japanese held to this stance despite the fact that Japan itself benefited from the abolition of South Korea's 'import diversification program' which formed part of South Korea's December 1997 standby agreement (Dow Jones, 21 March 2000). This stand would be consistent with previous Japanese attempts to influence, substantively, international financial institutions. The desired direction led toward a policy that would have greater sympathy with state intervention in economic life than that prescribed by the 'Washington consensus'.[29] Nevertheless, Japan appeared to fall into line behind the US and EU at the Okinawa Summit. The Japanese signed on to a reform program that strongly echoes the US Treasury line.

Japan is more supportive of a second aspect of US policy, however. The Treasury proposal recommends a recalculation of member quotas (the basis for weighted voting within the organization and in principle, determining the amount of resources that a country can call upon in a crisis).[30] This could have important implications for Asia, inasmuch as Asian countries would appear to be greatly underweighted (and European countries similarly overweighted). At least in this respect, the US and Japan (and

Australia) appear to be on the same side.[31] Nevertheless, it proved difficult diplomatically to allocate to the Japanese the second largest national quota within the Fund. Other Asian countries such as South Korea and Singapore are even further underweight, arguably constraining their access to Fund resources and limiting their influence in the Fund's Executive Board.

This issue came to a head in the struggle over who would succeed Michel Camdessus as Managing Director of the IMF. Traditionally this job has gone to a European, while the Presidency of the World Bank has gone to an American. A Japanese national has traditionally led the ADB. After protracted internal negotiations, the EU nominated a lightly regarded German, Caio Koch-Weser, for the post. In the meantime, while the Europeans were negotiating, in a break from previous practice, Japan put forward its own candidate, former MOF Vice Minister and promoter of the Asian Monetary Fund, Eisuke Sakakibara. Some other Asian countries (though notably not China) were convinced to give token public support to his candidacy.[32] A disparate coalition of developing countries would eventually nominate a third candidate, the acting Managing Director, Stanley Fischer. After no consensus was achieved in the IMF Executive Board, in a second iteration of the process the EU nominated another German, Horst Köhler. The US indicated his acceptability, and he received the endorsement of the Executive Board.

It is a bit hard to know what to make of the Japanese action. Under the circumstances, Sakakibara, a highly controversial candidate, was surely unacceptable to the US (and many others). It appears that the Japanese did not mean the nomination to be taken at face value, but instead as a signal of Japan's unwillingness to accept the continued European stranglehold on the Managing Director's job.[33] Indeed, if a Japanese national did secure the Managing Director's position, Japan would come under pressure to release its hold on the ADB presidency (to another Asian country, i.e. not to the US or the EU).[34]

This fiasco, coming on the heels of the Moore–Supachai debacle at the WTO, vividly illustrated the fundamental bankruptcy of the national 'reservation' system which selects senior leadership posts for international institutions. In this sense, the Japanese action should be regarded as a success, even if it did not yield short-run benefits.[35]

CONCLUSIONS

Japan may well have been the prime beneficiary of the liberal post-war economic order. Yet its ability to influence that order has been constrained by

US dominance, a lingering suspicion of Japan in the rest of Asia, and Japan's own internal politics. However, Asia has been shaken by its experience during the financial crisis. Among other things, this has led to a reappraisal of its relationship with the US government and the Washington-based multilateral economic institutions. There is a sense of disappointment with both aspects of 'Washington'. Together with US initiatives, which are likely to encounter opposition in Asia, this has created an unprecedented opportunity for Japanese diplomacy. An economic slowdown (and an accompanying rise in protectionism in the US) could widen this opening.[36]

In such an environment, it would be understandable if Asians intensified efforts at creating an alternative involving regional cooperation, either as a complement to, or a substitute for, multilateral cooperation. Yet Japan's ability to lead such an effort is uncertain. Ironically, one of the reasons that the US is so influential in setting the Asian agenda is that collectively the Asian economies remain dependent on the US market. This remains the ultimate destination of a significant part of their output, even if this dependence could be expected to lessen over time (Noland, 1994). If Japan wants to wield more influence in the region, it will have to learn to import more and establish better political and economic relations throughout the region, most importantly with China, the region's second largest economy.[37]

Such an effort, in turn, is impeded by lingering distrust of Japan in the region, especially in China. For its part, Japan remains understandably wary of China, particularly in light of its authoritarian political system. The kind of political exigencies that fueled the rapprochement between France and Germany after World War II appear to be missing in Asia and will continue to hamper regional cooperation, at least in the medium run.

Surmounting these obstacles is a hard task. From a Japanese perspective, remaining under the US security umbrella, continuing to export to the US and maintaining a focus on the WTO-centered global trade system is a path of less resistance. There is no guarantee that Japan will continue along in this manner, but it would take major domestic as well as international political and military changes to move Japan on to a significantly different trajectory.

NOTES

*Chapter prepared for the Centre for Japanese Economic Studies (Macquarie University) Fifth Biennial Conference, *Can the Japanese Change? Economic Reform in Japan*, Sydney, Australia, 6–7 July 2000. Hye Kyung Lee provided helpful research assistance, and Fred Bergsten, Jeff Schott and the conference participants offered useful comments on an earlier draft of this chapter.

1. See Allen (1946), Lockwood (1954), Hunsberger (1964) and Morishima (1982) for informative economic histories.
2. Ironically, the 'unequal treaties' that until 1899 severely limited the Japanese government's ability to impose import tariffs may have actually fostered Japan's development by forcing the country to specialize along the lines of its comparative advantage. The limitation on tariffs also encouraged the use of other policy tools, such as low-interest loans and government procurement preferences for 'strategic' industries, establishing a precedent that would continue for a century.
3. Takahashi's policy was similar to the one later advocated by John Maynard Keynes in his 1936 treatise *The General Theory on Employment, Interest and Income*, though by the time the Keynes book was published, Takahashi was dead, murdered by a group of rebellious young officers.
4. This was for several reasons. After the war, left-wing ideologies flourished in reaction to the nationalist ideology promoted by the military regime. Moreover, as a 'big country' and one without a lot of resources for study abroad, Japanese intellectuals adopted English to a lesser extent than their counterparts in smaller countries. This meant that they had relatively few opportunities for education abroad and direct exposure to foreign intellectual trends. As a consequence, some peculiar strains of Marxism developed in Japan, especially in the economics profession. The highly bureaucratic nature of the Japanese university system generated an enormous degree of inertia in staffing. As a result, many university departments of economics remained heavily Marxist. For these and other reasons, there has been relatively little interaction between professionally trained economists and those actually making economic policy in Japan.
5. A number of countries invoked Article 35, permitting them to withhold some membership privileges. Typically, the underlying purpose was to apply discriminatory quantitative protection. Australia was among these countries, and did not stop invoking Article 35 until 1964.
6. Welcome to the wild and wacky world of trade policy in which everything has a three-letter acronym. For those who think that there is anything new under the sun, see Hunsberger (1964), Table 7–10. This is a list of Japanese goods subject to GATT-inconsistent price and/or quantity restrictions in a number of markets in 1960, including those of the US and Australia.
7. Just the opposite: The developing countries believed that they had been taken to the cleaners during the Uruguay Round (the previous round of negotiations). They remained skeptical about taking on further trade liberalization commitments, and far better prepared to defend their interests in these negotiations. Similarly, Asia was still recovering from its financial crisis, and policymakers there believed they already had enough issues with which to grapple. Japan showed its lack of interest in further trade liberalization by blocking the Early Voluntary Sectoral Liberalization (EVSL) effort in the Asia Pacific Economic Cooperation (APEC) forum. It opposed forestry and fisheries liberalization. In the US, President Clinton was unable to secure 'fast track' trade negotiating authority from the US Congress.
8. The US also pushed for a number of 'immediate deliverables', such as a second information technology agreement, government procurement transparency and an e-commerce tariff moratorium.
9. The Clinton Administration's behavior in Seattle was perplexing. It sought to promote labor and environmental issues. But President Clinton's statement in Seattle that he would like to see economic sanctions used against countries not meeting labor standards took his cabinet members in Seattle by surprise, destroying any possibility of making progress on the issue. Indeed, conversations with a number of developing country negotiators indicated that the President's remark, together with the behavior of the demonstrators, strengthened their resolve to resist US demands. Some regarded the demonstrators as an officially sanctioned attempt physically to intimidate foreign negotiators.
10. The *de facto* Australian-led Cairns Group is an international coalition of self-identified non-subsidizing agricultural exporters. When China enters the WTO, it could be expected to side with Japan and the EU against agricultural trade liberalization.

Potential future supporters of agricultural liberalization could include Russia and the Ukraine.

11. See Kelly (2000) for an Australian interpretation of the renewed Asian regionalism.

12. Discussion of these possibilities preceded the fiasco in Seattle. Japan has maintained that it was approached by all of its potential partners, though in the South Korean case there is some disagreement on this point.

13. See JETRO (2000) for a discussion of a possible Japanese FTA with Mexico.

14. Lee (2000) contains a wide-ranging discussion from the Korean perspective, while Cheong (1999) summarizes the underlying technical model.

15. Yamazawa's model is a conventional Walrasian CGE embodying the assumption of constant returns to scale in production, with two alternative macro 'closures'. It has eleven sectors and seven regions. The underlying data are taken from the Purdue University GTAP project. This means that quantitative restrictions, such as those existing in the agriculture or textile and apparel sectors, have been converted to tariff-equivalents. Cheong provides even fewer details about his model.

16. Many in Asia regard the IMF as a front for the US government and do not distinguish between the actions and positions of these two entities. In part this reflects ignorance, but in part it is an understandable response to the predominate influence the US wields in the Fund. In the case of South Korea, the Fund program conditionality included items of direct mercantilist interest to the US and Japan. These conditions were of questionable relevance to the financial crisis.

17. Like many of us, the President later changed his tune. In a 14 September 1998 speech to the Council on Foreign Relations he described the Asian crisis as 'the biggest financial challenge facing the world in a half century'.

18. The US participated in the 'second line of defense' associated with the second IMF program in Thailand. However, even this participation was purely symbolic inasmuch as the US Treasury fought the actual use of 'second line' funds and has never disbursed a dime.

19. Joseph E. Stiglitz (at the time the chief economist of the World Bank) contemporaneously put forward serious criticisms of the IMF programs (Stiglitz 1998, 1999). See Noland (2000a), Chapter 6 for a detailed analysis of the Fund program in South Korea.

20. In the interests of brevity these statements blur distinctions among Asian countries. In Indonesia, in particular, some segments of the society actually welcomed the IMF, which was regarded as less cozy with the Suharto regime than the World Bank. At possibly the other extreme, there was a widespread view in South Korea that the IMF program was a deliberate attempt to subvert the South Korean economy that was believed to pose a threat to the US in sectors such as automobiles.

21. Apart from emergency lending by the Asian Development Bank, pre-existing regional institutions did not play major proactive roles in the crisis. Currency swap and repurchase ('repo') agreements among the central banks were swamped by the crisis. APEC not ASEAN were largely developed by their members' foreign ministries. Their finance ministries (in particular the US Treasury in the case of APEC) have remained unenthusiastic, and neither organization has a highly developed financial component. Rhetorically, at least, both organizations have continued to support liberalization, however, and they may have served to constrain backsliding.

22. The 'old' Miyazawa Initiative was a 1980s plan to promote domestic demand. The government of Japan subsequently announced that beyond the 'New Miyazawa Initiative' an additional ¥2 trillion would be made available for sovereign loan guarantees. This money, if disbursed, would offset the roughly $30 billion of net lending that Japanese banks withdrew from the region in 1998.

23. Japan followed this up in 2000 with proposals for debt relief for the world's poorest countries.

24. See Asian Development Bank (2000). ADB President Tadao Chino later tried to clarify this point by stating that there may be a role for an AMF, but that the IMF should remain the lead agency in handling future crises (IMF, *Morning News*, 12 April 2000).

25. Not surprisingly, Thailand has emerged as Japan's most reliable ally in this regard. See,

for example, the reported remarks of Deputy Finance Minister Pisit Leeahtham at the ADB's annual meeting (Dow Jones, 5 May 2000).

26. Prior to the Asian crisis, a number of central banks had established currency swap and repurchase agreements, but these were easily swamped by the crisis. Agreements among the members of the organization of East Asian and Pacific Central Banks and the organization of Southeast Asian Central Banks were deepened and expanded in January 2000 and once again in May 2000.

27. See, for example, Noland (1998).

28. Frankly, the Treasury position is unclear on this point. Some have interpreted this ambiguity as reflecting a desire by the Clinton Administration in general, and the Treasury in particular, to pre-empt the Meltzer Commission report while at the same time preserving support from Congressional members concerned about labor, human rights, etc. On this point, the Meltzer Commission report's majority statement would abolish policy conditionality. 'The IMF would not be authorized to negotiate policy reform.' The minority dissent defends this practice without specifying the policies appropriate as conditions for IMF lending.

29. Japan has a history of trying to push the international financial institutions toward more interventionist policies. In the late 1980s and early 1990s, the MOF co-sponsored seminars with the IMF in which Japanese representatives pushed the virtues of capital channeling to developing country policymakers. At the same time, the MOF underwrote World Bank research activities which yielded the controversial 'Asian Miracle' study (World Bank, 1993) and financed a second World Bank project along these same lines in the wake of the Asian crisis. Contemporaneously, the MOF underwrote the establishment in Tokyo, not Manila, of the Asian Development Bank Institute, a think tank charged with developing an alternative development paradigm.

30. The quota constraint on borrowing was bent for Mexico in 1994 under US pressure. It was broken dramatically during the Asian crisis, when South Korea was permitted to borrow nearly 20 times its quota.

31. In his speech to the Manila Framework group, Kuroda argued that 'a reassessment of the quota distribution to reflect the changes in the global economy is urgently needed' (*Financial Times*, 22 March 2000). Minister of Finance Kiichi Miyazawa and Bank of Japan Governor Masaru Hayashi reportedly reaffirmed this position in the IMF's International Finance and Monetary Committee the following month (Dow Jones, 16 April 2000). Australian Foreign Minister Alexander Downer joined the chorus, telling a German business newspaper that 'Europeans and Americans should finally see the world as it is, not as it was' (*Handelsblatt*, 24 July 2000).

The real problem appears to be the overweighting of Europe. Japan's economy is half as large as that of the US or the EU, but its quota is one third of America's and only 20 per cent of Europe's (Bergsten, 2000). The problem with a quota reallocation would not lie in presenting Asia with a greater share. Reducing the European share while preserving the historical prerogatives of individual countries would be the real difficulty. Simply treating the EU (or, alternatively, the ECB members) as a single member could result in the European quota exceeding that of the US. This would not only be unacceptable to the US on diplomatic grounds. In theory it would require moving the IMF and World Bank headquarters to Brussels (which no one wants) since the charter states that the organization's headquarters must be located in the capital of its largest member.

32. In the end only Thailand voted for Sakakibara, while China supported Koch-Weser, and the others, following the US example, abstained.

33. Sakakibara said as much himself, describing his candidacy as 'symbolic' (Reuters, 10 March 2000). He stated that Japanese authorities had launched his candidacy despite knowing 'that the chance of my getting the position was very low' (*Financial Times*, 24 March 2000). The fact that Japan promoted such a controversial figure could be interpreted as an indication of just how weak the Japanese pool of potential candidates for important international positions actually is.

34. The problem for Japan is that, given the quota-weighted voting system, there is not another Asian country (with the possible exception of China) that could provide major

support for a Japanese candidacy at the IMF in exchange for Japanese support in the ADB.
35. The IMF and World Bank subsequently established working groups to examine their top personnel recruitment procedures.
36. On this point, see Noland (2000b).
37. Ikenberry (2000) contains a useful discussion of these issues.

REFERENCES

Allen, G.C. (1946), *A Short History of Modern Japan, 1867–1937*, London: Allen & Unwin.
Asian Development Bank (2000), *ADB Clarifies Position on Recent Report*, News Release No. 26/00, Manila: Asian Development Bank, 21 March.
Bergsten, C. Fred (2000), *The New Asian Challenge*, Working Paper 00-4, Washington: Institute for International Economics. March.
Cheong, Inkyo (1999), *Economic Integration in Northeast Asia: Searching for a Feasible Approach*, Working Paper 99-25, Seoul: Korea Institute for International Economic Policy. December.
Hunsberger, Warren S. (1964), *Japan and the United States in World Trade*, New York: Council on Foreign Relations.
Ikenberry, G. John (2000), 'The Political Economy of Asia-Pacific Regionalism', *East Asian Economic Perspectives*, Vol. 11 (March), 35–61.
International Financial Institution Advisory Commission (2000), *Report of the International Financial Institution Advisory Commission*, IFIAC: Washington, DC, March.
JETRO (2000), *Report on Closer Economic Relations Between Japan and Mexico*, April, http://www.jetro.go.jp/ec/e/report/fta_mexico/index.html.
Kelly, Paul (2000), 'The Mega-Tiger is Now Our Main Game', *The Australian*, 8 March.
Kuroda, Haruhiko (2000), 'Speech', Canberra: Australian National University, 17 February.
Lee, Kyung Tae (2000), 'Economic Effects of and Policy Directions for a Korea–Japan FTA', paper presented at Toward a Korea–Japan FTA: Assessments and Prospects, Seoul, Korea, 24 May.
Lockwood, William W. (1954), *The Economic Development of Japan*, Princeton: Princeton University Press.
MITI (1999), *Is the Comprehensive Approach a Road to Success in Seattle?*, November, http://www.miti.go.jp/info-e/cw99113e.html.
Morishima, Michio (1982), *Why Has Japan Succeeded? Western Technology and the Japanese Ethos*, Cambridge: Cambridge University Press.
Noland, Marcus (1994), *The Implications of Asian Growth*, Working Paper Series 95-5, Washington: Institute for International Economics.
Noland, Marcus (1998), 'Statement', House International Relations Committee Hearings on The Financial Crisis in Asia, 4 February, http://www.iie.com/TEST-MONY/jmn2-3.htm.
Noland, Marcus (2000a), *Avoiding the Apocalypse: The Future of the Two Koreas*, Washington: Institute for International Economics.
Noland, Marcus (2000b), 'Economic Interests, Values, and Policies', paper presented to the National Intelligence Council – Federal Research Division, Library

of Congress conference on East Asia and the United States: Current Status and Five-Year Outlook, Washington, 17 February, http://www.iie.com/TEST-MONY/nic2000.htm.

Stiglitz, Joseph E. (1998), 'More Instruments and Broader Goals: Moving Toward a Post-Washington Consensus', *WIDER Annual Lectures 2*, WIDER: Helsinki.

Stiglitz, Joseph E. (1999), 'The Korean Miracle: Growth, Crisis, and Recovery', paper presented to the International Conference on Economic Crisis and Restructuring in Korea, Seoul, Korea, 3 December.

Summers, L. (1999), 'The Right Kind of IMF for a Stable Global Financial System', speech to the London School of Business, London, December 14.

United States Treasury (2000), 'Response to the Report of the International Financial Institution Advisory Commission', Washington, DC, 8 June.

World Bank (1993), *The Asian Miracle*, Washington, DC: The World Bank.

Yamazawa, Ippei (2000), 'Toward Closer Japan–Korea Economic Relations in the 21st Century', paper presented at Toward a Korea–Japan FTA: Assessments and Prospects, Seoul, Korea, 24 May.

COMMENT ON 'JAPAN AND THE INTERNATIONAL ECONOMIC INSTITUTIONS'

Colin McKenzie[1]

Noland's chapter examines the role that Japan plays in three international economic institutions: the World Trade Organization (WTO), the Asian-Pacific Economic Cooperation (APEC) forum, and the International Monetary Fund (IMF). There are two aspects to this examination: how Japan has worked to change the institutions and how Japan has worked within the institutions' existing frameworks. The chapter's discussion of the WTO, for example, focuses on what Japan did in an attempt to change the structure of the WTO during the recent Seattle talks and how Japan has used the new dispute settlement procedures set up as a result of the Uruguay Round. My comments will try to link Noland's discussions to some of the political science literature on Japan's international role.

Application to Other Economic Institutions?

Noland concludes that there are three factors limiting Japan in its attempts to exercise greater influence in the three international institutions he examined:

- Japan's relationship with the US;
- Japan's relationship with Asia;
- the agriculture sector in Japan.

In addition to the General Agreement on Tariffs and Trade (GATT), APEC and the IMF, there are, of course, other international institutions and organizations that could have been examined, for example the Organization of Economic Cooperation and Development (OECD), the World Bank, the Asian Development Bank (ADB) and G8. It is unlikely that the conclusions derived by Noland would be changed if these organizations were examined. Japan's recent success at the International Whaling Commission meeting in Adelaide, in leading the fight against the proposed South Pacific whale sanctuary plan, provides a test of the Noland hypothesis. An examination of the participants at the International Whaling Commission reveals that, with the exception of Korea, which abstained in the sanctuary vote, there were no participants from Asia.[2] The US has in the past strongly opposed and continues strongly to oppose whaling by Norway and Japan and, as a result, voted for the sanctuary plan. However, the US support seemed relatively restrained compared with Australia's. The difference of views between Japan and the US on the sanctuary issue was not threatening to the US–Japan relationship. Since the Japanese opposition to the sanctuary proposal was a 'pro-primary producer' move, Noland's third factor was not relevant. This superficial examination suggests that Noland's hypothesis fits the case of the International Whaling Commission as well.

'Japan Punches Below Its Weight'

There would be few who would disagree with the proposition that Japan punches below its weight, but this is not just a Japanese problem. Several important questions arise here: which countries punch below (and above) their weight? (Presumably the US (and the EU?) punches above its weight.) How do we measure this? Why does it occur and what is special about the Japanese case? While not answering all these questions, Noland suggests three important factors for Japan:

- US dominance and Japan's unwillingness to risk a rupture of relations with the US;
- Japan's historical legacy from the Second World War;
- domestic politics.

Building coalitions with similar countries would appear to be one way for countries to increase their punch. Through the Cairns Group, for example, Australia appears to have significantly increased its punch in multilateral trade negotiations. Perhaps Japan should consider coalition building with other countries seeking to protect their agricultural sectors (for example,

Korea) as a means to increase its punch. An alternative is to work outside institutions that are dominated by the US. Perhaps the correct interpretation of the Asian Monetary Fund proposal is that it is an attempt to work outside the framework of the IMF.

Japan as a 'Reactive' State

In his review of six books related to Japan, Calder (1988) characterizes Japan as a 'reactive state'. A reactive state has two essential features: (1) it 'fails to undertake major independent foreign economic policy initiatives when it has the power and national incentives to do so; and (2) it responds to outside pressures for change, albeit erratically, unsystematically, and often incompletely' (p. 519). Much of what Noland describes would appear to be consistent with this description of Japan. Calder also suggests several features of the domestic political structure in Japan that discourage proactive foreign policy behavior; for example, the fragmented nature of decision making within the bureaucracy and the role of domestic interest groups (including agricultural federations).

Decision making in the bureaucracy may change in 2001, when a significant rearrangement of ministerial arrangements is to occur. One of the most interesting features of the discussions leading up to this rearrangement is that a merging, splitting up or major reorganization of the Ministry of Foreign Affairs was never really seriously contemplated. Japan possibly missed a golden opportunity to come up with bureaucratic arrangements that would help it deal with future issues likely to arise in the international economic sphere. While not without its problems, the Australian example of combining its Department of Trade and Department of Foreign Affairs into a Department of Foreign Affairs and Trade provides one way to avoid fragmentation of decision making on trade issues.

A separate issue is how the Japanese Ministry of Foreign Affairs should be organized internally. For example, in its Economic Bureau, the divisions correspond to the respective international economic organizations such as the WTO and the OECD. The OECD group is usually given responsibility for those issues which are likely to arise but tend not to fit nicely into other areas. Still, there are no real satisfactory arrangements for dealing with issues that cut across jurisdictional lines.

Leadership Role

Young (1991) distinguishes three forms of leadership: structural leadership, entrepreneurial leadership and intellectual leadership (see also Young (1989)). According to Young (1991), leaders influence bargaining and negotiating by devising effective ways to bring their party's structural power to bear (structural leadership); by using its negotiating skills (entrepreneurial leadership); or by relying on the power of ideas (intellectual leadership). Noland implicitly suggests that Japan has not been able to exercise any of these three types of leadership. (Deng (1997) contains an application of these ideas to Japan in the context of APEC.) But, Japan's attempts to increase the number of 'pro-whaling' member nations of the International Whaling Commission could be interpreted as an exercise of structural leadership.

In terms of intellectual leadership, it should be noted that both domestic Japanese politicians and economists have failed to become involved in the international economic debate. For example, there is no Japanese equivalent to Jesse Helms. As a reason for the lack of political interest in the international economic debate, Calder (1988, p. 531) goes as far as suggesting that the re-election prospects for politicians specializing in foreign affairs and defense matters (and by implication international economic affairs) are not so good. Japan's economists were very silent during the course of the Uruguay Round, but perhaps some of this is due to being 'captured' as members of deliberative councils (*shingikai*).

As both Noland (2000) and Deng (1997) point out, liberalization of agricultural markets (particularly rice) provided a key test for the Japanese leadership role. It is a test that Japan clearly failed. But what type of leadership is expected and does it qualify as a fair test? One form of leadership might be for Japan to make an announcement unilaterally to reduce its agricultural protection (or even a preparedness to reduce its protection). Such an announcement could have killed three birds with one stone: acting outside the shadow of the US, increasing imports (of rice) from Asia, and making some fundamental and unilateral moves in agriculture.

Is it reasonable to expect this sort of policy? To put the question differently, would it be reasonable to expect the European Union or the US to make a similar unilateral announcement? While there are examples of countries making unilateral reductions in protection, for example Australia's 25 per cent across the board tariff cut in the early 1970s and its announced gradual reduction of protection of the automobile industry, these are probably exceptions. The standard case for free trade is that it is in a country's own interests to reduce protection regardless of what other countries do. This of course leaves us wondering why we need a WTO or multilateral trade negotiations (see Krugman (1997)). Is the multilateral framework of the WTO the best means for achieving reductions in protection? Politically it is easier to sell a reduction in protection if you get something in return (even if it is in a completely different sector) or you can say that you were forced to accept the reduction given the threat of being labeled a 'spoiler'. The reactive state paradigm for Japan highlights the importance of this type of external pressure as a mechanism for promoting domestic change. Of course, significant amounts of funds in the form of 'Uruguay Round Countermeasures' have been pumped into the rural sector to offset the negative effects of agricultural liberalization.

Appointments

In his discussion of the WTO and the IMF, Noland notes that there have been disputes recently about the appointment of the Director General of the WTO and the Managing Director of the IMF. National pride is obviously one important issue for the US, Europe and Japan in each securing a top position in the World Bank, the IMF and the ADB, respectively. Some crucial questions are:

- What difference does it make to the way the institution functions and approaches various issues?
- How important are the leadership positions of these organizations?
- Does the nationality of the top individual matter that much?

Surely the personality and ideological stance of the individual and the corporate governance mechanisms of each organization are far more important. This is an important area for future academic research.

While Sakakibara may not have been put forward as a serious candidate for Managing Director of the IMF, it is perhaps a signal of dissatisfaction with the current arrangements. Next time Japan may very well put up a more serious candidate (Takatoshi Ito?).

Prime Beneficiary of the Current Economic Order

'Japan has arguably been the *prime* beneficiary of the liberal economic order' (Noland (2000, p. 1, p. 21). I have heard and read this statement many times. It is repeated in the introduction and the conclusion. A statement repeated sufficiently often might take on the semblance of fact, but the individuals who make this type of statement present no substantial evidence in support of this position. It is often used to suggest that Japan is a free rider on the economic system (see Balassa and Noland (1988)). As Inoguchi (1988) indicates, free riding is one of the three contending images for Japan's role in the international community, the other two being 'supporter' and 'challenger'. Of course, there is no doubting that Japan has been, and will continue to be, a beneficiary of the liberal economic order, but can it be said that Japan is the *prime* beneficiary?

Notes

1. The author would like to thank Marcus Noland for his helpful comments.
2. *The Age* of 5 July 2000 reports the details of the votes for the sanctuary proposal as follows. Countries that voted in support of the sanctuary proposition were: Austria, Australia, Brazil, Chile, Finland, France, Germany, India, Mexico, Monaco, the Netherlands, New Zealand, South Africa, Spain, Sweden, Switzerland, the United Kingdom and the United States. Countries that voted against the proposal were: Antigua and Barbuda, China, Denmark, Dominica, Grenada, Guinea, Japan, Norway, St Kitts and Nevis, St Lucia, and St Vincent and Grandalines. Countries that abstained were: Ireland, Korea and Oman. Italy and the Soloman Islands were absent from the meeting.

References

Balassa, B. and M. Noland (1988), *Japan in the World Economy*, Institute for International Economics, Washington, DC.

Calder, K.E. (1988), 'Japanese Foreign Economic Policy Formation: Explaining the Reactive State', *World Politics*, 40(4), 517–41.

Deng, Y. (1997), 'Japan in APEC: The Problematic Leadership Role', *Asian Survey*, 37(4), 353–67.

Inoguchi, T. (1988), 'The Ideas and Structures of Foreign Policy: Looking Ahead With Caution', in T. Inoguchi and D.I. Okimoto (eds), *The Political Economy of Japan, Volume 2 The Changing International Context*, Stanford: Stanford University Press, pp. 23–63.

Krugman, P. (1997), 'What Should Trade Negotiators Negotiate About?', *Journal of Economic Literature*, 35, 113–20.

Noland, M. (2000), 'Japan and the International Economic Institutions', paper presented at a conference on 'Can the Japanese Change? Economic Reform in Japan', Macquarie University, Sydney.

Young, O.R. (1989), 'The Politics of International Regime Formation: Managing Natural Resources and the Environment', *International Organization*, 43, 349–75.

Young, O.R. (1991), 'Political Leadership and Regime Formation: On the Development of Institutions in International Society', *International Organization*, 45, 281–308.

Index